ArtScroll Series®

Rabbi Nosson Scherman / Rabbi Meir Zlotowitz
General Editors

Rebbetzin Esther Greenberg

Woman
to

Compiled and edited by
Aviva Rappaport

Published by
Mesorah Publications, ltd

Woman

Practical advice
and classic stories
on life's goals
and aspirations

FIRST EDITION
First Impression . . . September 1996
Second Impression . . . November 1996

Published and Distributed by
MESORAH PUBLICATIONS, Ltd.
4401 Second Avenue
Brooklyn, New York 11232

Distributed in Europe by
J. LEHMANN HEBREW BOOKSELLERS
20 Cambridge Terrace
Gateshead, Tyne and Wear
England NE8 1RP

Distributed in Israel by
SIFRIATI / A. GITLER—BOOKS
10 Hashomer Street
Bnei Brak 51361

Distributed in Australia & New Zealand by
GOLDS BOOK & GIFT CO.
36 William Street
Balaclava 3183, Vic., Australia

Distributed in South Africa by
KOLLEL BOOKSHOP
22 Muller Street
Yeoville 2198, Johannesburg, South Africa

Printed in the United States of America by Noble Book Press Corp.
Bound by Sefercraft Quality Bookbinders, Ltd., Brooklyn, N.Y.

*This book is dedicated
to my wonderful mother,
who, despite a life of hardship
and personal tragedy,
struggled unceasingly
to instill in her family
the enduring values of
the Jewish people.
Our appreciation for her
continued unstinting support
can never be fully expressed.*

✺ Contents

✄ *Preface*

It was late at night. Rebbetzin Greenberg had just given an hour-long talk on "The Jewish Home" to a group of women in a city far from her home. They crowded around her afterwards, eager to hear more, reluctant to let her leave. But tonight she had another appointment, despite the late hour.

The taxi made its way through the dark, near-empty streets to a neighborhood on the other side of the city. There, anxiously awaiting her, was a woman to whom many eyes in the community turned for advice and guidance, a woman whose husband held a position of public importance. Yet now she herself was faced with a pressing personal problem. To whom could she turn?

Like so many women, she found in Rebbetzin Greenberg the listening ear, the understanding heart and the womanly wisdom she needed.

There are women all over the world whose lives were touched in a profound way by their contact with the Rebbetzin. Many women have confided that they can separate their life into two parts: before meeting her and after.

She had a nobility of soul that bridged differences in age, background, ethnic group, and lifestyle.

With her passing in 5751 (1991), the sense of loss felt was not only for an individual, but for the repository of authentic Judaism as well, especially as it applied to women and their role in life. This book, which is based on tapes of an English lecture series the Rebbetzin delivered in the Mattersdorf neighborhood of Yerushalayim three years before her passing, is an attempt to preserve her legacy and thus give thousands of additional women access to her teachings.

The lecture series consisted of 31 sessions given over the period of a year, resulting in a total of 59 hour-long tapes on the subject of "The Jewish Home." The halachic material in those lectures has not been included in this book.

In adapting this material, every effort was made to adhere closely to the original, both in content and in order of presentation. For instance, the chapter on controlling anger appears early in the book because that is where the Rebbetzin placed the subject when she spoke. Wherever possible, the words are direct quotes; however, as any reader familiar with transcriptions will know, the spoken word needs adaptation in order to become readable.

Of prime importance in adapting the Rebbetzin's spoken word to book form was faithfulness to her meaning and intent, as well as accuracy in the presentation of her ideas. In addition, and of great importance, was the preservation of her "voice." Those who knew Rebbetzin Greenberg and have read the manuscript have commented that the "voice" they hear throughout is indeed hers.

It was my privilege to become close to the Rebbetzin, especially during the final year of her life. The Greenberg family's continued trust, friendship, and support gave me the confidence to undertake this project. The work was accompanied by fervent prayers that the Rebbetzin's message would be truthfully relayed and that no inaccuracies of meaning or content would find their way into the final product. Any shortcomings in the work should certainly not be attributed to the Rebbetzin.

May the remarks made by Rebbetzin Greenberg at the beginning of her lecture series serve as our heartfelt prayer as well: *B'ezras Hashem,* may these words be of benefit, and may everyone take away something which will help her and add to her knowledge, her marital harmony, and the sanctity of her home.

❧ *Acknowledgments*

הודו לה׳ כי טוב כי לעולם חסדו, מי ימלל גבורות ה׳ ישמיע
כל תהלתו

Give thanks to Hashem, for He is good, for His kindness is everlasting; Who can recount the mighty acts of Hashem or make heard all His praise. (Tehillim 106:1-2)

With every mountain climbed, it is only natural to look back down to our starting place and remember the beginning of the journey, to mentally retrace our steps, and think of all those who lent a helping hand along the way. We remember how high the mountain seemed and how hard it was to take the first steps, and we begin to appreciate the key roles certain people played in our climb. There is no doubt that this book would not exist if not for the devoted efforts of Rebbetzin Carol Weinberger of the "Lashon Marpeh Torah Tape Library" in Har Nof, Yerushalayim. She can truly serve as a model to be emulated by all who aspire to benefit others by taping Torah lectures and making them available to the public. Over the course of a year, she taped each and every lecture in the series; rain or shine, no matter how difficult the personal circumstances or how pressured for time, she was there.

R' Yaakov Branfman deserves our deep appreciation for graciously setting aside time from his busy schedule as writer and editor to transcribe a major portion of the tapes.

Mr. Shmuel Blitz of ArtScroll/Mesorah, Jerusalem, provided the professional vision, assistance and expertise needed to guide the project to its completion.

Above all, our heartfelt gratitude is extended to HaRav Yitzchak Greenberg *shlita*, and to his and the Rebbetzin's children, for authorizing this volume. May the merit of their endless devotion to Torah and Klal Yisrael be a blessing for the entire family.

For a married woman, nothing is more important in her life than her husband, as the Rebbetzin so often reminds us. May my husband, my lifelong companion on all journeys, whose encouragement, patience, and faith in this project carried it to completion, be blessed with continued success in Torah, and may we both merit, along with all of Klal Yisrael, to see our children, grandchildren and all our future generations immersed in Torah and *avodas Hashem*.

A. Rappaport

A Brief Biographical Sketch of Rebbetzin Esther Greenberg ע״ה

Rebbetzin Esther Greenberg was born over sixty years ago. Her father, HaRav Ha-Gaon R' Naftali HaCohen Shakovitzky, was the son of R' Binyamin, the renowned Maggid of Minsk, who, as a result of his inspirational talks given to communities far and wide, was exiled to Siberia by the authorities. Her mother, Rebbetzin Chaya Rachel, was the daughter of HaRav HaGaon Avraham Droshkevitz, the Mashgiach of Volozhin.

R' Naftali HaCohen was a leading disciple of both the Chofetz Chaim and the Saba of Slabodka, R' Nosson Zvi Finkel *ztz"l*. During the upheavals of World War II, HaRav HaGaon Avraham Shapiro, the Rav of Kovno, advised R' Naftali HaCohen to leave

Lithuania and become the rabbi of Gateshead, then a small town in England. As a going-away present, R' Shapiro gave R' Naftali HaCohen the top hat he had worn when he went to the United States at the behest of *gedolei* Torah. This was a tangible sign of his blessing for success in the undertaking, and indeed, the entire family was saved.

Gateshead was at that time a haven for refugees fleeing Poland and Lithuania. R' Naftali HaCohen, along with Rabbi Eliyahu Dessler and Rabbi David Drayan, established all the essential community institutions. When the now famous Gateshead Seminary for girls was founded by R' Naftali HaCohen, Rebbetzin Greenberg was the first student enrolled in the first class, becoming a devoted pupil of Rabbi Dessler.

During the war years, she formed a woman's *chesed* organization, one of whose activities was sending packages to those trapped in the camps. Sixteen-year-old Esther Shakovitzky remained awake until the early hours of the morning packing relief parcels, to the point where her hands bled — yet this did not deter her from continuing the lifesaving work.

When she made *aliyah* to Eretz Yisrael upon marriage to her husband HaRav Yitzchak Greenberg *shlita,* she began teaching. Waves of immigrants were then arriving from Yemen, and even though she was not yet fluent in Hebrew, she was one of the pioneering teachers who devoted themselves to the education of the Yemenite girls. She taught in the city of Rosh HaAyin for over thirty-two years. She was not only a teacher to the girls, but a mother to them as well. They turned to her with every problem, even long after they had graduated from school, and generations of girls were educated to Torah and mitzvah observance through her efforts.

About twenty years ago, Rebbetzin Greenberg realized that there was an urgent need for an all-encompassing transmission of the laws of *Taharas HaMishpachah.* With the approval of all the leading Torah authorities, she traveled the length and breadth of the country to teach Jewish women how to establish authentic Jewish homes based on values of education, *taharah,* and marital harmony. She educated generations of students in both Eretz Yisrael and abroad on how to instruct brides as well as married women on the subject of "The Jewish Home" and all that is encompassed therein. She also counseled couples privately, and many marriages were saved as a result of her efforts.

Several evenings a week were devoted to speaking to various groups of women, and, as one rabbi said: "A thousand rabbis could not have done what she did!"

Over the years her sphere of activities expanded and she traveled to Jewish communities all over the world — the United States, Canada, South Africa, and Europe. Her lectures, which were delivered in Hebrew, English, or Yiddish, drew large audiences of women anxious to hear her message. In every community she visited, she formed a core group of women to guide and counsel others on the subject of "The Jewish Home."

She also organized the annual national conference on *Taharas HaMishpachah* which was attended by approximately 1,000 woman from all over Eretz Yisrael who came to hear more about "the woman as the pillar of the home."

She had made plans to travel to the-then Soviet Union, but after a brief illness, the sun set at midday and she passed away. She was laid to rest on Har HaMenuchos in Yerushalayim. The gathering at her funeral — in the thousands — was something never experienced before in that city, and truly a tribute to an extraordinary woman.

May she awaken merit from her abode on high for all who continue her work and for all who merit to kindle the light of holiness and purity in Jewish homes. And may her memory be a blessing!

1
The Ideal Home

When a girl dreams of the kind of home she would like to have, she visualizes this home not only in the physical and material sense, but in the spiritual sense as well. Each one has her dreams. And whatever you really want and strive for with your whole heart will be attained.[1] If you have clearly defined goals in mind for the kind of home you would like, you will achieve them — because a home, in the spiritual sense, is entirely dependent on the woman and what she does.

A home is more than four walls, a ceiling, and a roof. Our Sages

---

1. Vilna Gaon, *Mishlei* 23:12.

tell us that the **woman** is the home. She is the mainstay of the home and without her, there is no home.[1]

A woman is likened to "ground," for she is the foundation of the home.

She is called a "tent," because she shields everyone.

She is called the "glory" of the home, for it is she who glorifies the home by doing her utmost to establish a home based on the foundations of faithful Judaism. It is she who puts into practice all the beautiful mitzvos of the Torah that are kept in the home, training herself and her children to follow in the right path.

A woman is also called the "essence" of the home. Unfortunately, the opposite can be true as well, for the Hebrew root of essence can also mean "to uproot." The woman can become the "destroyer" of the home — the choice is hers.

How is a home created? A lesson can be learned from Sarah and Rivkah, who showed us the way to build the ideal home. When Yitzchak took Rivkah for a wife, he first "brought her into his mother Sarah's tent and took Rivkah and she became his wife and he loved her and was comforted after [the death of] his mother."[2] Nowadays, people think the sequence of these events should be different, but this is the proper way a Jewish home is built and should serve as our model.

Yitzchak began building his home by bringing Rivkah into his mother's tent to show her the kind of home he grew up in and wanted to have when he was married. "When my mother was alive," he explained, "there were three very special characteristics which distinguished this tent. First of all, when my mother, Sarah, lit the candles for Shabbos, they burned from one Shabbos to the next. Second, when my mother kneaded the dough, there was such a blessing in the bread that whoever ate even the smallest piece was satisfied. And third, the Cloud of Glory was always present, showing that the Divine Presence rested on the tent." Yitzchak then asked Rivkah: "Do you feel you can create the same kind of atmosphere, the same kind of reality that my mother did?"

What was so special about this tent, the home Sarah created? It reminds us of another place where all these characteristics were

---

1. As Rebbi Yossi said, ". . . I called my wife my home and my home I called my wife" (*Gittin* 52a).
2. *Bereishis* 24:67.

found: the *Beis HaMikdash*, the dwelling place of the Divine Presence. In the *Beis HaMikdash*, when the *kohen* lit the candles of the Golden Menorah on *erev* Shabbos, they burned till the following *erev* Shabbos. Every Friday, the twelve loaves of bread were replaced with newly baked ones. The bread from the previous week, which had miraculously stayed fresh, was then divided among the *kohanim*. And although there were thousands of *kohanim*, our Sages tell us that even if a *kohen* received a small piece, he felt satisfied.

Yitzchak was actually asking Rivkah if she was capable of building a *Beis HaMikdash*! If she was, then she was the right wife for him.

After he showed her the tent and she agreed to follow in his mother's ways — and after he saw that she could be like his mother Sarah — then he took her, and she became his wife. Then — *after* she became his wife — he loved her, for love in Jewish marriage comes from giving. And finally, only after Yitzchak saw that his wife was like his mother was he "comforted."

Their home was a *Beis HaMikdash*, just as every Jewish home is a miniature *Beis HaMikdash* — and the builder of this *Beis HaMikdash* is the woman.

We have to work at making our home a place of happiness, of sanctity, a place where the walls sing with joy. Our home should be like a *Beis HaMikdash*, where people enter and feel the warmth enveloping them — like my first home in Israel, the house of R' Meir Chadash *ztz"l*. That home was a legend: The door never closed and everyone was welcome. You didn't have to look for the *shalom bayis*, the warmth and harmony, the pleasantness — you felt it the moment you walked through the door. R' Chadash and his wife lived together in absolute unity for sixty years, with never a harsh word spoken. You never heard a raised voice because they had such perfect communication and understanding. R' Shach *shlita* eulogized R' Chadash by saying that the outstanding legacy of Torah he left behind — two yeshivos and thousands of students — can be credited to the atmosphere of the home that the Rebbetzin created. This is what a woman can achieve.

One of our great Sages, Rabbi Yosef, was blind, but whenever he heard his mother's footsteps he would say, "I wish to rise in honor of the Divine Presence which accompanies my mother wherever she goes," and he would rise and stand. This applies to every Jewish woman — if you try to the best of your ability to build your *Beis HaMikdash*, the Divine Presence will go with you.

The home is actually a living mirror of the woman's entire personality. Her husband and children — everything in the home — reflects her. Everything she brings to it, all the warmth and love, permeate the house.

We cannot imagine how much a home absorbs our personality!

> *In Lithuania a rabbi once arrived in a certain town just in time for Minchah. After davening, he went up to the rabbi of the shul and said, "There must be something special about your shul, for I've never davened such a Minchah in my life! Can you explain this to me?"*
>
> *"Tell me," asked the rabbi, "where did you stand when you davened?"*
>
> *"In that corner."*
>
> *The rabbi turned to look at the spot the visitor pointed to. "I'll tell you why your Minchah was so special," he said. "One hundred and fifty years ago the Vilna Gaon stood in that corner and davened — that's why you davened such a wonderful Minchah."*

Since our home absorbs whatever we do — everything is recorded and nothing is lost — we want all of our actions to be worthy of the *Beis HaMikdash* we are building. If we understand and remember that we are always in the presence of Hashem, this feeling will monitor our actions and elevate them. We will conduct ourselves differently — with our husband, with our children, with everything we do.

"An eye sees . . ." our Sages tell us.[1] In the last one hundred years, says the Chofetz Chaim, modern technology has made it possible for even people who live in an era of weakened faith to see the truth of these words. After all, if a mere human being was able to discover the secret of television or video, where a person on one side of the world can view the actions of someone across the ocean, why wouldn't Hashem be able to see everything we do?

---

1. *Pirkei Avos* 2:1.

"An ear hears . . ." And if, by dialing thirteen digits, we can speak to anybody anywhere in the world through a device created solely by the limited mind of a human being, can't Hashem hear everything we say?

"And all our deeds are written in the book." Consider one simple electronic device, the tape recorder. A mere human being discovered the secret and put it together. We can put in a cassette and record, and later listen to everything that has been said. If a tape recorder can record someone, it is not difficult to imagine that Hashem must be able to hear and record everything we say and do.

> Once the Chofetz Chaim hired a wagon driver to take him from one town to another. On the way, the driver stopped the wagon in the middle of the road, got down, went into a nearby field and started taking produce. The Chofetz Chaim began shouting, "Someone sees you!" and the wagon driver fled the field in fear.
>
> When he climbed up onto his seat, the driver looked back at the field to see who was there. When he didn't see anyone, he turned to his passenger and complained: "Why did you tell me there was someone looking when there's no one there?"
>
> The Chofetz Chaim replied: "I'm sorry, but you are seen . . . from Above. Everything we do is seen."

In fact, we are told that every time we open our mouths to speak an angel writes down everything we say.[1] It's like having our own private secretary! So we must be very careful and weigh each word before it is said, for nothing is lost — not one single word. Our words actually remain permanently embedded in the atmosphere.

Our Sages tell us that after 120 years the walls of our houses will appear before the Heavenly Throne and the Heavenly Court, and they will bear witness to what was said and done in our homes. So let us make our walls sing with joy, contentment, and happiness. The impression will last forever.

Everyone in the world strives for immortality. We all want to be remembered forever. We find very great artists, sculptors, com-

---

1. *Devarim; Midrash Rabbah,* Chap. 6.

posers, authors, who want to create a masterpiece that will insure that they will be remembered always. They want their work to be so wonderful that in a thousand years from now it will be worth millions and millions and people will say, "He made that, he painted that picture, he wrote that book." A person is prepared to invest years and years of hard work into his masterpiece solely because he wants to be remembered.

Each of you, whether you realize it or not, is creating your own masterpiece. You are working on your life's work: building a home. It is your eternity, the creation of a lifetime.

If you think of your home as a masterpiece, as the work of a lifetime, then how much are you prepared to invest in such a creation?! Work at creating happiness around you, work at creating your home. It is the most wonderful creation there is. It is yours.

It Is Up to Us

In all generations, Jewish women have had a very great share in the redemption and the salvation of their people. "In every place where the men broke the wall, the women fenced and repaired it."[1] When the men made the Golden Calf, the women refused to contribute their gold jewelry. Later, when the spies returned and spoke disparagingly about Eretz Yisrael, saying it was a land that destroys its people, the daughters of Zelofchad came to Moshe and said, "We want an inheritance in Eretz Yisrael." It is always the women, the great women of the Jewish nation, who repair the breaches.

In Egypt, the midwives Shifrah and Puah rescued and cared for the newborn infants, although Pharaoh could have had them killed for disobeying his command. Because they feared Hashem more than a flesh-and-blood king, they were rewarded with the monarchy and priesthood for their descendants.

All women in Egypt were faced with terrible decrees. Their husbands worked as slave laborers. A man would be so worn out he never even came home — he just fell down in the field as he worked, slept a little, was beaten, and got up to work again. When a woman went to the well to draw water, she would find small fish which she cooked

---

1. *Midrash Tanchuma, parashas Pinchas.*

into a meal for her husband. She would make herself beautiful and then take the food she had prepared and bring it to her husband out in the field. He would be so exhausted he couldn't even lift up his head to look at her. She would take her polished copper mirror and hold it in front of him to let him see the two of them together in it, and then she would say, "Look at me." It was through these mirrors that our nation was brought into being.

When it came time for Moshe to build the *Mishkan*, the women came and offered their copper mirrors. Moshe hesitated to take them. After all, how could something that had been used for the evil inclination be used for a holy purpose? But Hashem said to him, "Take those mirrors. They are more precious to Me than anything else, for with those mirrors the women brought the Jewish people into being."

Moshe accepted the women's mirrors and fashioned them into the *kiyor*, the vessel that held the water for the ritual washing of the *kohanim*. This was a sign that the women had pure intentions, because this copper vessel — made from their mirrors — held the water which purified the hands and feet of the *kohanim* when they served Hashem.

We are taught that "all the generations are redeemed only in the merit of the righteous women, the *nashim tzidkanios*, of each generation."[1] Each generation has its righteous women in whose merit the nation continues to exist. This continued existence rests with the women, because they bear the torch of Torah and mitzvos to pass on to future generations.

---

1 *Midrash Zuta, Rus* 4:11.

2
Marital Harmony

arriage is our chance for perfection. "Male and female He created them, and called them 'Adam.' "[1] Man is a single entity, formed by male and female combined. Yet if Hashem wanted to create two human beings, male and female, why did he begin with only one? The Vilna Gaon explains that because Hashem wanted the woman to be a helpmate to the man, He created them as one and then divided them — only if the woman is part of her mate will she be able to truly help him.[2]

---

1 *Bereishis* 5:2.
2. Vilna Gaon, *Mishlei* 9:10.

Alone, neither half is complete. Both halves are needed to create one whole. Completeness comes when these two halves join together into one unit. Two can help each other; two can give to each other. The love and harmony between them should be greater than that between people in any other relationship. They should become like one body. When these two halves are joined, bringing completeness, the Divine Presence becomes a partner with them.[1]

Under the wedding canopy a blessing is recited which contains all the ten expressions of happiness. But that blessing — and the happiness to which it refers — is not only intended for the wedding night — it's for a partnership of a lifetime! And not only for this life, but for eternity.

Our Sages tell us that a wife is the light of her husband's eyes. She enables him to stand on his feet. She is like a wall, encircling him, taking care, watching over and guarding him.

When it comes to choosing a wife, it doesn't matter how much money a girl has. Money is like a wheel that turns round — one day it's there, another day it isn't. But a girl of good character, a girl with all the *middos tovos*, is herself the dowry. She can "make do," she can manage, she knows how to cope. Then you have the greatest riches there are in the world.

We are all familiar with the Mishnah where Ben Zoma says, "Who is called wise? He who learns from everyone. Who is rich? He who is happy with his lot in life."[2] Rabbi Akiva asks these same questions, and his answers, while not as well known, are of great interest to us. To the question, "Who is rich?" Rabbi Akiva answers: "He who has a wife whose deeds are beautiful."[3]

Who was more qualified to say this than Rabbi Akiva!? His wife had a plait of beautiful hair so long it reached the ground, yet she cut it off and sold it — so she could send the money to her husband to enable him to study Torah. Even though she grew up in the house of an extremely wealthy man, her father Kalba Savua, she

---

1. There is a well-known Gemara in *Yevamos* (63a) where Rabbi Elazar says: "He who has no wife is not called 'Adam,' for the verse says Hashem created them male and female, and he called their name 'Adam.' " The Zohar explains that the *Shechinah* cannot rest on something that is not perfect, for something that is imperfect is not complete.

2. *Pirkei Avos* 4:1.

3. *Shabbos* 25b.

laundered soiled clothing to provide for herself and the children. Who knew better than Rabbi Akiva that a wife whose deeds are beautiful is the greatest treasure a man can have!

In Judaism we have structure to the home and family. We expend every major effort to insure that this structure remains intact and does not suffer the breakdown which is happening all over the world. In the Jewish family, the father is the head of the family and the mother is his helpmate; he is the king and she is the queen, and the children are princes and princesses. There must be respect and *derech eretz*. If the mother respects and honors the father, then the children will respect and honor the father. When the father respects and honors the mother, the children respect and honor the mother. The whole conduct of the home is regal, because we are the daughters and sons of Hashem, the King of all kings. And sons and daughters of the King must conduct themselves accordingly.

There is a wonderful teaching of our Sages which succinctly reveals the secret of *shalom bayis*:

"A wise mother said to her daughter: My child, if you will be your husband's maidservant, he will be your servant and will respect you like a noble woman. If you lord over him, then he will rule you as a master, regarding you as a lowly servant."

Modern counseling courses talk about the "balance of marriage." For us, this is nothing new — over 2,000 years ago our Sages said there must be a balance in marriage! If you treat your husband as a lord, as a king, then he is going to treat you as a queen. But if you think that you can lord over **him**, then he is going to lord over **you** — he'll be your lord and master with force.

Every woman must be the doctor of her marriage. She must keep her finger on its pulse to see if she is keeping the balance. If you sense friction, if there is lack of understanding, it is a sign that something is wrong. You may have made your husband feel that you are destroying his self-image. Since you are not building him up enough, he is retaliating by pushing you down. That creates friction and a vicious cycle of tension, quarrels, and, of course, lack of *shalom bayis*. But if you keep the balance, always respecting your husband, always honoring him and treating him like a king, as if you were his subject, he will treat you like a queen.

Once there was a couple who lived happily until they began quarreling often. The friction became so great that they went for counseling. When they came to the counselor the wife complained that her husband had become so stingy she had to ask him at least ten times for every single penny she needed. She was fed up and couldn't stand it any longer. From the conversation, the counselor discovered that this woman's husband felt inadequate. He felt that since his wife was much more educated and gifted than he was, the only thing that gave him importance was that she had to ask him for money — so he made her ask for everything at least ten times! The minute she realized how this gave him a feeling of self-importance and self-respect, she didn't mind asking ten times. And marital harmony returned to their home.

That is keeping the balance of the marriage.

The balance of marriage changes constantly. When you first get married, there are only the two of you. During the first year of marriage you build a very close relationship together, especially if you have had guidance beforehand. Then the first child comes along and the balance changes. If you are wise, it then becomes a close-knit family and you share the baby. But some women are not that smart. They think the baby is theirs alone and they shut their husband out. That's one way to create a very big gap in the marriage. If you act that way, your husband will find other interests while you busy yourself with the baby. A mother like this becomes very possessive, living through her children and tying them to her apron strings. Her children don't like it and can hardly wait to grow up and leave home. And they won't be in a hurry to return.

Each new child will change the balance of the marriage slightly. It is up to you to do your best to recreate the balance, to widen the circle, not to push your husband away by always busying yourself with the children that actually are part of each of you.

Children stay at home for twenty years or so, but eventually they do leave the nest to get married, and then husband and wife are back to being a couple again. There have been cases where women have gone through a terrible crisis when the children left home because they had built no relationship with their husband. Instead, they had centered their entire life and all their interests on their children. When the children eventually do leave home, this type of mother often has a breakdown. All of a sudden she starts complaining to her husband, "Why don't you ever stay home with me?" and he doesn't know what's the matter with her! For the last twenty years she's told him to go away, and he has — he's busied himself with work, *shiurim*, and other interests. Now all she has left is a vacuum, complete emptiness. Don't ever forget that the most important thing in life for you is your relationship with your husband. You have to build that relationship. Work at it daily. Don't lose contact, and never let communication break down. It cannot be said strongly enough: **The most important thing in your marriage is your husband.**

Sometimes we are called upon to take an elderly parent into the home. That can also change the balance of the marriage. Often it is very hard to make ends meet — this too can affect the balance of marriage. Or there can be, *chas v'shalom*, illness in the family. Every change can upset the balance of your marriage; but if there is a real closeness, a true partnership, then husband and wife become a united front. Every challenge should draw the partners closer together. If the communication between them isn't strengthened, the gap between them will widen and pull them apart. Don't let this happen to your marriage. Instead, do everything together, sharing and caring. As King Solomon said, two people working at a problem are much better than one, because together they learn to cope and overcome, together they adapt to change and rise to meet the challenge. And if there is perfect trust between the two, then leadership can pass from one to the other without either person being fearful that the other partner will take advantage of his weaknesses. For instance, one of the partners might be more capable of managing the budget and paying bills, but sometimes, if he cannot, the other partner takes over. Likewise with educating the children. Sometimes one partner is more talented with running this aspect of the home, but leadership in this area — and all areas of the home — can pass from one to the other with perfect understanding, trust, and sharing.

We want to respect our partners and never intentionally hurt them. We want to be givers and not takers. In Judaism, we define love as giving: The more you give, the more you love. When you give to another person, you are giving a part of yourself; you are actually investing yourself in the other person. The more you give, the more you invest of yourself; and the more the other person becomes a part of you — the more you love him.

The Hebrew word for **love**, *ahavah* (אהבה) has the numerical value of 13, as does the word *echad* (אחד), which means **one**. Husband and wife should love each other so much that they become like one. *Ahavah* (13) and *echad* (13) together equal 26, which is the *gematria* of Hashem's Name: If there is such togetherness, such communication, such *shalom bayis*, such oneness, then the Divine Presence, the *Shechinah* is in the home. That's the meaning of love!

A loving relationship is one in which individuals trust each other enough to become vulnerable, secure that the other will not take advantage, neither exploiting nor taking their partner for granted. This involves much communication, much sharing, and much tenderness. It is a relationship where selfishness gives way to selfless giving, where the language of communication is kept open, where the good in it is maximized and the bad minimized.

Trust is being secure in the knowledge that you are each other's best friend and that no matter what happens, you will stand by one another. It is seeing the other partner as a friend who can be trusted, depended upon and enjoyed. You are happy to be together. Such trust offers unlimited strength and support upon which one can always draw.

Such a relationship is defined not by the length of time but by the quality of caring. It is a home for one's soul, a place to be ourselves and explore our deepest inner yearnings, hopes and fears, without fear of condemnation, rejection or being abandoned. It is an environment where we gain the strength to fight daily battles. It is a blending of oneself without loss of one's uniqueness. It allows the other to be all that he or she can be.

Don't be afraid of giving — you can never give too much, if you give willingly. Never force anyone to do anything for you in the name of love. Love is not to be bargained for. Remember that the relationship is a pooling of resources. That means that you are not only giving, you are becoming more.

— anon.

Work on yourself, and you will develop into a more shining personality. Try completing these three assignments and you will see the immediate benefit to your home and your marriage.

1. Keep your finger on the pulse of your marriage.

For a week, pay special attention to what goes on in your home. Ask yourself these questions: Is there tension in the home? Is my husband dissatisfied with something? What have I said or done to destroy his feeling of self-importance?

Whenever you feel tension or anger, or if there is an exchange of words, it is a sign that one person is not showing enough respect to the other. These unpleasant feelings always occur when one partner destroys the other partner's self-image, self-respect, and sense of self-importance. If this happens, change direction. Start to build the other person up. Give him back his feeling of importance — you are going to be the winner, not the loser.

2. Write down all the reasons why your husband means so much to you.

Write down all your husband's good qualities. Write down only virtues — no failings whatsoever. You can even write down all the wonderful qualities you saw in your husband before you married him — because they're still there and he's still got them!

Listing your husband's good points will bring you back to seeing things in the right light. The next time you begin to feel annoyance and a lack of appreciation, read the list. You will instead feel happy and full of gratitude to Hashem.

3. Make a resolution to get up every morning and say: Today my home is going to be a *Beis HaMikdash.*

Every time you want to let off steam, remember that your home is a *Beis HaMikdash* and the walls are listening and will bear witness. The *Shechinah*, the Divine Presence, is called the "Mother of Peace." When there is *shalom bayis*, the *Shechinah* dwells in the home. When there is friction and quarreling in the home, the *Shechinah* can't bear it and departs. But the home is not empty; something else comes in its stead — the Satan himself! Say to yourself: Today, I am not going to throw the

Shechinah out of my home. Today I am going to keep the *Shechinah* in my home.

The next day get up and say the same thing. Keep it up for a week. It's going to be easier every day. Make the effort to turn your home into a *Beis HaMikdash* where the *Shechinah* dwells and from which it does not depart.

You are creating your masterpiece — your *Beis HaMikdash*.

3

Communication

When I ask you to listen to me and you start giving me advice, it shows you don't understand what I asked you to do.

When I ask you to listen to me and you start saying, "You don't need to feel like that," you are trampling on my feelings.

When I ask you to listen to me and you feel you have to help me solve my problems, you disappoint me.

Tell me with a look, with deeds, that you care . . . and don't assume that I know.

And even if you think or feel it may sound confusing, don't worry — please do express your caring.

I need constant appreciation, for appreciation encourages me to continue doing my job.

Let me know when you don't feel well, when you are worried about something, when you are misunderstood,

because it encourages me when I know that I can help,
comfort, and encourage you.
So please listen to me.
And if you want to talk, please wait a while — I
promise I will listen to you too.
— anon.

One of the problems of our generation is that people don't listen. When you walk into a room full of people you can see that no one is really listening to the person he's speaking with; instead, he's listening to himself!

There is a very simple scientific reason for this: If we speak quickly, we can say about 250 words a minute. On the other hand, our minds can process about 500 to 600 words per minute. What are we doing with the extra time? Traveling to Europe! Most people are so busy thinking about what is *about* to be said that they don't listen to what is being said. True listening is thinking about what was said and how it applies to oneself. True listening is staying with the speaker. Otherwise, you fail to absorb his thoughts and your mind flies away elsewhere.

Communication means first *listening*, without judging whether or not what the other person has to say is worth listening to or not. Instead of thinking, "This is pointless, I'm not interested at all," keep an open mind.

Listen with your heart, not your ears. Give the other person your full attention. He should feel you are fascinated with what he is saying, that you are there with him, not far away. And we can all sense whether a person is with us or not. So really listen.

Make a rule that no day should go by without you and your husband sitting down together, for at least half an hour, to talk things over. If he comes home late, the conversation could even take place in the middle of the night. If you are too tired to wait up, take a nap when he is out and then get up when he comes back. Prepare a hot drink and some cake, sit down together and talk.

You must find time to be married, because otherwise it's not marriage — it's a 24-hour grind with no communication. He's got complaints, you've got complaints, and you never get a chance to talk to each other! It is essential to make time for your marriage. No matter how busy a man may be, even if he is the most dedicated and diligent Torah scholar or the most pressured businessman, he must make time for his wife and family. In fact, the greater the man, the more wonderful a father and husband he is.

Some wives seem to think that giving their husband a report of what they've done during the day is communication, but it's not. It's more like a newspaper article. Communication means discussing problems and solving them together. Communication means sharing your dreams and hopes for the future. That's the way to create togetherness.

So let us ask ourselves: How do we go about creating this communication? It is very easy to talk about, yet so hard to do. There are so many husbands and wives who have lost it somewhere along the way. They may have been married for a long time, but they stopped communicating years ago. Some don't even speak to one another any longer! One of the best suggestions for improving communication between husband and wife is for them to sit down and learn something together. Sit down, just the two of you, for half an hour, and read something. It might be a *halachah* or a *mussar sefer*, or a Torah commentary — it doesn't matter as long as it's something fulfilling. Then start discussing what you have read. Soon you will find yourselves sharing thoughts and talking about all the problems that need solving.

We create a spiritual bond when we learn together and talk things over. Sometimes there is a problem which you find difficult to discuss. But if you sit down to learn together, you begin talking together, which opens the door to solving those problems you had found to be formidable.

You *must* talk for at least half an hour daily. Never miss this, because you are working on your marriage, an eternal partnership.

What do we mean by "eternal" partnership? Although we know life is short, we find eternity a concept difficult to grasp. R' Simchah Zissel of Kelm described it this way: Picture a large hall filled with sesame seeds from floor to ceiling. Once in a thousand years a bird comes in and takes one seed. How long will it take for the bird to empty the hall? That gives us some idea of what eternity is. In this world, we are on a journey, preparing ourselves for the future. Every day has a purpose — don't waste it! Life is precious, so do your best to create an eternal partnership. Start communicating.

The most important thing for a woman, especially after marriage when she has already finished school, is to study Jewish thought. It helps us work on perfecting our character. When we study, we put on a pair of Torah spectacles and see the world in the light of *daas* Torah, and this is very important.

Never stay in one place — work on yourself endlessly. You can, for instance, elevate yourself by listening to lectures on tape. There are plenty of tapes and tape libraries. If this isn't feasible, at least once a week attend a lecture. A human being is always moving, either up or down, from one level to another, and if he doesn't work on elevating himself, then he will, *chas v'shalom,* move in a downward direction. Learning is a way to elevate ourselves.

If you don't work on yourself and your husband does, then not only are you not standing in one place, you are losing what you had — and it's tragic. You will have nothing about which to communicate with you husband, and you will lose your connection with him.

There are four basic types of people whose way of "communicating" is very destructive, especially in marriage:

The Pressure Cooker: There is the type of person who can be defined as a pressure cooker. Every time this type of person feels aggressive, he bottles it up, until the steam rises right to the lid and bursts out. When something happens to aggravate this type of person, he doesn't say much at the time. Instead, he accumulates the aggression. This is one of the worst possible things a person can do! It is *very* dangerous to be a pressure cooker. It is much better to get your feelings off your chest in the proper way. If you learn to communicate properly, you'll get rid of resentment daily.

The Sniper: The second type of partner in marriage can be called a sniper. Snipers take aim from a distance. Many women are guilty of doing this without realizing it. A mother will get up in the morning and start making critical remarks left, right, front and back — and then the children start crying because their feelings are hurt. She says, "What's the matter?" Her husband gets upset and can't wait to escape. "What's the matter?" she asks. "What did I say? I didn't say anything."

A person who is a sniper doesn't realize how terrible it is. It ruins the marriage, it ruins the *shalom bayis*, it destroys the husband's and children's self-image. A sniper thinks she is innocent, but she is really hurting her husband and destroying their marriage.

The Scapegoater: The third type of marriage partner is the scapegoater. He or she is like a *tallis* made entirely of *techeiles*, entirely pure and blameless. No matter what happens, the other partner is always to blame for anything that goes wrong in the house. This type turns his or her spouse into a dishrag without even realizing he or she is doing it. A couple like this is not even capable of talking to each other. The scapegoater can destroy entire personalities, shattering them and leaving only a broken shell.

The Lock: The fourth type of partner is the person who is a lock. He locks his spouse up. How does he do it? The minute his partner wants to say something he says, "Oh, I can't bear you lecturing me!" He doesn't let the other person open his or her mouth — the minute they begin to speak, he cuts them off. You can't communicate with a person like this.

If you feel you may bear some sort of resemblance to any of these four types, start putting it right, because marriage is a partnership. True partners care for each other, understand each other, and help each other. Love can be demonstrated in a million ways. Seeing that the house is warm on a cold wintry day, or having a hot meal ready, is an expression of caring. A couple can reach a stage of so much mutual sharing and caring that the other partner feels it every minute of the day.

Every human being longs for a friend in life. Everyone longs for a partner with whom to share his dreams, ideals, and whatever is important to him. Your greatest friend and partner is your husband. There is no closer human relationship. The more capable we are of loving our partner in life, the closer the relationship between man and wife, the more capable we are of loving Hashem.

A husband needs a wife who is prepared to listen to him, someone who cares so much that she will always balance him so he won't get off the track. It's detrimental for a person to be alone. He can feel guilty when he shouldn't, and praise himself when perhaps he shouldn't. When there are two, they balance each other. Each partner shows the other person the right perspective, by saying, for instance, "You're not as bad as you think; you're not to blame." That's the meaning of partnership in marriage.

In order to attain such closeness, husband and wife should direct themselves to building and strengthening the partnership. They need to base their relationship on the assumption that sharing the problems and experiences of marriage is preferable to living a single life. People who are single or have been left alone often tell us how lonely they feel because they have no one with whom to share. Sometimes people don't appreciate what they have when they have it. So care for and develop your partnership — it is very precious.

Take the other partner into your private world of thoughts and feelings. Be open with each other. Some people think being open means telling the other partner all the silly things you've done in your life. This is not necessary. As Jews, we don't confess to a priest; we say *vidui* and confess to Hashem. So don't feel you have to confess to your husband and tell him all the foolish things you did before you met him! You must know when to keep quiet. Don't ever tell your husband things which will cause him to lose respect for you. If you are disturbed by something in your past, go to a rabbi — but don't talk to your husband about it, for it can ruin your marriage. Never let him lose respect for you.

What *should* be shared is everything that is part of your marriage. Being open with each other means — and this is especially important to understand — being open about everything that is *mutual.*

From the minute you meet.

When Rivkah first saw Yitzchak, she covered herself with a scarf out of modesty and fear. She felt unworthy, and stood in awe. From the beginning, this was the nature of their relationship. It may be that because she interacted with Yitzchak in this way, Rivkah was never able to tell him that Eisav was not what Eisav seemed to be and was therefore undeserving of the blessings.[1]

True partners never assume or presume. Wouldn't it be fantastic if one's husband was a mind reader? In the meantime, don't assume that your husband knows exactly what is going on in your mind, because he is not as yet a mind reader!

One of the first things a girl should realize even before marriage is that a man thinks logically, but a woman thinks with her emotions. Your thinking and his thinking may be entirely different. If you think a certain thing should be this way, often he cannot even grasp why. You must explain it to him, because his mind works differently.

Many couples ruin their *shalom bayis* because the wife assumes her husband should know certain things. For instance, one day, when a newly married husband comes home from *shul* in the morning, his wife says, "Where's the milk? Did you buy bread?"

He: "What milk? What bread?"

She: "Where's your common sense? You know there isn't any bread or milk in the house! Why didn't you bring milk?"

He: "You didn't ask."

She said one thing and he heard another, or she didn't say anything at all, so of course he couldn't know. She assumes he is a mind reader, but he isn't. Never assume — just say what you mean.

Of course, a wife shouldn't act like a general giving orders. Some women give orders right and left all day long. Usually when people are ordered to do something they resent it and refuse to do it. It is always much better to speak as if you are asking for a favor. That is the way you should talk to Hashem as well, like a poor man asking for a favor. If you ask your husband to do something in a very polite way he will never refuse. Let us say his name is David. Try saying, in a nice tone of voice, "David, I would like to ask you a favor. I hope you don't mind, but I would really appreciate it if you would please take the garbage with you when you go out." Now is there a husband in the world who is going to refuse such a wife? When he feels he is doing you a favor, he will do it gladly.

---

1. *Bereishis* 24:55. This was, of course, part of Hashem's plan so that Yaakov could receive the blessings.

The following twenty questions will deepen communication between husband and wife. Many couples have been helped by using this list as a tool to improve their marriage. A couple can work on one or two questions an evening. Each one of the partners should answer each question fully while the other partner either listens and/or writes down the response.

1. **What do I expect from you? What do you expect from me?**

2. **How do I feel about you? How do you feel about me?**

   A woman once said that although she is married and has six children, she and her husband have no *shalom bayis*. She said she has never told her husband she loves him because she is too shy. What kind of a marriage is that?! After eight or ten years of marriage she is too shy to tell him she loves him?

3. **Do I give and receive enough emotional support?**

4. **How does each one of us feel about things that are important to us?**

   Sometimes people have been married for twenty years and still don't know these things about each other because they have never gotten around to talking about them.

5. **What are our mutual aims and our mutual plans for the future?**

6. **Is it easy for us to decide things together?**

7. **What are our hopes and aims for our children?**

   Sometimes partners don't agree about how to raise the children. This is very bad. One of the most important basics of good parenting is a united front.

8. **What are my obligations to you? What are your obligations to me?**

   There are no "rights" in marriage, only obligations. Only when you have fulfilled your obligations have you then earned rights.

9. **Do I fulfill my obligations?**

10. **Do I reveal my true feelings to my partner?**

    Some of us are very good actors. We never tell the truth. It's as if we can't be bothered. Lots of people keep their marriage going but they couldn't care less. Their attitude is one of: Let him get on with his business and I'll get on with mine. That's not a marriage!

11. What duties and responsibilities do each of us have in the home?

Everyone should know what his duties and responsibilities are. A woman should not do everything in the home while the husband and children act like guests. Sometimes you see a woman who works day and night while the other members of the family come in and eat whenever they please, as if they were living in a hotel. The family doesn't respect her because they see the home as hers and expect her to take care of it. But the home belongs to everyone, and everyone has a share in it. Each member of the family must bear the burden of the home by carrying out his duties and fulfilling his responsibilities.

12. Is there something I do which always annoys my partner? Write down the things you do which make your partner angry.

Two people get married and each has his *meshugasin* (idiosyncrasies) — plenty of them. If there are certain *meshugasin* that drive the other partner crazy, drop them — you can live without them. Adjust. Being flexible is part of being a proper wife. The same standard applies to the husband as well. There may be, for example, a husband who the minute he walks in the door takes off his shoes and leaves them in the middle of the hall. When a young couple gets married and the wife discovers that her husband does this she should handle the problem intelligently. She certainly doesn't want to start arguing. The first time it happens, she picks up his shoes and puts them where they should be and doesn't say a word. Then there's a second time and a third time, and still she keeps quiet. The fourth time it happens, she can wait for a time when they are sitting and talking, and say in a voice dripping with honey, "I have a very big request to make of you. I want to ask you, I hope you don't mind, but it upsets me very much when you come into the house and leave your shoes in the middle of everything. Would you mind, please, doing me a big favor, I would be so obliged, I would be so grateful and appreciate it so much . . ." Use the whole dictionary! ". . . if you would be so good as to put your shoes in the corner." She has him laughing and he will do it — there will be no anger.

If there is anything *you* do that annoys him, drop it. Decide it is something you are going to work at because you don't want to annoy him. Ask him what about you annoys him; then you can tell him what annoys you.

13. What bad habits and *middos* do you feel you need to correct?

Everyone has bad habits and bad *middos.* It is a lifetime job to strengthen the good *middos* and repair the bad ones.

14. What good *middos* should I acquire?

15. What value and meaning does our marriage have for me?

You should feel there is a special meaning to your marriage.

16. Who or what would I miss most if it was lost? What is the most precious thing in my life?

17. What gift can I give you to cause you the greatest joy? What makes you happy?

It doesn't matter how much money you spend, as long as you show you care. Let's say you are out shopping and you see a piece of cake. Your husband happens to love cake but you don't usually bake because you don't want to gain weight. Now you buy two pieces and in the evening when he comes home you make it a special occasion. Sit down together, share the cake and have a little chat — it's a pleasure! Remember: It doesn't matter what the gift is — it's not the monetary value that matters, it's what you put into it, your showing that you care.

18. What can we possibly do to make our mutual life happier and more joyful?

19. What is a perfect partnership?

Answer: Sharing with all your heart and soul the worries and joys; sharing every minute, every day, and all of your life.

20. How should I conduct myself always?

With flexibility, with gentleness, and with forgiveness.

Learn to be forgiving; know when to give in. Stubborn people say they are always right. Even at best we are not always right. As one saying has it: "Be clever, be wise — don't be right." The person with the right answer isn't always the winner.

A woman once related a most remarkable story:

Even as a girl I already knew I wanted to become religious, but my family was adamantly opposed. One day, my mother, who was dying of cancer, called me over and told me that if I became religious I would never be able to marry. My mother made me swear that I would not become a ba'alas teshuvah before I got married.

While I was in college, I met a Jewish boy I liked very much. When he asked me to marry him, I agreed . . . on one condition: I wanted to become observant. I told him I wanted to keep the three main tenets of Judaism — family purity, kashrus, and Shabbos — and be allowed to raise the children the way I wanted. He agreed, and we married and came to live in Israel.

For sixteen years I was observant while my husband was entirely non-religious. I used to go with him to a restaurant and sit beside him watching him eat treif — but I stayed patient and kept our marriage together. One day a co-worker of his dragged him to a seminar (I would never have suggested it, because he would never have agreed). My husband eventually became a ba'al teshuvah, but did only the minimum. For instance, he only davened at home and didn't want to go to shul or any shiurim.

I decided to ask for advice on how to improve the situation, and was told to organize classes in our home — that way he wouldn't have any choice but to listen. I did, and I invited the best speakers from the ba'al teshuvah movement. After a period of several years, I began to notice a gradual change.

And then, a dream came true: my son was accepted at one of the best yeshivos in the country! I could hardly believe it. I never thought one of my children would be accepted into such a prestigious yeshivah. Why, there must be at least ten applicants for every place — it's one of the hardest to get into. They don't accept just anybody, only the best boys in the country. The mashgiach told me that I have such a wonderful son, every yeshivah would be proud to accept him.

How did this remarkable woman achieve this triumph in the home against such odds? Through gentleness. You cannot achieve anything by fighting. You'll only rub the other person the wrong way and awaken resentment, opposition, and aggression. If you want to achieve something, it can only be achieved through ways of pleasantness.

Having the last word won't make you the winner, but letting the other person feel he is right, will. The main thing is that the marriage be fantastic — that's what really matters. Once a woman said, "I'm always right." I thought to myself, after you finish arguing with him he gives up! For the sake of *shalom bayis,* let *him* be right — that's womanly wisdom.

4
Faithfulness

he next step in creating communication is faithfulness. It is important to know what we mean by this for it can express itself in various ways. Lack of faithfulness means, for example, that you come home and say to your husband, "Why can't you be like Shoshi's husband? He's so handy around the house, he can fix anything." Faithfulness means that you **never** compare your husband with anyone else's husband. Remember: Your husband probably knows things that her husband doesn't know. You have to accept him the way he is and take it from there. He has his virtues and his faults. If he's not handy around the house, then you should be!

There are seven conditions to a true contract between man and wife at the time of their betrothal: It is a bond which is everlasting, righteous, just, kind, merciful, faithful and cognizant of Hashem. These seven correspond to the seven blessings of the wedding ceremony. There is an especially close relationship between the sixth condition and the sixth blessing. The sixth condition mentioned at the time of engagement, *I betroth you in faithfulness*, declares that the husband will rejoice with his wife and never look at another woman. Similarly, the sixth blessing uttered during the marriage ceremony states: "You shall gladden beloved companions like You gladden Your creations in Gan Eden of yore." Why does the blessing refer to the joy of Adam and Chavah rather than the joy of Avraham and Sarah, Yitzchak and Rivkah, or Yaakov and Rachel? The answer is that the joy of Adam and Chavah was unsurpassed. There were no other human beings in the world to come between them or dilute their pure happiness. So too, we hope that the bliss of every couple will be as complete, with their eyes, hearts, and thoughts fixed only upon one another.

In other words, your home should be a Gan Eden, with you being Chavah, and your husband Adam. Nobody else exists for a woman except her husband. For a husband, nobody else exists except his wife.

Adam and Chavah's wedding in Gan Eden was very beautiful. Hashem decorated Chavah for Adam with twenty-four jewels; there were ten wedding canopies, each one more beautiful than the next. Hashem Himself was the *mesader kiddushin* and the whole Heavenly Court came to the wedding. The angels escorted them to the wedding canopy and all the heavenly host danced and sang, just like people do at weddings.

Every man should feel on the day of his wedding that he is Adam, and every woman that she is Chavah; they should both feel as if they are the only people in the world. Every husband should tell his wife, all his life, as Adam did: "You are part of my flesh and part of my bone." You should feel that you are living only for each other, and every man should feel that the only woman in the world is his wife — all other women do not exist for him. And every woman should feel that the only man in the world is her husband — all the other men do not exist for her. If you think that way all your life, if no one else exists for you except your husband and no one else exists for him except you, you are going to live in Gan Eden all your life!

Some people make a big mistake — they think Gan Eden begins after 120 years. They're wrong. Gan Eden starts in this world. We are creating our Gan Eden here; it's an eternal relationship. It's part of the World to Come and you are working on it now. When we move on, after 120 years, it will be like moving from one place to another together. It's up to you to create that kind of relationship. Happy is the person who has the sense to know how to live in Gan Eden all his life. So feel that you exist only for each other. Don't make any comparisons — her husband can do such-and-such and my husband can't. Remember the assignment to write down all the wonderful traits you saw in your husband before you married him? Were you surprised to find he still has them? One of our problems is that the minute we get married we start looking for the bad traits instead of seeing the good ones. Look at all his virtues, not at his faults. Maximize his good points by encouraging them. When we tell somebody he is worthless, he begins to feel that he is worthless. If we build him up, the sky's the limit.

The story of Devorah the prophetess can teach us a great deal:

> Devorah's husband was a not a very learned man, and this pained her. "How can I elevate him so that he will have a portion in the World to Come?" she wondered. After careful thought, she came up with an idea. "Let us make a partnership," she suggested to him. "I'll work at making wicks for the golden candelabra in the Mishkan and you'll take them there. That way, we'll both gain merit." Her unspoken thought was that if he would spend time at the Mishkan, he would be changed by the sanctity of the place.
>
> Devorah had an additional motivation. "My husband will meet such wonderful, righteous people there," she reasoned. "Being in close proximity to greatness will surely have an influence for the good."
>
> Devorah could have just taken a few threads, twisted them, made some wicks and been finished in ten minutes. Instead, she put her whole heart and soul into the wicks she made. They were so wonderful that she was called "the woman of the torches," for each wick gave the light of a torch.

Hashem then said to her, "Devorah, you wanted to make his light shine, I will make your light shine throughout Klal Yisrael." And she became a prophetess and a judge in an era when Pinchas the grandson of Aharon was the Kohen Gadol![1]

Nowadays, if a wife wants her husband to go somewhere she says, "Oh, GO!" If he doesn't want to, she starts arguing: "What are you sitting around for? Pick yourself up and go!" His response is: "I don't want to!" and right there a quarrel starts. Devorah, though, used her womanly wisdom to elevate her husband without pushing.

✍ A Sense of Humor

Another necessary ingredient for communication is a sense of humor. It is an absolute necessity for any marriage and if you weren't born with one, then cultivate it. Get people to explain jokes to you in the beginning until you catch on, then learn to laugh and see the funny side of life. Laughter is very healthy for us. When we laugh we inhale a lot of air, and it's very good to get all that oxygen into the body. A person who can see the funny side of life is never going to be unhappy because there's humor in everything. It's like a seasoning: If you cook something without salt, you can't eat it; it's tasteless. The salt of marriage is a sense of humor.

If you have a sense of humor, you can always get by. Let's say there is tension between the two of you and one of the partners has a good sense of humor and starts cracking jokes. Can you get annoyed and start screaming? You'll start laughing instead, and the minute you laugh all the tension goes away. So first try to look at the funny side of everything and see if you can make a joke about it. Then there will be nothing to fight about.

---

1. Based on *Tanna d'Vei Eliyahu*, Chap. 1.

5

Keep Growing

Communication with one's self is the beginning of personality growth. A person who is honest with himself can reach endless heights. King Solomon, the wisest of all men, always communicated with himself: "I gave to my heart . . ."; "I took notice with my heart . . ."; "I told my heart to understand . . ."; "I said within my heart . . ."; "I took everything to my heart . . ."; "I spoke to my heart."[1]

Everyone must learn to speak with his soul. A person may be capable of talking to others, yet not be capable of being alone with himself. When he finds himself alone, he becomes afraid and lonely,

---

1. *Koheles* Chap. 1.

and feels as if the world is empty. He feels like a stranger to himself and runs away from meeting himself face to face.

They say that a person who is afraid to be with himself is really shaming himself.[1]

We are our own greatest friend, yet we turn our backs on ourselves. Without the ability to communicate with ourselves, we remain strangers to ourselves. Instead of living with our own dreams and thoughts, we think only of our friends and their reactions to what we're going to say.

Make an appointment to talk to yourself. Imagine your soul standing alone in front of the Heavenly Throne,[2] as did Avraham, who went out "early in the morning" to be alone with his Creator; Yitzchak, who "went out to meditate and pray in the field"; and Yaakov, who "encountered" Hashem, a reference to prayer. They knew the secret of being alone with their soul.

Many *gedolim* kept a notebook to further their self-communication and self-knowledge. Every evening they would sit down with their personal notebook and go over every hour of the day, asking themselves: What did I do at this minute? Did I waste a minute when I could have been learning? The Vilna Gaon knew exactly to the minute if he had made use of every minute of the day, and the Chofetz Chaim would cry over a minute or two if he felt he had wasted the time. We may be far from their level, but we can turn ourselves into wonderful people by acquiring the ability to communicate with ourselves.

Reb Yosef Yoizel of Novarodok was a successful entrepreneur while still a young man. One day he met Reb Yisrael Salanter and they began talking. Reb Yosef Yoizel explained that he was working instead of being in yeshivah because, as he put it, "You need with what to live." Reb Yisrael Salanter looked at him and said, "You're looking for something to live with, but what have you prepared to die with?"

Reb Yosef Yoizel was a very deep person and these words hit him like a bomb. He went straight home, sold his business, settled all his affairs and shut himself in a little hut

---

1. *Chovos HaLevavos, Sha'ar Cheshbon HaNefesh* 1:1.
2. *Rabbeinu Yonah, Sha'arei Teshuvah* 1:21.

in the middle of a forest. He arranged to have food placed on his windowsill once a day, and went outside only to go home for Shabbos. He stayed there alone for fourteen years!

After fourteen years, Reb Yisrael Salanter told him, "Enough. You have to start doing something for Klal Yisrael." Reb Yosef Yoizel left his isolation and went on to found 200 yeshivos in pre-war Europe.

It's very easy to say that we should communicate with ourselves, but how exactly is it done?

The first step is to find the time and place. Decide that tomorrow morning, after everyone is out of the house, you're going to let everything else wait so that you can spend half an hour being alone with yourself.

Once you've made the appointment and you are alone with yourself, what's next? What are you going to talk about?!

If you think for a minute, you'll agree that there is an inner dialogue going on within us all the time. Without being aware of it consciously, our minds are constantly carrying on a conversation. Sometimes we're annoyed with someone, and then our thoughts are filled with negative comments about that person. Or we think about recent events, community news, etc. Our thoughts come and go as they please because our thinking is unfocused.

The minute we realize we can take this inner dialogue and direct it rationally to make use of it, we will discover how constructive and positive it can be.

Thinking has a great deal to do with our feelings and our functioning. If you think you can, you can. By directing and clarifying our aims and plans in life we will be able to focus our thinking, making it very constructive and productive.

First, **choose your subject**. Then, **gather your facts** in a very orderly way. Write down all the ideas that come up. One idea may connect with something you've thought of before. Our mind is like a computer and has already amassed a tremendous amount of knowledge. If your knowledge is orderly, it connects with other things. It is essential to feel interested and relaxed while you're doing this.

For instance, you might decide to think about your family vacation. Or, ways to bring up the children, make the home function better, improve health or manage income. Gather information in an orderly way. It will enter your subconscious and then, if a problem arises, your mental computer — the subconscious — will work on it.

Study your problem and **analyze it in depth**. Be creative.

Then **leave it**. You've done everything you can.

Not every problem will be solved immediately. You may wake up in the middle of the night with an answer. Or, one morning you'll suddenly think of a new idea. What's happening is what is called *binah*, understanding one thing from the other. Your mind is automatically taking the new information that you set into place and trying out all kinds of variations. You will become very creative and your inner computer, which is coordinating all your ideas, will help you solve your problems. Suddenly thoughts will click into place, giving you a solution to a problem.

Be open with yourself. Talk to yourself about your dreams. You can't live in a daydream, but you *can* put your dreams into practice. Remember, if you're capable of dreaming it, you're capable of turning it into reality. Let's say you have a dream about a certain thing you'd love to do. Don't think it's unattainable. Take a piece of paper and write down, "This is my dream. How can I possibly achieve it?" Systematically write down ways of turning your dreams into reality.

Get started — even if it takes you ten years, it doesn't matter. Just get started now and work systematically to realize your dreams. A person who knows how to direct this inner dialogue in a highly creative, constructive, and positive way can gain tremendous achievement in personality development.

Rehearse How To Act

Another advantage we get from this inner dialogue is that it prepares us for the future. For instance, if a shy person comes to a meeting unprepared, he may become so nervous that he forgets everything he planned to say. But if he has rehearsed beforehand, saying to himself, "If I'm asked this question, this will be my answer . . ." he will be self-confident and inspire the confidence of others. Or, a mother can think, "If the children act in such-and-such a way, this is how I'll react . . ." If you mentally rehearse your reaction to various situations, when that situation occurs you're ready for it. You won't lose your head, and you won't feel ashamed afterwards.

Use the following 13 points to work on becoming a wonderful person:

1. Never stop educating yourself as a human being. Study *mussar*, learn more about Judaism and the Torah perspective on life.
2. Work on perfecting your character. Always, day in and day out.
3. Develop your powers of concentration. Nowadays, when people ask for advice they don't hear the answer because they're so busy hearing what they want to hear. Then they'll go to a third person and tell him you said something else entirely.

> *Two people came to the Chazon Ish to ask the same question. The first one went in and the Chazon Ish answered him. The man left, then told his friend what he'd heard from the sage. The Chazon Ish, standing near the window, overheard the exchange. Later the Chazon Ish commented: "He didn't say what I said. He repeated what he wanted me to say, not what he heard me say."*

4. Be interested in every task and every subject. Whatever you're doing, give it your maximum attention and interest, no matter how trivial it may seem. If you're interested and you do it enthusiastically, you will enjoy it.
5. Be orderly. Live by the motto: "A place for everything, and everything in its place." Bring order to your mind, and organize your life.
6. Be relaxed. If you're tense, you paralyze your thinking. You can go to a relaxation class to learn the basics of relaxation. You will function 100% better. Whatever you do will be done in a calm manner, more easily and without stress. Relaxation enables us to make the maximum use of our time and should be part of every woman's life.
7. Don't spend your life crying over spilled milk. Most people are always busy regretting what they did yesterday. They often say, "If only I hadn't done such and such, this never would have happened."

Stop regretting the past. At the most, say to yourself, "I'll do better next time." Some people get all worked up over what they said and did. "Why did I say that to her?" they ask themselves repeatedly. "I should never have said that." They can't fall asleep because they're so busy thinking about what happened. "She probably thinks I'm . . . .," they worry.

Don't do it. Leave it alone, it's over and finished. Instead, plan your next conversation with that person.

Some people spend a lifetime on regret, talking about nothing but yesterday. But yesterday is dead. At best you can say that next time you'll try to do better. Stop regretting all your past errors and blaming yourself. Otherwise, you'll ruin your life. It's time consuming and health consuming, distracting and self-destructive.

8. Sit and don't do anything. This secret, revealed to us by our Sages, is one of the best pieces of advice ever given. Let's say you've tried to solve a certain problem and you haven't been able to. You've gotten as much information about it as you could, and now you've come to a dead end. Leave it for now. Often, problems solve themselves. Sometimes time solves the problem. Sometimes, if you leave it alone and stop churning it in your mind, the solution may come to you on its own.

9. Ask yourself, "What kind of person would I like to be, spiritually and physically, and with what character traits?" Remember, if you think you can, you can. Get started. Make your plan and systematically start turning yourself into the kind of person you want to be.

10. Persevere. In other words, stick with it. The person who sticks with it and is determined to achieve what he set out to do doesn't quit in the middle. He won't become discouraged, and he will *never* give up. Don't say, I can't do it, it's not working. What's the sign of genius and character? When you come to a point where you can't proceed anymore yet you say, "I'll give it another try. I'm not giving up yet."

Of course, if a person has decided that he's going to insist on a certain foolishness, that's nothing but stubbornness. If a child has a strong will, you have to channel it in the right direction and make sure this trait is not used for foolishness. If he's strong-willed in learning, he'll be the *gadol hador*. There were *gedolim* who were so determined not to fall asleep learning that they used to put their feet in cold water — in the winter! That's perseverance.

11. Never become discouraged or depressed. You can't become perfect overnight, so don't decide you're going to become the most wonderful personality by tomorrow morning. It won't work. If you are already a wonderful person, decide that by the time you're a grandmother, you hope to be somebody very special — that's a realistic aim. For now, work on being the best wife and mother you can — and don't get discouraged.

    There will always be setbacks. Perseverance means continuing to try even if you have setbacks and even if you think you're failing. You failed?! Who says you failed? It may just be time to start again in a different direction. Failure is sometimes very good indeed. It may force us to focus on something else. So get started again.

12. Develop skills. Ask yourself, in a practical way, "What do I need to know in order to be the most perfect wife and mother?" And then write it all down and get started. If it's connected to the home, learn it, work at it. The more skilled you become, the more it will help you build up your self-image.

    Many women become depressed about not having certain skills. "I always wanted to learn . . . I always wanted to know how to . . ." How many women cry that they're terrible at homemaking, that they "can't even sew on a button." None of this is *kabbalah*! It's something you can learn. Start finding a way to acquire all the skills that cause you to have an inferiority complex. Make a list of what you always wanted to know but still don't. Then prove to yourself that you're capable of doing the things you thought you couldn't. Don't say, "I'm a nothing and a nobody." Who says so?! Prove to yourself that you're a something and a somebody. You should be able to respect yourself as a wife and a mother.

13. Begin turning yourself into the shining personality you want to be. Dedicate yourself, focus yourself, and discipline yourself.

✒ Believe in Yourself

If you think you are beaten, you are.
If you think you dare not, you don't.
If you like to win, but think you can't, it's almost certain you won't.
If you think you'll lose, you're lost. Success begins with a strong will — it's all in the state of mind.
Life's battles don't always go to the stronger or the faster man, but sooner or later, the man who wins is the one who thinks he can.

— anon.

We have free choice — it's in our hands.

Create a perfect self-image, because the minute you do, you are encouraging yourself further, focusing on inner controls and attaining an inner discipline.

Once Eliyahu was walking in the fields when he saw a man plowing with twelve oxen. He looked at this farmer and through ruach hakodesh saw that he had within him the ability to become his most outstanding disciple.

Eliyahu removed his cloak and threw it down at the feet of this man plowing the field. When the cloak fell at his feet, the young man looked up from his plowing and their eyes locked. This farm worker then said to Eliyahu, "Please wait for me. I shall return home to kiss my parents good-bye, and then I'll come with you."

This farm worker was Elisha. He took the twelve oxen and sacrificed them to Hashem, went home and said good-bye to his parents, and then followed Eliyahu to serve him. He eventually became Eliyahu's greatest disciple.

When the time came for Eliyahu to ascend to Heaven while still alive, he said to Elisha, "You can ask me whatever you wish before I leave you." Elisha said: "I want to be a prophet twice as great as you." Eliyahu answered: "If you have within you the ability to elevate yourself and foresee what will happen within the next few minutes, that will be a sign that you will be a prophet twice as great as I am. It all depends on you!"

Elisha looked into the future and saw the chariot of fire and the horses of fire, and Eliyahu going up alive in fire to Heaven. And Elisha did become a prophet twice as great as Eliyahu, even reaching the level where he revived the dead.

Even as great a prophet as Eliyahu couldn't give such an exalted level to his disciple. He told him clearly, "It's up to you. You'll have to be able to elevate yourself." [1]

The ability to build a fantastic personality and become a great person, to focus on your inner dialogue and build your self-image, depends on you. If you can envision it, you can achieve it. Make the effort and turn your dreams into reality. As King Solomon said: "Drink the waters from your well; they are for you alone and not for any others." [2] If you "drink your own water," i.e. draw from deep within yourself, you will do a kindness to yourself.

"I want you to know," began the well-known rebbetzin admired for her extensive community activities, "that of all the lessons I learned, the one that made the greatest impression on me was the one about not blaming the past.

"You see," she continued, "I grew up in a vehemently anti-religious environment. My whole upbringing was secular in the extreme. I didn't think I would be able to shut the door on my past.

"But then I heard you say that the minute we stop blaming circumstances and other people for our faults and failures, that's when we free ourselves. I decided to begin again."

Once this woman realized she could forget the past, she was able to start anew. And she did. She married and raised a wonderful family, becoming an outstanding woman able to help and inspire others.

Everyone can build anew. Make yourself into a fantastic person.

---

1. *Melachim I* 19:19, Radak.
2. *Mishlei* 5:15.

6

Controlling Anger

Listen my child to the
mussar of your father, and don't
forsake your mother's Torah. Accustom
yourself to speak whatever you say
calmly to every person at all times . . .
— *Iggeres HaRamban*

voiding anger is so important that the Ramban begins his famous letter of advice to his son by telling him how to avoid anger: ". . . speak whatever you say calmly to every person at all times . . ."

We all know how terrible anger is. The *Zohar* says that a person who loses his temper loses his soul and is given a lesser one instead. If he goes so far as to throw things — on the ground or at people — or if he breaks things, it's as if he brought a sacrifice to Satan!

Controlling anger should be at the top of everyone's list of character traits to perfect. Here is a way to work on anger, or any other area you wish to improve:

Each week choose to work on a different character trait:

1. Take each day as a unit.
2. Break each day into smaller units of two or three hours.
3. Find verses or sayings which refer to these character traits and repeat the chosen verse endlessly — at least 1,000 times. If it speaks to you, it's yours. You can take, for instance, the verse from the *Iggeres HaRamban:* כל הכועס כל מיני גיהנם שולטין בו — *All kinds of Gehinnom control an angry person.* Or, as one woman did, the verse כי כעס בחיק כסילים ינוח — *Anger rests in the heart of fools.*[1] Then, every time you feel yourself wanting to get angry, you say, "I'm not a fool!" This technique has helped many people — it's literally saved their marriage and children. But the verse must be repeated at least 1,000 for proper effect, Rabbi Yisrael Salanter tells us, because only then, if you repeat it with enthusiasm at least 1,000 times, does it becomes part of your subconscious and enter your inner being. It then begins to work on you and change you. The next time you feel like losing your temper you will be in control because you will hear the verse like a tape playing in your mind.

> *Reb Yisrael Salanter would take a different verse each day and repeat it endlessly. There's a story told that once he was traveling with another great Torah scholar who slept in a room adjoining his. Reb Yisrael spent the whole night walking back and forth. He would always take his shoes off so as not to disturb others, but people would put their ears to the door to hear what he was saying and learn from it. This night, his neighbor heard him repeat the last verse in*

---

1. *Koheles* 7:9.

Koheles over and over again: *"Fear Hashem and keep His mitzvos because that is all that a human being is about."*

In a small personal notebook, write down the verse you are going to say at least 1,000 times during the coming week. At the top of the first page, write down: "1,000 points." Keep a day-to-day record of your behavior with respect to the character trait you have chosen to work on. If you are working on anger, for instance, watch your reactions during the day. If you slip and get angry, write down the incident and deduct some points. If you go through a whole day without getting angry, reward yourself with some small treat. If by the end of the week you still have at least 700 points, you deserve a prize — buy yourself something special. It may sound like a joke, but by rewarding yourself you will not only become convinced that you are achieving your goal, you will also become convinced of your self-worth. Try it! You are going to improve.

The *Chovos HaTalmidim*, a popular guide for students written by a great Torah scholar in pre-war Poland, offers two very effective techniques for controlling anger:

1. Instead of letting off steam — giving back to the other person what you think he deserves and thus ruining the relationship — sit down with a pen and paper. Paper is very patient; you can write down whatever you like. So take pen in hand and write a letter to the person who made you angry and give him the biggest telling off you can possibly think of. He's a this and a that and you'd like to give him . . . Just write it all down. Then, when you've finished, don't send it, keep it. If you feel a little bit less angry but still haven't gotten it out of your system, read the letter aloud to yourself and put it in a drawer where nobody can see it. Wait. After a few hours read it again, and the next day read it again. By writing it all down you are getting rid of your resentment. Do this until you no longer feel angry. Then destroy the letter. The next time you meet the person you'll be able to say, "Hello, how are you!" with no anger at all. You have gotten rid of it in the best possible way without doing any harm or damage to anyone.

2. Develop an automatic response to instinctively refrain from anger. Every night we sleep in a bed and no matter how narrow that bed is, we don't fall off — it's remarkable! When a person is fast asleep, he may turn over many times a night. Actually, he should roll out of bed, yet he doesn't. Why? Because we have already developed an automatic response so that the minute we reach the edge of the bed we turn over and don't fall off. Who falls out of bed? Only a very young child who hasn't developed this instinct, or an elderly person who has lost it. If a person who is asleep can control himself, how is it possible that a person who is awake can't control his anger? What anger shows is lack of control. Decide that the minute you want to get angry you'll say to yourself, "I am not going to fall out of bed." And you won't.

A wonderful story is told about a woman in the marketplace selling apples. She got into an argument with one of her customers, lost her temper and started screaming, shouting, and cursing. The whole marketplace was in an uproar. The customer turned and walked away while the seller was still shouting and screaming after her . . . until suddenly, the apple lady spotted a new customer approaching. In a flash she was all smiles, "Madam, please buy my apples — they're so beautiful."

What tremendous powers of control a human being has if it is worth his while!

Rabbi Elya Lopian had nine sons, and when he had to discipline them he would say, "Wait a minute, first of all I have to put on this special coat." The children knew that he was always in control. This can help you too. Get yourself a red robe and leave it hanging on the bathroom door. When the need arises, say (not as a threat) to the children, "Children, I think Mommy might have to put on the red robe in order to get angry." This way the children see that if you do punish them it is not because you are getting rid of your anger but because you are trying to discipline them for their own good. That's the right way to educate children.

Another good suggestion for curing ourselves of anger is to have somebody tape us when we lose our temper. Arrange it beforehand, and then have somebody make a tape, and listen to how you sound when you are shouting. It's a cure for life!

Count to twenty before you begin speaking, or take ten deep breaths.

Lower your voice. Force yourself to speak in a calm tone. As soon as you raise your voice you lose control; the minute you lower it, you gain control.

Agree beforehand that the minute one partner starts raising his voice, the other will take a step or move his chair backwards. The minute he calms down, start coming forward again.

Fine yourself. Have a special *pushke* for fines; every time you lose your temper put in two dollars for *tzedakah*. (This is what the *gedolei mussar* would do.) You'll have a lot of money for charity! But once you see that getting angry is a very expensive business, you'll stop.

Accept whatever is happening to you. If it's *min hashamayim* (Divinely ordained) then what are you angry about? And everything is *min hashamayim*! Accept the message you are being given. This is part of *bitachon*. If I have *bitachon*, trust in Hashem, then I know that everything that happens is *min hashamayim*. So what am I getting angry about? The child broke something? It was *min hashamayim*. The baby spilled her food? *Min hashamayim*. It was only a *nisayon*, a test for me. Everything Hashem does is for the good, so what are we complaining about? Who and what are we angry at?[1]

We are not angels, we are human beings. You get up early in the morning and go to bed late at night, and during that busy day many things happen which may irritate you and arouse resentment. It may have been that your spouse didn't act as you would have wished and he annoyed you. When you sit down to talk things over, get it off your chest — use the "balloon method." Every time you are annoyed and find yourself pushing down your resentment so as not to show it, it accumulates — your balloon is blowing up. Once it's stretched to its limit, it bursts. Make sure to let the air out of the balloon every day. Get rid of accumulated resentment. For instance, you can say, "Moshe, today when you said this, it hurt me a lot. I was very upset about it." Talk it over. But make sure

---

1. There are three excellent books which deal with the subject of anger: 1) *Sidra Tikkun HaMiddos*, by Rabbi Avraham Tobalsky, is a series of books on character improvement, and the volume on anger is called *Haser Ka'as MiLibecha*. The title is taken from a verse in *Koheles*: "Remove anger from your heart." 2) *Alufeinu Mesubalim*, by Rabbi Teharani; 3) *Erech Apayim*.

your timing is right. After you have already talked about various other things, and after you have solved problems together and reached a stage where the atmosphere is right, then you can say, "This is something that upset me."

You *must* work things out together because if things upset you and you are not working them out you are spoiling your marriage. Never let your balloon accumulate resentment — let the air out daily. Otherwise it can burst and ruin your *shalom bayis.*

End each day by reviewing it. Make an accounting and work out what went on. A group of women in America once had a sticker which summed it up: "Never put out the light on a fight."

Once Rabbi Abba went out from the gate of the city. He saw a poor worker in front of him who looked very tired. The man went over to a building whose walls were on the verge of collapse. Although the building looked as though it would fall down any minute, the poor man went into the building, lay down, and fell asleep. Rabbi Abba was very upset when he saw this. Why, the man could be killed any minute! He decided to watch over him. While sitting there, Rabbi Abba saw a huge poisonous snake come out of the ground and approach the man. He was petrified, but at the very last minute a wild animal jumped out from among the stones of the broken-down building and killed the snake. The poor man slept through the incident, blissfully unaware. When he awoke, he got up and walked away from the building . . . and the entire ruin collapsed!

There is no such thing as coincidence, so Rabbi Abba went over to the poor man and asked him, "What are your good deeds? In what merit were you saved?"

"I am just a plain ordinary person," the man replied.

But Rabbi Abba knew there must be a deep meaning to the events he had witnessed. "It is not possible. I just saw two obvious miracles — they weren't even hidden. Why did Hashem do two obvious miracles for you? How are you worthy of that? What are your good deeds?"

"Well," answered the man, "I am very particular about one thing. I never go to bed at night without forgiving everyone

*who offended or hurt me, or without asking forgiveness of any
person I may have hurt. I finish accounts every day."*

This is called making a *cheshbon hanefesh,* a spiritual accounting. Be a good bookkeeper. Finish off the day's accounts, work them
out — don't carry over the minuses of yesterday to the next day.
Take each day as a unit and live each day anew, for each new day is
a new creation and you are a new person. When you work out the
accounts and start each day anew — taking the air out of the balloon — you are going to have a wonderful marriage.

7

A Shining Countenance

"**M**ay Hashem bless you and keep you safe, may Hashem make His Face shine upon you . . . may Hashem lift up His face to you and give you peace."

A "shining" face means a smiling face.[1]

We ask Hashem to smile at us because we have been told that everything good that happens to the Jewish people happens when He shows us a shining countenance. When Hashem hides His Face, it is called *hester panim*, and is considered one of the greatest tragedies possible. All the calamities and misfortunes that happen to the Jewish nation happen at a time of *hester panim*.

---

1. *Brachos* 7a, Rashi.

The Torah describes Jewish suffering in Egypt: "It happened in those days that the king of Egypt died and the children of Israel cried from the labor and they cried out. Their cries rose to Hashem from the labor and Hashem heard their oppression and He remembered His covenant, and Hashem heard the Jews and Hashem knew."[1] Our commentators explain that at first Hashem hid His face from the people and they became oppressed.[2] Then their cries reached Him and He saw them, and understood their suffering and felt their pain. Hashem made known that in His anger He will remember His mercy.

We are told that herein lies the secret of the shining of the Divine Countenance (he'aras hapanim) and that it is related to Divine knowledge. Although this subject is profound and beyond our comprehension, the connection between Hashem's shining countenance and the secret of knowledge has been revealed to us. We can infer that human knowledge also contains an element of "shining countenance." We too have been blessed with knowledge, and although there is no comparison and value between man's knowledge and the secret of Heavenly knowledge, some small resemblance does exist.

When Hashem created man in His image, He not only imbued humanity with a degree of His honor, crowning it with the advantages of intelligence and good traits, but He also endowed man with His form in the aspect of His shining countenance. A wealth of blessing and grace is hidden in the illumination of man's face. We have been given the power to look with understanding, to shine our countenance on other people. We've learned it from Hashem.

If you know how to smile, you know the secret.

Moshe lived in Pharaoh's palace where he was surrounded by servants and dressed in royal garments. He lived a princely life and could have stayed at home without interesting himself in the affairs of the Jews. Instead, he saw their suffering and went out to help them. When he saw someone carrying heavy pails of water, he lifted them up; if he saw someone carrying a heavy burden of sand, he carried it with him. He did not turn his face away — he set his eyes

---

1. *Shemos* 2:23-25.
2. Ibid., Rashi, Ramban.

and heart to share in their distress. In other words, Moshe knew the secret of knowledge and a shining countenance, and this made him worthy of being a messenger of the Redemption.

We are also told that before his death, "Moshe separated three cities on the eastern bank of the Jordan."[1] East is where the sun rises. Moshe prepared cities of refuge, places where anyone who has accidentally caused the death of another can live a normal life. If, for instance, a student must go to one of these cities of exile, his teacher is sent along with him. That is the extent of shining countenance one shows to a person who accidentally killed somebody!

The father of all the prophets did not find a more important mitzvah to perform before his death than this one, to shine the sun upon such unfortunates. Moshe began by taking note of the burdens and suffering of his fellow Jews, and he ended by establishing the cities of refuge. Like a brilliantly shining sun, his entire life was one of illumination for his generation and for all generations.

This is man's total purpose: to be an illuminator. This is the basis of all the mitzvos and of the entire relationship between man and his fellow man. Our Sages tell us: "Whoever brightens his teeth to a friend," i.e., flashes a smile, "is greater than one who gives him milk to drink."[2] A person who smiles pleasantly is giving a greater gift to his friend than if he gave him food! We are also told: "Always be first to greet every person."[3] The person who returns a greeting is being polite and courteous, but the one who greets his friend first makes the sun shine for him.

Every person hopes for and expects the shining of the sun from his friend. Each one of us must consider herself to be that very sun and shine upon everyone with whom we come in contact.

These two forces are the basis of human social interaction:

1. Every person's hunger for a smile from another; and
2. the power of granting this shining countenance, which is imbedded in the heart of every sensitive person. The same applies to mutual relations between groups, classes, countries, and regions.

---

1. *Makkos* 10a.
2. *Kesubos* 111b.
3. *Pirkei Avos* 4:20.

Every human being wants to be smiled at. It begins with a little baby lying in his crib. If you go up to the baby and smile at him, the baby smiles back at you. But if you show the baby an angry face, he'll start crying. This holds true with children of all ages. Children long for a smile and a kind word of encouragement or praise from their parents. Parents long for a word of appreciation from their children. It's mutual. There is no human being who doesn't need a smile and a good word.

Every student wants his teacher — from kindergarten on up — to smile at him, to encourage him, to give him a compliment. Our Sages told us 2,000 years ago that this is what makes a child develop properly. They say: "If you've met a student who hasn't succeeded in his studies, it is because his rebbe did not smile at him."[1] A child won't learn from a parent or teacher he's afraid of, but if he likes them, they can get him to do anything.

Teachers also long to be appreciated by their students and by their students' parents. Even the best teacher in the world wants a word of encouragement. It might very well be that it's the kind word said to him twenty years ago that's still keeping him going. One good word, one word of praise and appreciation, can keep a person going for a lifetime.

And what happens when you shop? Let's say you go into a store to buy a pair of shoes. You say to the saleslady, "I'm looking for a pair of shoes in such-and-such a size and color . . ." She brings out two pairs of shoes and says with a sour face, "This is what we have. Take it or leave it." Would you ever go back to that store again? Never! But what happens if you go into a store and the saleslady brings out twenty pairs of shoes, and tries very hard to please you. She's so patient and calm that in the end you may buy a pair of shoes just because she's been so nice. Even if you don't buy now, you'll always want to go back to that store because they've been so pleasant.

In every aspect of life, if people are nice to you, you go back. Even countries must be diplomatic and careful about what they say and how they say it — because human beings hunger for appreciation and a smile.

---

1. *Taanis* 8a.

Sometimes people live side by side without finding common ground or language. How bitter and angry are their lives because of this mutual misunderstanding! If we look for the source of this, we will see that it comes because people wait for the other person to make the first overture. Sometimes we wait in vain. Why don't we want to make the first move? Pride. Give it up, and you can be the first to say hello.

Sometimes neighbors can pass each other for years without exchanging a greeting. Instead of becoming closer to one another with the passage of time, the chasm between them widens. Each one imagines that the other has hidden reasons for maintaining his distance when actually no such reason exists at all. All that's lacking is the basic knowledge that each person is obligated to make the first overture and show a shining countenance to his fellow man. Each one of us should emulate Moshe, and instead of turning our heads away, look at the other person with understanding. It's so easy to turn away. We're afraid that if we start a conversation it will take up time we can't afford to spend. But you can smile and greet the other person in less than a minute, and still make him feel good.

> R' Avraham Grodzinski ztz"l, was the mashgiach of Slobodka Yeshivah before the Holocaust. For two years he worked on perfecting this middah of shining countenance. Widowed while still a young man, left with a large family of motherless children to raise, the youngest but an infant, he nonetheless always radiated happiness. Even at the worst of times, in the ghetto, under the greatest of pressures, he always showed everyone a smiling countenance.[1]

Our Sages teach us: "Greet everyone with a shining countenance";[2] and, "Receive each person with joy."[3]

"We learn from this," R' Shlomo Wolbe shlita explains, "that if a person gives his friend all the riches of the world with a downturned, angry face then it's considered as if he has given him nothing." He may have given him a million dollars, but if he didn't do it with a

---

1. Rabbi Shlomo Wolbe, Alei Shor.
2. Pirkei Avos 1:15.
3. Pirkei Avos 3:12.

smile, he hasn't given him a thing. "But he who receives his friend with a shining countenance, even if he hasn't given him a thing, the Torah considers it as if he gave him all the good gifts of the world."[1]

When other people try to be friendly, be friendly in return. Some people misconstrue everyone else's good intentions. Even though the other person wanted to help them, the first thing they think of is: "Oh, she's doing it because she wants to say that she's done me a favor."

One of the commandments given in the Torah admonishes us not to vex or annoy other people. This is usually understood to mean not to annoy people with words, but there is an additional dimension: Don't cause pain to another person by showing an angry or unfriendly face.

It's the way you say it and the way you do it that counts.

Especially in marriage, be very generous with sincere compliments to your partner. Don't think, "I'm too shy," or, "I can't say it." Make the effort, even when you feel tired — you'll save your marriage and give your husband a gift of life. A marriage where husband and wife compliment and praise each other thrives. When the husband thinks his wife is the most wonderful woman in the world, and the children know he feels that way, and where Mommy keeps telling the children there's no one in the world like Daddy, then both parents are built up in each other's eyes and in the eyes of their children. Children who come from such a loving background can go through anything in life and come out whole. They have a firm foundation for a lifetime, and the stamina to bounce back no matter what.

Look only for the other person's virtues, and never mention the shortcomings. After all, you've got plenty of your own. Everyone has, because if we didn't, we wouldn't be here. If you're still here it means you're not perfect, so let's not demand perfection from those closest to us. Just accept them as they are and give them a tremendous amount of encouragement. If you do, they'll turn into the people you want them to be.

"Just as water reflects a face, so does a heart feel another heart."[2]

---

1. *Avos DeRabbi Nosson* 13:1.
2. *Mishlei* 27:19.

A man from a small village arrived in the big city for the first time in his life. He came to a big, beautiful office building and was shown into a waiting room where one entire wall was a mirror. Now, this country bumpkin had never seen a mirror before in his life. He sat down to wait on one of the lounge chairs, tired and tense from his long day.

As he looked around the room, his eyes met those of an angry-looking man across the room staring straight at him. "What are you so angry about?" he asked impatiently. No sooner had he spoken when the fellow across the room became even angrier.

"What! You dare show me faces like that? I'll show you." He jumped up, strode across the room, and gave a solid punch to the figure in the mirror.

The mirror shattered and people came running. "What have you done?" they asked him.

"What kind of place is it here? People have such angry faces!"

Patiently, they pointed to an unbroken section of the mirror and suggested: "Try smiling at this man and see what happens."

— *from the teachings of Novarodok*

When you smile, the world smiles back. Smile! You'd be surprised at what happens.

8

Priorities

There was once a family with ten children. They were so poor the children often went hungry. One day, the mother found an egg. She thought to herself, "If I boil this egg and divide it up into ten pieces, each child will get practically nothing!"

She took the egg home and cooked it. Then she went into the bedroom, locked the door . . . and ate the egg.

Her children knocked at the door and said, "Mommy, what are you doing in there?"

She told them, "Children, I am making you a mother."

*Y*our first priority is **you**! Only if you care for yourself will you be able to be a wife to your husband and a mother to your children.

Some women think it's smart to be an object of pity. But a person can feel pity once, twice, even ten times, and then he's going to get fed up with it. If a wife is always sickly and not feeling well, with a pain here and an ache there, her husband will soon lose patience. But a wife who is happy and coping with life, a wife who feels healthy, dresses well and looks good, will be appreciated. Her husband will think she is the most wonderful wife in the world, and the children will think they have the best mother in the world.

Get organized so that you have time to take care of yourself. Don't neglect yourself even if you have fifteen or sixteen children. It's no excuse — there are people who have seventeen or eighteen children and they look fantastic, as if they've just had the first baby.

✍ *Be Good to Yourself*

A woman has to know how to be good to herself — that's part of getting her priorities straight. Organizing your day is part of being good to yourself.

Start the day right:

1. Get up at least fifteen or twenty minutes before the children get up.
2. Get dressed. R' Elya Lopian used to instruct all the women in his family never to come downstairs without being fully dressed. You will feel better about yourself if you are not seen running out to put your children on the school bus while still wearing a robe!
3. Say *brachos*. This shouldn't take you more than ten minutes.

4. Eat breakfast. Our Sages say that the most important meal of the day is breakfast. Take a slice of bread with cheese or eggs, have a hot drink — it will take you no more than ten minutes.

Take care of your health. It's a precious gift, so easy to maintain, yet so hard to regain. Exercise, fresh air, and good food will help you be on top of the world, functioning at 100% efficiency. Don't think it's smart to forgo food; instead, be health conscious and eat well, because good nutrition will put you one step ahead of the game. And don't eat junk food or bring it into the house; give yourself and your family only healthful food. If you're not currently in the best of health, work at building yourself up. Make it a project. Taking full care of your health means you'll be able to function at peak capacity.

Take care of your body too — it's also a gift. For instance, when you take a shower, smooth some body lotion over the rough spots. Rub cream into your feet before you put on your stockings, and instead of feeling tired, they'll feel fresh and loved. These may seem like small things, but you'll feel like a different person.

Try to look your best every day; a woman should always be well-groomed. Find time to have your wig set and have it set regularly. Ask professionals how to care for it in-between visits. If you take care of it properly, it will last longer.

Many women drag themselves through the day like a car without gas. If you come to certain houses at two o'clock in the afternoon, the woman will open the door still wearing her nightgown with a robe over it. "Oh, I've had such a hard day," she sighs. "I haven't even had time to have a cup of coffee." Who's to blame? What does she mean she didn't have time?! It's not because she didn't have time, it's because she doesn't know how to organize her life.

Some remarkable women can raise even fifteen or sixteen children in two-and-a-half rooms. The table gets taken out of the room at night so the beds can be pulled out. You should see the closets, the order and cleanliness, the way the children look, and the way the mother looks, always serene and never rushed — because she's organized.

There are only twenty-four hours in a day. A person who is organized can get a lot out of them because time won't run away from her.

✍ Orderliness Is the Key

What does a disorderly household look like? The mother drags herself out of bed in the morning at the last possible minute. Nothing is ready. One child wanders around looking for a pair of socks, but can only find one sock and doesn't know where the other one is. The husband needs a clean shirt, but it's nowhere to be found. The ten-year-old can't find clean clothes and she's late because she didn't get up on time. Now she has to rush, so she has no time to eat breakfast. Then she remembers that she needs a special notebook today, but she can't find it, so she turns all the drawers upside down. Everything's on the floor, yet she still can't find what she wants. If she doesn't rush, she'll miss the bus, so she leaves everything as is. She gets to school late looking hungry, tired, worn out — and all because of a lack of order in the home.

No matter how hard it is for you — even if a child has kept you up at night — stick to your schedule and get up on time. Otherwise, you'll ruin the day for yourself and your family. If you're very tired, then once everyone's out of the house go back to sleep for half an hour or so.

In a disorderly home, family members don't clean up after themselves.

Let's say you haven't yet trained the members of your family to be orderly. You have left the kitchen spotless, with absolutely nothing on the countertop, when someone walks in to make a cup of coffee. First, he heats up the water. Then he takes out a cup and saucer, the spoon, and of course, the jar of coffee. Then he takes out the sugar. By now the water has boiled and is poured into the cup. Two teaspoons of sugar are added to the coffee (some spills along the way and stays there). He takes the milk out of the refrigerator, pours it in the cup of coffee and leaves the container sitting on the counter along with the coffee and sugar. For one cup of coffee, the kitchen is a shambles!

In an orderly home, items are put away after they're used. One woman used humor to help her family learn to put things away. She bought colored labels for each item. On the one for the milk, for instance, she wrote, "I belong in the refrigerator." On the coffee she wrote, "Please put me back in the cupboard." Everyone had a good laugh and the orderliness in the kitchen improved.

In a disorderly home, it can take a whole evening to clean up after the children play.

In an orderly home, when children finish playing with a toy or game, they know they're not allowed to take out another until they put the first away. When they bring friends home to play, their friends help them clean up too.

In a disorderly home, children throw their clothes wherever they please.

In an orderly home, the mother trains her children to care for their clothing. If a child throws his clothes around, she'll put them high up on a closet shelf and say, "If you don't know how to put your clothes away, they're going to go to sleep. They're very tired from being thrown around, so they need a vacation." The child will plead to have them back and promise to take care of them and put them away in the future.

In an orderly home, everyone has obligations to fulfill. The home belongs to the whole family, and together they carry the burden with a smile.

An orderly person lives by the motto: "A place for everything, and everything in its place." Before she goes to bed, she prepares clothing for the next morning. If she's a teacher, the lessons are prepared and in order. Orderliness is a reflection of our state of mind as well. The thoughts of a disorderly person are mixed up and unclear, whereas those of an orderly person are clear and organized.

If you achieve orderliness, you'll have time for everything.

Punctuality: Part of being organized is being punctual. In England they say, "Punctuality is the courtesy of kings." If you are late, it's a sign that you disrespect the other person. A person who is punctual can be relied upon, at home, in school, and at work. If you ask her for a favor, you know it's going to get done because she's a person who gets things going and meets her commitments.

Learn To Relax: When you feel stress or tension, when you're afraid or worried, sit down and relax. It's a shame that most people don't know how to relax, because relaxation is the secret of mental and physical health. Sometimes a woman sleeps eight or ten hours at night yet wakes up in the morning so tired and worn out she'd like to go right back to sleep again. This is because even her sleep was tense. If you learn to relax, even ten minutes worth of relaxation or an hour of sleep will leave you feeling as refreshed as a full night's rest.

Practice relaxation. Sit in a comfortable chair, close your eyes and breathe deeply. Let go of each limb. Feel your eyes, mouth, feet, hands, arms and legs all become soft, warm, and heavy. Allow your thoughts to drift by like white clouds in a blue sky. In the beginning, it's not that easy, but if you practice, it will become a wonderful way to refresh yourself — you'll have the energy to go on for hours afterwards.

Budget Your Time: Time should be budgeted just like money, because time, like money, is limited. You don't have more than twenty-four hours in a day, so live within your means. Make sure you have time to take care of yourself — including time to rest — and your family.

You may have to learn to say, "I'm sorry, I can't." Pesach won't wait for you, nor will Shabbos. You may be a tremendous do-gooder — that's fantastic. But . . . must people get used to the idea that you do it all? There must be somebody else besides you who can help out! Share the *chesed* — and do something for yourself too.

If you're well organized, you can do *chesed* every day. For instance, an organized mother can easily have neighbors leave children with her without it bothering her. She has trained the neighbors' children to pick up after themselves (just as her children do), so they don't leave a mess.

A person who is organized always has time, while a person who is disorganized never has time. That's why they say, "If you want something done, ask a busy person." Never ask a person who has time, because she'll never get around to it. The woman who is so organized that every minute of her time is budgeted, is the woman who has time for everything, and is the one who will be able to help others.

Without being tense about it, organize your time. If you do, you'll find you have a lot more of it, and you'll find life much easier.

For efficiency and productivity in the kitchen, make a two-week menu plan listing three meals a day. A weekly menu plan is boring, but a two-week plan creates more variety. Make a list of salads and a list of sandwich fillings and let your family help choose the menu plan. Children love doing this.

To help you budget your time, make a weekly plan for household chores, and schedule the work day by day. Make your daily plan a feasible one, so that you can pat yourself on the back and feel you're an achiever. Avoid the pitfall of deciding that as long as you're going to start planning, you might as well catch up on the things that haven't been done in the last six months. Take into consideration how much time you have available and estimate how much time it will take you to complete your household tasks. Leave yourself ten or fifteen minutes between each job for resting or sitting down to relax so that in case a job takes you longer than you estimated, you'll have time to catch up. Aim for efficiency and alacrity. You can fall asleep watching some people — they can hardly move! Learn the most efficient method for getting each job done well, and don't forget to clean up after yourself as you work.

The secret of an efficient home is to pretend Friday doesn't exist. Make believe there are actually only five days in the week: Sunday, Monday, Tuesday, Wednesday, and Thursday. By not including Friday as a workday, you'll be sure to finish everything by Thursday night. Don't worry — you'll have plenty to do on Friday anyway, even without scheduling anything.

Some women mistakenly think Friday is a fast day. When Friday comes around in their house no one eats because the mother of the house is in such a frantic rush she's forgotten to make sure there's food around! It's a mistake to leave the family hungry. Make sure to prepare Friday's meal in advance. Then give the younger children a nap in the afternoon so that they will be fresh for Friday night. You can't force them to sleep, but you can have them rest with a book so that they will be able to sit at the Shabbos table. You should lie down to rest too. Remember, you're not only a cook and a cleaning lady; you too deserve to go into Shabbos feeling rested and ready to get the most out of this day. Shabbos is like opening a window into the World to Come. A woman who's not organized, who starts her cooking at Friday noon, has nerves that are sky high. She's busy shouting and screaming at everyone, the whole place is in an uproar, and then Shabbos is not a Gan Eden, it's a Gehinnom! She won't be walking into Shabbos, she'll be falling into it holding on for dear life.

Friday afternoon is the worst time of the week for peace in the home. Evil forces are very hard at work fomenting quarrels and marital disputes. In other words, the Satan has a lot of business on Friday afternoon — it's his most profitable day. He will go from one Jewish home to the other to cause arguments. To keep him out of your home, try your best to finish all your preparations by Thursday.

Think of our grandmothers who had to cook and bake everything from scratch and managed with no refrigerators or freezers. My mother-in-law, for instance, grew up in Jerusalem's Old City without any modern conveniences, yet by ten o'clock on Friday morning one could eat off the floor — not of the house, of the courtyard! It was spotless. She would get up at two o'clock in the morning even when she was eighty-five years old! By the time my husband would stop by to visit her on Friday morning, she was sitting and reading *Tz'enah Ur'enah*, with all her preparations finished, ready to offer him a piece of cake. That's an *eishes chayil*.

It's a pleasure to go into Shabbos rested. Enjoy lighting the candles, saying a prayer afterwards, *davening Shir HaShirim* and *Kabbalas* Shabbos, and then sitting down with the family at the Shabbos table, with everyone rested.

Some women say that while it's very easy for them to plan their day and stick to the plan if the children aren't around, it's almost impossible when the little ones are home. The secret of success — even when the children are home — lies in being organized. If you're organized, your children will be organized too. Children need a schedule. Very young children, for instance, need both a morning and an afternoon nap. Plan your day in such a way that when the little ones are sleeping, you get a lot done. Also, let your children work with you as much as possible. They will enjoy it and keep busy with you. If you feel it's unbearable to have the children underfoot, it will be. But if you have patience and you teach them as you work, you can do anything with children around, because children love helping. I've seen many two-year-olds helping to clean the house — they love it.

Even getting enough sleep is a matter of planning. You may have a large family, or work full time outside the home. Maybe you can't get eight hours of sleep at a stretch, but you can break your sleep into units. Take a nap here and there — it all adds up. Sometimes just lying down for ten minutes is very refreshing. And remember, ten minutes of perfect relaxation is sometimes worth more than eight hours of far-from-perfect sleep. Also, if you learn the right rhythm of working, you won't get as tired. Ask other women how they pace themselves throughout the day to make the most of their time.

A woman needs to recharge her batteries and stay fresh. Make sure to go out to a lecture once a week. Even a woman who is working outside of the home should do so to refresh her mind. A woman who is at home should go out twice a week, not necessarily in the evening. It's also very relaxing to listen to a tape. Don't think that you always have to work while you're listening to a tape — you can make time, when nobody's at home, and give yourself that hour of pleasure without feeling guilty about it.

A woman needs to get out and enjoy herself. Attend social events and evenings to benefit yeshivos and other worthy organizations. You'll be less tired and have more strength for your family.

Say "No" with a Clear Conscience

There is a certain type of woman who is so busy with everyone else's needs she forgets to run her own home. Her husband and children have no food, the laundry doesn't get done, the house doesn't get cleaned — all because she's so busy doing for others. Yes, it's wonderful to build a home of *chesed* — it's important to build a home of *chesed*, but it is also important that it not be done at the expense of your family. Start by doing *chesed* with yourself, with your husband and with your children. There are families where the children feel deprived because they don't have a mother — she's always somewhere else. She has no time for the family because she's always running around. Many times a woman will be busy with everything except what she should be doing. You have to ask yourself: Will my home and children turn out to be less than the way I want them to be because I'm too busy helping others? The children should not feel for the rest of their lives that they suffered because of other people. Everything must be done in the right measure, even *chesed*. Every woman should give of herself to others outside her family — if she can handle it properly, without letting people impose on her.

Don't be a slave to the telephone — make it your servant. When it's time to put the children to bed, disconnect the phone. Your children come first. When your husband comes home for supper, sit down with him and take the phone off the hook. Otherwise, there will be constant interruptions and you'll never communicate. Don't worry — they'll call back. Everyone may need you, but you also have to have your own life. Anyone who really needs you will eventually reach you.

Remember, too, that no one is indispensable. What would happen to all those people who call you or knock on the door if you went away for a two-month vacation? Do you think they wouldn't manage?

❧ Be Good to Others

We can do *chesed* all day long, yet it's not true *chesed* if we turn the other person into a cripple by helping him too much. True *chesed* means guiding the other person to become independent. When another person is not functioning and we do everything for him, that's not *chesed*. It is a kindness to help people stand on their feet and function. If you *always* help them out, they'll never be able to help themselves out because they won't be prepared to; they'll become emotional cripples.

What the outside world calls mercy and kindness is not as we define it. Sometimes what may look "cruel" is actually the greatest kindness:

> *A professional, single woman became a ba'alas teshuvah. She had a brilliant mind and began studying privately with a learned rebbetzin. Their study sessions often lasted for six hours at a stretch and they became close friends.*
>
> *Months passed, and, naturally, this woman was a frequent Shabbos guest at various homes in the community. One day the rebbetzin said: "You're missing out on having*

the beauty of Shabbos in your own home. Why be a person who is always invited out to other people's homes? Be a person in your own right."

Now she doesn't need to wait for invitations — she gives invitations. She makes her own Shabbos . . . and invites other people to join her.

This rebbetzin did true *chesed* for her new friend. Our yardstick should be to help the other person be healthy in body and mind, to be a normal, functioning human being. Sometimes it might be a kindness not to be too kind. You must learn to evaluate each situation to discover how you can best help the other person while still encouraging him to become a successful, independent human being.

Don't Ruin Your Marriage

Some husbands are very much opposed to their wife doing *chesed* outside the home because when they come home they find her all worn out. Instead of coming home to a wife, they come home to a dishrag!

Take your husband's feelings into consideration. Don't go running around to do *chesed* if it will be at his expense.

Every woman wants to do *chesed* and we're all for it, on the condition that it is done in an organized manner. If she budgets her time — and her *chesed* — she'll have plenty of time for both.

Try to get one step ahead of everything. Look for ways to find more time for yourself during the day. You are your first priority — being a fantastic wife and mother.

Focus on priorities. Ask yourself the following questions which will help you focus on priorities daily:

1. What do I regret not having done recently?

What are some of the things you'd very much like to do but haven't managed to get to and keep putting off? It may be you'd love to visit certain relatives, yet never find the time for it. You keep thinking, "Oh, I wish I could find the time to visit them," yet you keep putting it off again and again.

Maybe you have a neighbor or someone you know who's been through a hard time and needs encouragement. Take the time to make that brief phone call to say, "Hello, I just called to wish you a good Shabbos." If there's a close friend or family member who's going through a rough time, find the time to call and say, "Hello, I'm thinking of you, how do you feel today?" If someone's been through a terrible tragedy, call her. She can use the support and encouragement. Even a few words can make a difference: "We're with you — is there anything we can do?" It's doesn't actually *take* that much time, it's *finding* time that's difficult. Once you make up your mind that you're not going to put it off, and you go ahead and do it, you'll feel a warm glow inside.

> *The wife of a renowned rabbi said that when her husband was alive she got 2,000 New Year's greetings.*
> *The year after he died she received only three.*

Never put off these important kindnesses, because later you might be sorry. Why spend a lifetime regretting not doing what you could have or should have done?

If you want to go to a *gadol* to ask for a blessing, go ahead and do it. Don't wait for an opportunity, for it may never present itself. Do it now, so that you won't feel sorry afterwards that you missed your chance.

Tell those close to you how much you love them. Children in particular need a great deal of encouragement, yet too few mothers are lavish with praise and expressions of love. A child needs touching and warmth; a child needs to be told verbally that he's good. Remember to take the time to give words of encouragement to those you love.

Whenever you feel the need to do something, make the time for it. You'll discover that it takes less time than you thought it would.

2. When do I feel happy?

Material pleasures are short-lived. After you've worn a new dress once, your pleasure in wearing it is automatically less. But when you say a kind word to a heartbroken person, you feel a lasting sense of satisfaction. Perhaps you have an elderly neighbor who is very lonely. You can invite her in for a cup of tea, and — even while you're working — sit her down at your kitchen table with some cake and let her help you peel the vegetables. It will give her the feeling that she's still useful and important. By giving her the feeling that she can still contribute, you'll feel wonderful too.

Sometimes, just paying someone a sincere compliment can make you happy. Tell a friend how nice she looks, thank a saleslady for being considerate, look for ways to encourage and praise others, as this woman did:

> *My mother-in-law was living with us and I didn't think I could take it anymore. I felt fed up and ready to ask her to leave. You can't imagine how hard it was — she was driving me crazy.*
>
> *On the other hand, I had a guilty conscience, because she was in the terminal stages of cancer. My frustration came because I wanted to be good to her, but she wouldn't let me. She criticized everything I did for her. It got so I dreaded going into her room.*
>
> *Then a friend said, "She's being that way to you because it's a way of asking for attention, just like children do when they misbehave. She desperately needs warmth and affection. For a week, try being warm and loving to her no matter how she acts towards you. See what happens."*
>
> *It was a miracle. In a short time, my mother-in-law became a sweet and pleasant person to live with.*

Elderly people can live for months on the memories of one visit:

> *Twice a year, on chol hamoed Pesach and Succos, Rabbi Aryeh Levine used to take a wagon and go to visit all the widows of Torah scholars in Yerushalayim. He would come to the door with a smile and a warm greeting. Once inside, he would sit down as if he had all the time in the world, and ask about the family. His visit may have lasted only minutes, yet he never appeared rushed. After a few minutes chat, he would rise and wish the widow "a gutten Yomtov," and leave.*

He used to make about seventy or eighty calls like that in one day! His visits probably kept those poor widows alive for the next six months . . . until his next visit.

3. What would I want said about me after 120 years?

In order to focus on what you really want to be and achieve in life, consider what you would like said about you. Praise for the kind of home you made and the kind of children you left behind? Or that you were very busy cleaning the house? Some women make cleaning their major occupation. They have no time to educate their children, because to them a child is just an object to be moved from one place to the other. He isn't allowed into the living room because he'll mess it up; he can't play downstairs because he'll bring in dirt. He has only about four square yards in the whole house in which to move! There are women who'd rather see their children out in the street all day than to have them inside dirtying the house. We're all for a clean house, *but . . .*

One woman replied to criticism that not everything in her home was always perfectly in place because of her *chesed* by noting: "I have visited a lot of cemeteries and I have yet to see a monument that has written on it, 'This woman excelled at cleaning.' " Don't neglect your house, but don't overdo it.

9
Holidays

The secret of making the most out of every holiday is planning ahead. An organized woman will look forward to every Yom Tov on the calendar — and her family will too.

✎ *Pesach*

Many women have told me that the following hints on how to plan for Pesach saved their lives. They might save yours too.

Begin by taking a look at your calendar to see when Pesach is due. Then, mark the day by which you want to be out of your kitchen. Also ask yourself: By which day do I want to finish the rest of the house before I get to the kitchen? A good answer is: by the first of Nissan. If you work with that goal in mind, your preparations will be much easier — and your children will enjoy being your children. They won't feel neglected and sorry for themselves, and you won't be endangering their lives. Terrible tragedies can happen to small children when their mothers are so busy and tense over Pesach preparations to the point where they neglect their children.

Begin cleaning with your bedroom, and start with the closets. Remember: There's a difference between "kosher for Pesach" and going crazy. "Kosher for Pesach" doesn't mean you have to scrub the ceiling! There's no *chametz* on the ceiling — unless the pressure cooker exploded! Cobwebs are not *chametz* and dust is not *chametz*. Here too, you have to be smart and know what your priorities are.

The first list to make well in advance of Pesach is the list of household repairs. Don't wait until *erev* Pesach to fix a banging window or leaky faucet. Get furniture repaired at the same time as well.

Your second list should be of the clothing needed for the entire family, from head to toe. Buy what needs to be bought and mend what needs to be mended.

Your third list: dry cleaning and washing. Send out the dry cleaning as early as possible. Of those items you wash yourself at home, do the heavier ones early so that you won't get exhausted right before Pesach. Curtains can be washed in advance, heavy bedspreads as well. If you start ahead of time, you'll be able to work gradually.

Fourth, prepare a list of cleaning materials: rubber gloves, floor cleaner, etc., from the many cleaning materials on the market. One of the best tools is a big piece of sponge cut from an old mattress or foam pillow, used instead of rags. It's very soft and gets into every crack in the refrigerator. If you wring it out and wipe down the doors after you've soaked it with a cleanser, you won't need to dry them because it doesn't even leave water spots. It's good for everything. A chamois cloth, kept in an air-tight container, will make everything shining clean. Prepare your cleaning materials in advance and get started. Who says you have to wash windows a week before Pesach?

Keep a special Pesach notebook that you use from year to year. You can't imagine the amount of worry, money, and extra work it will save you. Write down everything you buy for Pesach, and afterwards, everything that is left over. This way you can see what needs to be bought and shop throughout the year. For instance, if one of your china cups broke, write it down. Then next year, weeks or even months before Pesach, you can buy a replacement. With a notebook, you'll know what you need in advance, instead of suddenly finding you have to rush out at the last minute.

Make lists: How many people will be at the Seder? How many during the entire week? How much wine and grape juice will you need? How much chicken, meat and fish will you need? Calculate how many meals you will be serving during the week and how many people you expect for each meal. Calculate the number of portions you will need and buy accordingly. If you have a deep freeze, clean it first so that your meat, chickens, and fish can be in your freezer as early as possible before the holiday.

Make a list of grocery items and buy them right after Rosh Chodesh Nissan. Non-perishable items can be kept in a carton in a place you've already cleaned. By shopping early, you'll feel less pressured because you'll avoid the last-minute rush. You also won't have to spend hours shopping at a time when the stores are overcrowded.

Remember to buy kosher-for-Pesach cleaning materials, disposable tablecloths and disposable dishes. From Purim on, don't let your children walk around with *chametz*. Babies and toddlers who don't know the difference can be given kosher for Pesach matzos so they won't carry *chametz* all over the house. Once you've cleaned your kitchen, don't use regular dishes; if you can, buy pita instead of bread, because it does not leave crumbs. You can cook in your kosher-for-Pesach kitchen and serve the food on paper plates to eat with pita in another room.

In our family, we like to start cooking ten days before Pesach. Here is our favorite recipe for potato kugel:

In a Pesach food processor, process 3 onions with 3 eggs. Add salt. Then grate 4 fresh potatoes separately. Add 3 cooked, mashed potatoes (they make the kugel stay white inside). Add matzo meal to hold the mixture together. Heat a small amount of oil in a frying pan until it is smoking hot. Add kugel mixture, and cook on a very low flame for one hour. Turn the kugel over, and continue cooking on the other side for another half hour to an hour.

✎ *Purim*

If you are organized, you'll enjoy Purim, instead of being worn out.

Children's costumes should be number one on your list of things to prepare. Make a list of what each child is going to wear and then check off the items once you have them ready. If you have five or six children to dress up, use a separate page in a notebook to write down what each child needs. Get started early on the costumes. For instance, if you have a costume that is small for your children, call up a friend and offer to exchange. "Sarah, I've got a beautiful dancing girl costume, but it's too small for my children. Your daughter is two years older — what did she wear last year?" Be careful to take care of what you borrow from your friends; don't allow your children to eat in costumes that don't belong to you.

Are you sewing something new? Don't sit up nights the week before Purim sewing until you're ready to collapse. If you prepare well in advance, it's a pleasure to sew a costume.

Whether the costume is made or bought, take good care of it so that it can be used year after year. After Purim, wash it, iron it, and fold it carefully. Place it in a plastic bag and put it away in a special Purim box or suitcase. Each year, you can add new items. If you take care of them, costumes and accessories will last for a few generations. Not only does it save a lot of money, but it will be fun for the grandchildren years from now.

You don't have to go out the day before the school party and spend a fortune for each child. Think about Purim all during the year. Before you throw out that skirt, consider whether you might not be able to use it for a costume. Save it in your Purim box — you never know. With the addition of a few paper frills and some paper flowers, it might make a flower-girl costume.

A few days before Purim, take out each child's costume. Iron it and hang it on a hangar so it will be ready and waiting.

The second thing you have to prepare is *shalach manos*. By giving, we show love. Giving *shalach manos* multiplies love and friendship among the Jewish people.

If you receive a lot of candy and cakes that you'd rather your children not eat, take a positive approach. There's no need to shout at them. It's better to change their habits gradually. Make a decision that you're going to provide the children with a healthy snack, like nuts, raisins or fruit. On Purim morning, before you start sending *shalach manos*, give them a very good breakfast, so they won't be very hungry and snack too much. Tell them to leave room for the beautiful Purim meal that the family will have later.

Leftover candies and cakes shouldn't be thrown out. They can be donated to a school, where they can be used for special occasions.

❧ *Rosh Hashanah*

Some women think it's wonderful to run to *shul* and leave the children home alone. The famous story about how R' Yisrael Salanter came late to *Kol Nidrei* because he stopped to soothe a crying baby teaches us what a mistake this is. Other mothers drag their children with them. This, too, is a mistake. If children are too young to understand what's going on, they'll be bored and restless.

You go to *shul* to *daven*, not to have somebody pulling at you, and certainly not to spend the time serving food and drinks. It is inconsiderate to have children running around and crying, making such a commotion that those sitting nearby don't even know where they are because of all the noise.

Children should come to *shul* when they know how to pray. Before they reach that stage, they should come to *shul* to see others praying, but remain only five or ten minutes.

Prayer is heard everywhere. If you have small children, stay at home.

On Rosh Hashanah, when your children are young, you might want to take turns with a neighbor. She can go one day, and you the next. If your husband is not a *rosh yeshivah* or *rosh kollel*, you can do what many families do: The husband goes to *daven vasikin* (with the sunrise) and finishes by 10:30; then the wife goes — without the children — to hear the *shofar* and pray *mussaf* undisturbed while her husband stays home with the children. This is ideal. If it's not possible for you to stay in *shul*, you can go just long enough to hear the *shofar*.

If your husband must be present in *shul* for the main service, you can do it the other way around. You can get up early to *daven vasikin* while he stays home. People who find it hard to leave home for either service can have someone come and blow the *shofar* for them in their home.

If you are going to pray at home, get up early when the children are still asleep and complete *Shacharis*. Then devote yourself to the children. *Daven* with them whatever they are used to saying in nursery school. Later, take them to *shul* just to hear the *tekiyos*. When you bring your children to *shul* on Rosh Hashanah, explain to them, even from the age of four or five, that they shouldn't speak from the beginning of the first *tekiyos* until the end. After they hear the *shofar*, take them home and put them to bed for a nap. Then you can *daven Mussaf*. If your children aren't ready for a nap, sit them down to play quietly while you pray. Settle them down with something to do before you start. Well brought up children don't tug at their mother all the time. Get them busy with toys, games, and puzzles. Prepare snacks like pretzels and crackers in advance — that too will keep them busy.

If you have spare time, say *Tehillim*. In our family we try to finish all of *Tehillim* on Rosh Hashanah and Yom Kippur because *Tehillim* has 150 chapters, so twice *Tehillim* equals 300, which in *gematria* is כפר, forgiveness. If you can finish *Tehillim* twice over the days of Rosh Hashanah and Yom Kippur, by saying a certain amount every day, you have forgiveness.

Throughout the generations, all great people in Klal Yisrael have made resolutions at the beginning of the new year. Of course, it isn't realistic to resolve to become an angel by tomorrow, but you *can* resolve to improve. For instance, you can decide that you're going to say the first paragraph of the *Shema* — even the first verse alone, that Hashem is One — with all your heart. Or, you may choose to say the first blessing of the *Shemoneh Esrei* with special concentration. Don't make a resolution to say all nineteen blessings with special devotion because it will be too difficult. Instead, choose one in particular and stress it. Even little children can make resolutions, such as saying the first blessing in *Birkas HaMazon* carefully.

Make a list of ten resolutions that you're going to try to keep. During the year, read this list several times every day to remind yourself to keep it up.

One of the supplications we say in *Avinu Malkeinu* is: "Hashem, in Your great mercy, please blot out all the documents of our debts of sins." R' Neiman *ztz"l*, Rosh Yeshivah of Yeshivah Ohr Yisrael in Petach Tikvah, gave a beautiful explanation: In olden days, when people wrote on paper and wished to blot something out, they needed to take a very sharp knife and scratch the paper in order to remove what they wanted to delete. Their actions, though, left a hole in the paper. Later on, erasers were used. If you wanted to blot something out, you erased it . . . but the paper became thinner, more delicate, and could tear easily. Nowadays, if you want to blot something out, you need only cover it with some white-out; the paper stays strong. This, he says, is the way we ask Hashem to blot out our debts, i.e., our sins. We pray: Please Hashem, blot out our transgressions, not with a knife or an eraser, but with liquid white-out, our tears and prayers.

10

Prayer

he young man turned white as a sheet. It was during the Ten Days of Repentance, and Rabbi Yaakov Neiman *ztz"l*, Rosh Yeshivah of Yeshivah Ohr Yisrael in Petach Tikvah, had just asked him as they were leaving *shul*, "What about your *teshuvah*?"

"Please tell me," he asked solemnly, as if he faced sentencing for the most terrible crimes, "what *teshuvah* should I do?"

The next day, an elderly man walked out with R' Neiman as he left *shul*. R' Neiman turned to him and said, "We are now in the midst of the Ten Days of Repentance." The elderly man replied indifferently, "I don't need to do *teshuvah* — everything's all right with me." R' Neiman was amazed. He knew that this man, who was in his seventies, had children who didn't attend *shul* and grandchildren who had left Torah and mitzvah observance altogether. Yet the elderly man felt he had nothing to put right! R' Neiman said to him, "I am surprised that you say everything is all right. I myself couldn't sleep all last night, knowing that a few hours earlier in the evening I had said something I shouldn't have."

"Rabbeinu Nissim Gaon," R' Neiman continued, "wrote in his confessional prayer: '*Ribbono shel Olam*, I stand before You to recount my sins and to confess before You. Time will end, yet I won't be able to finish enumerating all my sins.' Rabbeinu Nissim, who was like an angel, felt he had so many sins," R' Neiman said with feeling to the elderly man, "there wasn't enough time for him to enumerate all of them." The implication was understood: How can you, or any of us, feel that "everything is all right"!

It is no secret that the Chofetz Chaim used to talk to himself out loud, giving himself *mussar* as well as praying out loud for other people. When he spoke to Hashem, it was like one person talking to another. One day, a student in the yeshivah in Radin overheard the Chofetz Chaim say to himself: "Yisroel Meir, today you are eighty-four years old and you haven't yet done *teshuvah*! What's the matter with you? What's going to happen to you? What will be the end? Yisroel Meir — wake up!"

Everyone has to start thinking about what he can do to put things right. With this in mind, we can approach the subject of prayer.

How do we serve Hashem? By praying. We know, however, that Hashem does not need anything, so what is the purpose of praying? R' Neiman explains that it is **we** who need to serve Hashem through prayer as a means of drawing closer to Him.

A person who is poor, prays for a livelihood. A person who is sick prays for a complete recovery. A person in business prays for success. Yet poverty, illness, and lack of success in business are also from Hashem. Hashem decrees everything, so why should we pray? If we are poor or ill, it is only because He decreed it — are we going to ask Hashem to change His will in order to do our will?

The truth is, we are saying to Hashem, "We want to give honor to Your Name." We are asking of Hashem *perfection*, not success.

We want to perfect ourselves, and the basis of perfection is faith. Every Jew who keeps Torah and mitzvos knows that there is a G-d. But there is a higher level of faith, and it is to that which we aspire. We strive for the perfect understanding that only Hashem exists in the world, nothing else: a faith so absolute within our hearts that we know His Presence is with us always. With such faith, we see that everything that happens in the world is from Hashem.

How can we reach such faith? By teaching ourselves to turn to Hashem for everything we need, because we feel there is no one on earth we can turn to to give us what we lack — everything comes from Him. R' Neiman says that our purpose in prayer should not be that Hashem fulfill our desires, but that we learn to trust in Him to do what is good for us. It is enough that we ask Him to strengthen our faith. Our desire is to perfect ourselves, and *that* is what Hashem wants.

Hashem gave us prayer for our own good, and it actually does work and achieve for us. It has an influence on what is happening because Hashem wants our prayer. The world can be compared to a huge clock, explains R' Neiman. Within the clock there are many wheels, with each one connected to another, and that one in turn connected to the next. When you wind the spring, all the wheels start moving. The spring that makes everything work in the world is prayer. Our prayer makes all the wheels turn, and the world continues to exist.

Don't think that prayer is an easy thing to understand. It's not. Our Sages say that a person doesn't even bend his finger without it being decreed in Heaven. If so, how can prayer come into the picture and change things?

The answer is that you can change your *mazel* by praying. The Jewish people are above *mazel* because we have prayer, and through it we can elevate ourselves above nature. With tremendous faith, the minute we start praying we take flight to Heaven. When *tzaddikim* such as the Steipler Gaon, the Chazon Ish, or the Chofetz Chaim turned to the wall and prayed, things happened. They changed the course of events.

One of the greatest Torah sages was still childless after years of marriage. Since his father-in-law was a disciple of the Chofetz Chaim, he asked the sage for a blessing. The Chofetz Chaim gave him a blessing, and he and his wife had their first child. A few years passed, and they longed for another child. The man went back to the Chofetz Chaim, and the Chofetz Chaim prayed again — and the couple were blessed with a second child. When the man came for a third blessing, the Chofetz Chaim said, "I can do no more."

This is the power of prayer: Through the prayers of the Chofetz Chaim two children were born to a woman who otherwise would probably not have had any children.

When Hashem created the world, nothing grew; only after Adam prayed did rain fall. Our mothers Sarah, Rivkah, and Rachel were barren; only after they prayed did Hashem grant them children.

Our Sages say that one who prays should see himself as if he is standing opposite the Heavenly Throne. Rabbeinu Yonah says he should divest himself of his body, and feel himself to be an unadorned soul standing in Heaven, talking to Hashem. When praying, you should feel as if you are talking to your Father in Heaven. Before you start praying, prepare yourself. Concentrate for a few minutes on the fact that you will soon be entering the presence of the King. Try to think of what you are about to say. Don't begin to pray with sadness, say our Sages, nor in a lazy way, nor with lightheadedness or laughter. Pray with the happiness of knowing you are doing Hashem's will.

R' Avraham Grodzinski *hy"d*, *mashgiach* of Slobodka Yeshivah, said: "Prayer is not just saying words with your mouth — it is an outpouring of the soul; it is speaking to Hashem from the depths of your heart." You must realize that whatever happens to you, whatever you have, whatever you are, is from Hashem. That is perfection in faith. This realization will purify your heart from all negative character traits. If you attain perfect faith, you feel that everything is from Hashem and that nobody can take a single thing away from you, or anybody else. Everything a person has is meant for him. If Hashem will not help us, then we cannot achieve anything; only if Hashem helps us can we succeed.

R' Grodzinski advises us to pray for the rebuilding of the *Beis HaMikdash* and for the coming of *Mashiach*, because the minute we begin to pray for higher goals we will be able to obtain the other things we need as well. We should feel a tremendous longing for perfection, for cleaving to Hashem. Even in our times you will sometimes find women who have reached such a state of trust and faith in Hashem that as a result they experience daily miracles in every aspect of their lives. It's because they say, "I'm leaving it all to Hashem. He'll take care of it."

The Chofetz Chaim says we have to pray to Hashem to give us what *He* thinks is good for us, because what we think is good for us is not always good for us.

Every day we say, "Hashem is near to all who call Him, to those who call Him in truth,"[1] meaning those who call him from the depths of their heart. This verse refers to the children of the raven. The raven is a very cruel bird: Once its chicks hatch, the raven deserts them. They cry out, and Hashem provides for them.

R' Dessler tells us to "seek Hashem where He is to be found, and call Him when He is near."[2] During the entire year, only one gate of Heaven remains open — the gate of tears. During the Ten Days of Repentance, though, all the gates of Heaven are open. All it takes is a small effort on our part: "Just make a little opening like the hole of a needle and He will open for you gates like those of huge palaces, big enough for carriages to pass through."[3]

Our sins cause a partition to form, explains Rav Dessler, and this partition covers over our feelings of purity. To break through such a partition would take five hundred light years. But we receive special Heavenly assistance (*siyata d'shmaya*) if we call Him when He is near. It's as if we are at one end of a long tunnel and are trying to reach Hashem at the other end. We start digging from our end, and Hashem comes towards us. We don't meet in the middle, though. Hashem doesn't only come fifty percent of the way towards us, he comes even ninety-nine percent of the way! We just have to make a small effort in prayer to receive an abundance of Heavenly help.

---

1. *Tehillim* 145:18.
2. *Yeshayahu* 55:6.
3. *Shir HaShirim Rabbah* 5:3.

Two thousand years ago when the Beis HaMikdash still stood, every Jew who was able to made the trip up to Yerushalayim three times a year. The journey was often long, the road hot and dusty, and many travelers became thirsty on the way.

One man was responsible for digging the wells along the road to Yerushalayim. He became known far and wide as Nechunya Chofer Shichin (Nechunya, Digger of Wells) for these wells, which gave clear water to refresh so many.

One day, Nechunya's daughter fell into a well and no one present was able to descend into the well to rescue her. Her heartbreaking cries could be heard from the depths.

Bystanders ran to the nearest tzaddik, Rabbi Chanina ben Dosa, to tell him that Nechunya's daughter had fallen into the well. Rabbi Chanina said, "All will be well." They came back a while later saying she was still in the well. Rabbi Chanina said, "All will be well." The third time they came to the tzaddik, he told them "She is already out!"

Rabbi Chanina asked that the girl be brought to him. "My daughter," he asked her when she arrived, "who brought you out of the well?"

"It was a ram, being led by an old man."

It had been Avraham Avinu who came to rescue her from the well!

The people then said to Rabbi Chanina, "You must be a prophet — you said that she would be saved."

"No," he replied, "I am not a prophet nor the son of a prophet, but I know one thing: If a tzaddik does a mitzvah, it is impossible for his children to die through that same mitzvah."[1]

Some time later, one of Nechunya's sons died of thirst. How was it possible that the son of the Digger of Wells died, when his sister was saved? Why didn't the merit of their father's great deed save both of them equally?

Commentators offer an answer — one that you should remember your whole life: When Nechunya's daughter was in distress,

---

1. *Yevamos* 121b; see *Etz Yosef.*

Rabbi Chanina ben Dosa invoked her father's merits on her behalf. The son of R' Nechunya died because there was no one to pray for him. There was no one to awaken his father's merits in Heaven. Without that, the merit lay dormant and was unable to save him.

Even the prayers of animals can evoke mercy. The *midrash* states: "Just as a deer longs for running water, so my soul thirsts for You Hashem."[1] The deer is considered the most righteous of all animals, and is one of the few wild animals that is kosher. When the other animals are thirsty and have nothing to drink, they go to the deer and beg her to pray, for they know she is righteous. What does she then do? She takes her horns and digs in the earth until they bleed, praying to Hashem to bring up water from the depths. When Hashem sees her praying, He tears the depths open for her and water wells up to meet her. All the little creatures then have water in her merit.

Prayer, if said without proper intent, does not reach the Heavenly Throne immediately. Although no prayer is ever lost, it can sometimes take years to rise. There are prayers which take forty days to become purified until they can go up to Heaven, and there are prayers which take twenty days. Prayers can be answered after fourteen days, after seven days, after three days, after a day, and even after approximately twelve hours.

There is also a prayer which is answered even before you manage to finish saying it. This is true prayer that comes from the depths, and Hashem hears it immediately.

The Steipler Gaon said that even if years have passed and you feel your prayer hasn't achieved anything, don't stop praying.[2] In the end, you will merit to see that your prayer *has* accomplished a great deal for you.

The Chofetz Chaim also mentions this: "He who prays endlessly will not have his prayers returned empty." Prayer is more powerful than good deeds and sacrifices. If a person sees that he has prayed and hasn't been answered, he should go and pray again, because in the end he will be answered.

The story of Iyov and his suffering teaches us the greatness of prayer. Iyov was tested — he lost his entire family, his wealth, and

---

1. *Tehillim* 42:2.
2. *Chayei Olam* 28.

suffered the agony of sores all over his body — and he said certain things he shouldn't have said. When three of his friends came to visit him, they accused him of complaining against Hashem, and self-righteously criticized him for it. Hashem then said to them angrily, "When a person is suffering as much as Iyov, how can you add to his suffering? Don't you feel for him? Your sin is a terrible one!" The three decided to go together to ask Iyov for forgiveness. Weeping, they begged his forgiveness for the wrong they had done him.

Iyov's suffering was the greatest expression of suffering there is; a human being cannot suffer more than Iyov suffered. Yet not only did he forgive his friends, he prayed for Hashem to forgive them as well. When Hashem saw this noble deed, that Iyov, despite his personal suffering, prayed for his friends, He gave back everything to Iyov — his family and double the riches he had before — all in the merit of his prayers.

The Chofetz Chaim said that when we stand in prayer before Hashem, we should feel as if we are talking to our mother, the one who gave birth to us, for a mother will always have mercy on her children and will always forgive. That is the way we should stand and beg from Hashem.

11

Charity

Every woman has her own ideas as to how much charity she can give — she knows her limitations. Yet the minute we realize that nothing is ours, that everything belongs to Hashem and we are just treasurers, it's easier to give.

Charity saves from death, as this wonderful story which is hundreds of years old shows us:

> *One of the great sages foresaw (with Divine inspiration) that his wife was destined to die on a certain day when she would go up to the roof to hang up the wash.*
>
> *Wash day arrived, and the sage sought to avoid the decree. "Today," he told his wife, "I don't have any money to give you to buy soap or any of the other essentials for doing*

the wash, so please put it off for a day or two. I'll see if I have the money then, but for now, don't do any washing." They were quite poor, and all he was able to leave her for the day until he returned that night was a loaf of bread and some cheese.

After her husband had gone, the sage's wife began to think: "How can I put off doing the wash? I'll search through the house — perhaps I'll find a coin here or there that I've hidden away." She looked in all the cupboards and managed to gather enough money to go to the market to buy a piece of soap. When she came home, she gathered sticks and put up the water to boil. Carefully, she shaved the soap into slivers and added it to the boiling water. After working all morning, she finished the washing. With a feeling of satisfaction, she placed the damp wash into a basin and started climbing the stairs up onto the roof to hang the wash.

She had only climbed one or two steps when she heard someone knocking at the door. Setting the basin on the floor, she went to open the door. In front of her stood a poor man. "Please — I haven't eaten yet today. Can you give me something to eat?"

"My husband left me a loaf of bread and a piece of cheese. Let's share it. I'll give you half my loaf of bread and half of the cheese and a glass of water. Is that all right with you?"

"Thank you very much. You've saved my life." The poor man sat down to eat, and then continued on his way.

As soon as he was gone, she started going up the steps again with the wash. Once more, there was a knock at the door. And again, there was a poor man standing there.

"I haven't eaten for three days and if you can't give me something to eat, I'm going to die here."

"I only have half a piece of a small loaf of bread left and a piece of cheese, which was going to be my food for the day," she answered him. "But I ate yesterday, and you haven't eaten for three days. I can wait until tonight when my husband comes home. Perhaps he will have money for us to buy food.

"In the meantime," she said, handing him the bread and cheese, "you may eat everything I have." After he finished eating, she went up on the roof and hung out the wash. A few hours later, she went up again and took it down. She folded it and put it in the closet and the day passed.

In the evening, her husband came home. "Baruch Hashem, I see you didn't do the wash today," he said.

"Oh yes, I did," she replied.

"Where did you get the money?" he asked.

"I looked in the cupboards and found a coin and it was enough."

"Tell me," her husband asked, "what else did you do to-day besides the wash? You must tell me."

"Oh, nothing special. I haven't eaten yet because I gave away the loaf of bread and the cheese to two poor hungry people who came to the door."

"What a z'chus you have! Now I can tell you — I didn't want you to do the wash because I foresaw that you were going to fall off the roof and die. But you gave away everything you had and saved those poor people. Because of that, nothing happened to you and Hashem added years to your life."

Charity saves from death — it's literally lifesaving. When we give charity, we don't do the other person a favor, he does *us* a favor. In the days of our Sages, when a poor man knocked at the door, he didn't ask for a handout. He used to say, "*Zachei bi* — earn merit through me!" Instead of the poor thanking us, we should be thanking them. By giving to them, we annul a bad decree and earn merit for life.

A woman who understands this can earn merit for her whole family. This remarkable story shows us what a proper wife can do for her husband:[1]

Once upon a time there was a pious, wealthy man who became very poor — so poor, that in order to earn a living he would hire himself out by the day to plow fields. One day while he was working in the fields Eliyahu HaNavi appeared

---

1. *Yalkut Shimoni, Megillas Rus* 4:607.

to him in the guise of a simple Arab and said, "You have six good years coming to you. When would you like them — now or at the end of your life?"

The poor man barely looked up from his work. "Excuse me please," he said, "but I am very busy and I'm being paid for my work. Please leave me alone."

Eliyahu came back a second time and again the poor man paid no attention. When he returned yet a third time, the poor man agreed to consider his proposal. "If you're so determined," he told him, "wait here. I never do anything without first consulting my wife. I'll go home and ask her, and we'll see what she says."

He went home and told his wife what had happened: "He won't leave me alone! What should I tell him?"

His wife thought for a minute and then said: "Tell him to give us the good years now."

The farmer went back to Eliyahu with the answer: "My wife said you should give the good years now."

Eliyahu then began arguing with him: "Right now you're able to work. When you get old, you might not have the strength; perhaps you should leave the good years for later."

"I never asked you for anything," the farmer replied. "It was your suggestion to begin with! My wife says 'now.' If you want to give the six years, give them now. Otherwise, good-bye."

"Fine," Eliyahu agreed. "Return home and you will find a treasure."

When the poor farmer returned home, his children came running excitedly to meet him. They told him they'd been playing in the yard and had suddenly discovered a great treasure. In an instant, the family became extremely wealthy.

"This money is sacred," the woman told her family. "We shall continue living exactly as we do now. We will not be as hungry as we have been, but that will be the only change."

She called over one of her children and told him, "Your responsibility will be to write down whatever I tell you to." She began giving money to the poor and needy, and told her son to record each charitable donation in a special notebook.

Their lives continued in this way for the next six years. They did not move to a bigger and better home, nor did they buy new furniture — they didn't even whitewash the walls. In fact, the farmer even continued working in the fields.

One day, Eliyahu reappeared. "Do you remember me?" he asked the farmer. "I have come to reclaim the treasure I gave you."

"And do you remember that I didn't take it without consulting my wife?" the farmer replied. "I never do anything without conferring with my wife. Please wait here — I'll go home and ask her."

He went home and told his wife that the stranger had returned to take back the treasure.

"Here," she said calmly. "Give him our account books. Tell him to look them over and see what we did with the money. Then ask him if he has better caretakers for his treasure. If he does, he can take it away. But if we've taken good care of his money, let him leave it with us."

When Hashem saw all their charity and good deeds, the tzedakah and chesed they did with the money, not only did the treasure remain with them, but it increased many times over.

All in the merit of a wise woman.

12

What Are We Really Like?

Rabbi Chanina ben Tradyon was a great sage, one of the ten martyrs killed by the Romans, about whom it was said: He found favor in the eyes of Hashem and men, neither cursing, nor saying an unkind word to anyone.[1]

When the Roman emperor issued a decree that all Jews were forbidden to study Torah, Rabbi Chanina openly defied the decree. He assembled large groups of Jews and taught them Torah while holding a sefer Torah in his arms.

When his rebbe, the famous Rabbi Yosi ben Kisma, became ill, Rabbi Chanina went to visit him. Rabbi Yosi spoke strongly to his student: "Chanina, my brother, don't you realize that it is a heavenly decree that these people, the Romans, are allowed to rule over us? They are the same

---

1. *Pirkei Avos* 3:3.

people who destroyed the Beis HaMikdash, burned the Sanctuary, killed so many holy, pious people and destroyed everything good — and they still exist! Yet I have heard it said that you sit and teach Torah publicly in huge assemblies while holding a sefer Torah in your arms."

Rabbi Chanina answered, "Heaven will have mercy on me."

Rabbi Yosi answered sharply: "I am telling you that your defiance is common knowledge and you answer me that Heaven will have mercy!? I would not be surprised if you are burned alive together with the Torah."

When Rabbi Chanina heard his rebbe's prediction of his death as a martyr, he knew immediately that it was true. Instead of panicking, he asked, "Rebbe, what will be my portion in the World to Come?"

"Have you ever in your life done a good deed?"

"Yes. Once I prepared two purses of money for Purim. One was for the Purim meal, and the other contained money to be given to the poor, so that they, too, might enjoy a festive Purim meal. The two purses got mixed up and I didn't know which purse was for what purpose. So I took all the money I had in both purses — all the money I had — and gave it away to the poor."

When Rabbi Yosi heard about this deed he said, "If so, I wish that my portion would be as your portion, and that your fate be mine."

W hy did Rabbi Yosi ask his student if he had ever done a good deed?! Rabbi Chanina was risking his life to teach Torah in public — what greater deed of self-sacrifice could there be? "It appears remarkable," says Rabbi Dessler, "that an individual who has thrown caution to the winds and risked his very life for the sake of propagating Torah should cite such a comparatively insignificant act as one that would justify his admission to the World to Come."

Yet Rabbi Yosi knew, Rabbi Dessler explains, that a person's essential character is exposed with the utmost clarity through the less significant actions, through the little things he does every day. "One is elevated to artificial heights and grandiose gestures by momentary inspiration, but true values are reflected only in the day-to-day routine of an individual." Rabbi Yosi wanted to know what his student Rabbi Chanina was like in *everyday life*.

We only get to know the real person by seeing how he conducts himself in daily life, how he acts in everyday life, how he performs his mitzvos daily, how he interacts with the people he meets each and every day.

✎ *Sanctify Yourself*

A soul born into this world can bestow sanctity, *kedushah*, to each limb of the body through doing mitzvos. "Rabbi Chanania ben Akashia says: Hashem wished to bestow merit upon (לְזַכּוֹת) Israel, so he gave them Torah and mitzvos in abundance . . ."[1] *To bestow merit*, in Hebrew, is similar to the word זַךְ, *pure*, so we understand that we were given mitzvos as opportunities to sanctify ourselves.

If we are careful to do mitzvos with our hands, our hands become sanctified. If we are very careful not to listen to *lashon hara*, our ears become sanctified. If we are careful with our speech, neither cursing, swearing, nor using unclean language, we can sanctify our mouth. Every limb can become sanctified, turning us into a vessel of *kedushah*. The more effort we make to do the will of Hashem, by performing the mitzvos we were given for this purpose, the closer we will be to Him.

As King David said: *I find proximity to Hashem very good for me* — that's the one thing I want, nothing else.[2]

Each and every mitzvah we do sanctifies us. The *Sefer Chareidim*, written over a thousand years ago, lists each of the 613

---

1. This is the *mishnah* at the end of each chapter of *Pirkei Avos*.
2. *Tehillim* 73:28.

mitzvos according to the limb of the body to which it relates. We can see from the following story how direct the connection is:

> *Achav was king of Judah. His non-Jewish wife, Izevel, was very wicked. She was so evil that the prophet foretold that she would die and be eaten by dogs.*
>
> *Despite all her evildoings, Izevel was careful in performing two mitzvos: She would look down from the window of her special chamber onto the main road and whenever she saw a funeral procession, she would go down, shake her head and say, "Oh, poor man. It's a pity a good person died." And whenever she saw a bride being led to the wedding canopy, she would go down, dancing and clapping her hands in front of the bride to make her happy.*
>
> *When Izevel died and the dogs ate her flesh, they didn't touch her skull, nor her hands and feet. Because she imbued these limbs with kedushah, they were guarded from harm.[1]*

The following remarkable story reveals the extent to which a person can sanctify himself:

> *Elazar bar R' Shimon was considered a very great sage, but his contemporaries disagreed with many of his halachic opinions. They considered many of the rulings he issued to be radical, and refused to accept them. Thus, when he felt his end was near, he said to his wife, "My father, Rabbi Shimon bar Yochai, is buried in Meron and my colleagues will not allow me to be buried beside him. When I die, don't bury me. Instead, take me upstairs to the attic and put me there. Don't be afraid; nothing will happen to you."*
>
> *When he died, his wife had him taken upstairs to the attic as he had wished. Each time she would come up to the attic she examined his hair — and whenever a hair had fallen out she found a drop of fresh blood.*
>
> *At first, his death was hidden from the townspeople and people continued to come to the house of Rabbi Elazar with their disputes. His wife would tell them to say whatever they*

---

1. Based on *Pirkei DeRabbi Eliezer* 17:1.

had to say in front of the door to the attic. They would argue their cases and then hear a voice from the room saying, "This one is in the right, and this one is at fault."

Once, when his wife went upstairs on her daily visit, she saw a worm coming out of his ear and she became very upset. "It seems that the body is starting to decay," she worried. That night, her husband appeared to her in a dream. "Don't worry," he said, "you only saw that worm because once I saw someone insulting a Torah scholar and I didn't protest adequately. Because I listened without issuing a proper protest, a worm came out of my ear."[1]

There are people even in our time who reach such levels. One esteemed righteous woman, who died in America and was buried there, was brought to Israel, after seventeen years, for reburial. The *chevra kadisha* was amazed to find that the body was perfect, as if she had died the day before.

"The nature of sanctity is two-fold," the *Mesillas Yesharim* explains: "It begins in labor, and ends in reward; it begins as an effort, and ends as a gift. Man begins by striving to sanctify himself, and in the end sanctity is bestowed upon him."[2]

For example, Chanah, the wife of Elkanah, did not have children for over nineteen years. All through those long years of childlessness, she was busy working on herself to reach perfection, sanctifying every single limb of her body. She waited nineteen years to ask Hashem one question: "*Ribbono shel Olam*, I have sanctified all my limbs, except one: the womb. Won't you please let me sanctify my womb as well?" Imagine how hard she must have worked to be able to say that 247 limbs were already sanctified! And we know that her prayers were answered and she was granted her wish and given a child, Shmuel, who grew up to become one of the nation's greatest prophets.

Our Sages tell us that when a person makes a small effort towards sanctity here in this world, it is granted to him in large measure from above.[3] It all depends on us — our reward will be

---

1. *Bava Metzia* 84b and *Ben Yehoyada* there.
2. Ramchal, *Mesillas Yesharim*, Chap. 26: "*Kedushah.*"
3. *Yoma* 39a.

according to our effort. If you make your mitzvos beautiful by doing them with love and joy, they will sanctify you and make you beautiful to Hashem.[1]

Rebbe Meir says: If a person does one mitzvah, he is given one angel to guard over him; if he does many mitzvos, he is given many angels.[2] The angels that accompany us, watching over us, are our own, the ones we have created with each mitzvah we do. We might imagine that when we leave this world we'll be accompanied by millions of angels, but our Sages teach us otherwise. We are told that the quality of the angel depends on the quality of our mitzvah. It's a long way to the World to Come, and sometimes a person can arrive there with only one angel because all the others fell by the wayside, too weak to complete the journey. In order to create a powerful angel, we have to do each mitzvah "like fire," in Hebrew, באש, ב = kavanah, א = ahavah, and ש = simchah, with deep intent, love, and joy.

Even one mitzvah done "like fire" can save us after 120 years. Even if 999 angels appear before the Heavenly Court as witnesses for the prosecution and testify against us, and only one angel out of the thousand comes and defends us, that one angel can save us from all the others![3]

One of the great chassidic leaders was once sitting in his room studying and teaching Torah to his students when suddenly there was a knock at the door and a poor woman rushed into the room.

"Rebbe, please," the woman begged tearfully. "Please come and see my husband now. He's dying and begs you to come and see him before he dies."

The Rebbe could not refuse such a request, and so, accompanied by his students, he arose and went to the house of the sick man. He opened the door of the sick man's room, but quickly withdrew and shut the door behind him. His students wondered at the Rebbe's strange behavior. What could have given him such a shock?

---

1. Vilna Gaon.
2. *Midrash Tanchuma* on *Vayetzei, siman* 3.
3. *Yalkut Shimoni, Iyov* 32:23.

After waiting a few minutes, the Rebbe opened the door again and went into the room.

"How are you feeling," he asked the simple Jew lying before him. "What can I do for you?"

"Rebbe, I haven't been a good person. I've spent my life doing so many bad things . . . please pray for my soul. That's why I called you. Please. Pray for me that I should find rest in the World to Come."

"Haven't you done some good in your life?" the Rebbe asked. "Try to remember."

But the poor man only sighed. "I have so many sins. I can't think of a single good thing I did in my whole life."

"Please try to remember — even one good deed. Perhaps you saved someone's life . . .?"

"Yes," whispered the dying man, "I do remember one thing that might be good. I don't know whether it's worth anything, but I'll tell you the story . . .

"I used to earn my livelihood by skinning animals after they were killed. I would leave the house very early in the morning, at about four o'clock. One day I left the house and was walking uphill to the slaughterhouse, when I saw horses galloping towards me with a wagon full of men, women, and children. They were Jews coming home from a wedding. I heard them all screaming with fear, and I straightaway realized that the driver was obviously drunk and that if the horses couldn't be stopped in a moment, everyone would be lost, for they were headed straight for the ravine. So I decided to risk my life. I was very strong, and I realized that if I would grab the reins and hold the horses everyone could jump out. And that's what I did. I gathered all my strength, ran towards the horses, pulled the reins as hard as I possibly could, and all the passengers jumped out. Then I let go, and the horses jumped into the ravine.

"That's all I remember."

The Rebbe said, "First of all, I promise you that I will pray for you. But I want you to promise me that when you come to the World to Come, after you've been to the

Heavenly Court, you will come and tell me what happened. Promise me."

The dying man, of course, promised. When he died, the Rebbe and his students attended the funeral, and the Rebbe told the burial society to give the poor man a very important place in the cemetery.

A few days later, the poor man came to the Rebbe in a dream, and told him: "Rebbe, I came to the Heavenly Court and I want to tell you what happened to me. They had a big scale and they put all my bad deeds on one side of the scale and it was weighed down heavily against me. Then they asked if there was anything to say in my favor. An angel came and said, 'Where's the justice? Isn't it written that he who saves one life, it is as if he saved a entire world?'

"So the Heavenly Court said to the angel, 'You're right. Justice is with you. We were waiting for you to come and be a defender for this person.'

"Then the angel told the court the story of how I saved the wagonful of Jews on their way back from a wedding. He went and brought all the men, women, and children who were in the wagon and put them on the scale. Still, the sins outweighed them. So the angel went away and brought the horses and the wagon and put them on the scale of merits. Still, the scales on the other side slightly outweighed them. But the angel didn't give up. He went away again, and came back with all the mud that was stuck on the wheels of the wagon and put it on the scales on the side of merit. And then the merit outweighed the debt and it was decreed that I could enter the World to Come. But first I had to come and tell you because they wouldn't let me into Gan Eden until I kept my promise."

Even the mud on the wheels counted!

There are two ways to do a mitzvah: You can do a mitzvah just to get it over with and feel you've done your part, or you can elevate it by imbuing it with extra beauty, with what is called *hiddur*. For example, you can buy a good kosher *mezuzah* for about $30. But some people want to do more. They realize the importance of the mitzvah, so they're very particular about it and will even pay many times more for a *mezuzah* of the best quality.

Likewise, some people buy *tefillin* several months before their son's Bar Mitzvah; as long as it's a kosher pair of *tefillin*, they're satisfied. But other people begin thinking about their son's *tefillin* when their little boy is only four or five years old. They will find out where the best *tefillin* are to be found and place an order years in advance. They are prepared to wait and pay thousands of dollars because they know that a Bar Mitzvah is not the party or the *kiddush* in *shul* — it's the moment when their son becomes an adult Jew who is responsible for his actions. They know that he will need the best possible *tefillin*, because *tefillin* written by a scribe imbued with holiness have the power to sanctify the thoughts of the person who wears them. For parents who understand the meaning of the mitzvah, the hall and the music aren't primary, and they don't need to copy or compete with their next-door neighbor. Their entire focus is on the *tefillin* their son will be wearing for the rest of his life.

So don't just do something to get it over with. Hashem rewards us for the amount of effort we put into a mitzvah, so use your creativity to do it to the best of your ability and give it everything you've got. Even the simplest movement of a hand deserves a reward . . .

> *In the time of the Vilna Gaon there were two women who would go collecting money for the poor and needy. They were well-known in the community and highly successful in this endeavor. Once the Gaon was asked if he thought they would have a share in the World to Come. He replied: "There is no doubt about it. But the one who holds out her hand to take the money will get a greater reward."*

Every woman should choose one mitzvah to pay special attention to — one mitzvah in particular that she always does heart and soul, so that it becomes hers — but without making herself "crazy" over it. Some people think that being exacting in performing a certain mitzvah means to make yourself crazy over it, but that's not what the Torah had in mind. It's written that a person should do the mitzvos and "live by them," not die by them. Hashem wants us to love our mitzvos, and do them in a normal way to the best of our ability. If we become obsessed, we won't love the mitzvah, but the opposite.

Did you ever see a woman who looked radiant? One of those special women with a glowing countenance? You are seeing the impression the mitzvos have made on her soul.

✍ *Light Up Your Soul*

The Chozeh (Seer) of Lublin lived about four or five generations ago and was renowned for his gift of being able to see what is ordinarily hidden from human eyes. People came from far and wide to receive his blessings.

One day a group of chassidim hired a wagon driver and his horses to take them to Lublin to visit the Chozeh. The group set off in high spirits, planning and discussing what they were going to ask for in their kvitlach (notes of request to the Rebbe).

When they reached a resting place along the way, the wagon driver turned to them and said, "When you go in to the Chozeh, I'll have to stay behind with the horses to look after them. Could you please do me a favor and take along my note too?"

"With pleasure," they replied. "Just write down whatever you want."

The wagon driver wrote out a note and gave it to them. They rode on and soon came to Lublin. When they arrived at the inn, the driver stayed behind with the horses. He watered and fed them and washed them down after the dusty trip.

Meanwhile, the chassidim arrived at the Chozeh's house where they received a warm welcome. Each one in turn presented his written request. After each had received his blessing, they handed the Chozeh the wagon driver's note.

"Oh!" exclaimed the Chozeh. "His name shines! He is a very great man."

The chassidim smiled. "It's only our wagon driver. He's a very simple person."

"His soul is shining," the Chozeh repeated. "I see him doing a very great deed. Go and look for him."

The chassidim went back to the inn to look for the wagon driver but he wasn't there. When they went out into the street again they noticed the town was strangely quiet. In the silence they heard the sounds of music coming from a distance.

They walked in the direction of the sounds until they came upon a wedding. People were dancing joyously around a bride and groom and there, in the very center of the circle, dancing in ecstasy, was none other than their wagon driver!

"You look so happy," they said to him when the dance ended. "You must be related to either the bride or the groom."

"No, not at all," he replied straightforwardly. "Let me tell you what happened. After you left me and I finished taking care of the horses, I decided to take a walk to see if there was anything going on and I came upon this wedding. I joined the celebration when suddenly — before the chuppah — I heard somebody crying, such heartbreaking crying! I said to myself, 'What's going on here?! A wedding and somebody's crying like this!'

"So the people explained to me: 'The bride is a spinster, and an orphan at that. The groom is an old bachelor and he too has no parents. The bride is very poor and has no dowry, but she did promise to give the groom one thing — a tallis. Now that the time has come, though, she doesn't have the money, so the groom said he's not going through with it, the marriage is off. That's why the bride is crying.'

"I thought to myself, 'The poor girl! Who knows if she'll ever find another husband! I must help her buy a tallis.' "

The wagon driver had begun searching all his possessions, all the secret hiding places where he had hidden a few extras coins in case of emergency. He took off his cap and found a few coins inside the band; he emptied one pocket and dug deep into another and managed to scrape together all the money he had on him. He bought a tallis and sent it *to the groom, telling him to go ahead with the ceremony. And so he did.*

Now the wagon driver said to the chassidim, "Can you imagine how I feel? I'm like the father of the bride!"

The chassidim went back to the Chozeh of Lublin and told him the story. "One single mitzvah," he told them, "one single mitzvah that you do with joy can light up your soul."

13

Happiness

appiness is not a destination — it's part of the journey. *We* are the people who create happiness, making ourselves happy by making others happy around us. The more moments of happiness you create, the happier you will be.

Happy people are creative. And making a home is one of the most creative jobs there is because a homemaker has to know something about everything — she has so many different roles and tasks.

Happy people are committed to their work, and their commitment makes them feel needed and useful. Be committed to your home.

Happy people don't ever want to be somebody else. They appreciate themselves for who they are. Never want to be somebody else; be **you** to the best of your ability, for happiness is within **your** reach.

Happy people use their talents and potential to the fullest. Most people in the world use only about 20 to 30 percent of their potential. They put the remaining 80 percent of their potential in a suitcase, lock it with a key, and write on it: "Not For Use," and store it in the attic. Make use of your potential to the fullest — you'll be surprised at what you can accomplish.

Happiness and creativity will add an extra dimension to every task you do in your home. Practice feeling happy and grateful when you do even the most routine chores, like making the beds, preparing meals, or sending the children off to school. Instead of complaining to the whole world that you have to make the beds again, thank Hashem for giving you the opportunity to care for your home. Those who spend their days sighing and complaining — "I've never had a good day in my life" — are missing the point. Each day has its moments of joy. Gan Eden isn't something you're waiting for — it begins here and now.

Some people think that happiness is something "out there," something you have to go looking for. They think, for instance, that buying a new dress every few weeks will make them happy. They find, though, that once they've bought the dress they again feel an emptiness inside.

There are those who search for happiness by continually redecorating their home. The minute they finish with the floors, they redo the bathrooms. When they finish the bathrooms, they order a new kitchen, and on and on, never satisfied.

Others are unhappy in their work. They think they'll be happy if they change jobs, so they go from one job to the other, yet happiness eludes them. Those who feel dissatisfied with where they live are always moving in a continual search for happiness.

Happiness does not lie in fleeting pleasures, it lies within us.[1] It's not something you "work on" for fifty years only to find you're still

---

1. *Orchos Tzaddikim, Sha'ar Simchah* 1.

looking for it. What is commonly considered pleasure is nothing but an illusion. Even those items you feel you want very much — will buying them really give you permanent happiness, or will it just make life easier for you?

Many women are unhappy because they've been fed the wrong kind of information. They've been told that they have their rights, that they should be "liberated." Don't worry — there isn't any religion that gives as many rights to a woman as the Torah does. If you approach your work in the home with love and joy, then the work just flows. But if you feel it's awful and a chore, and you've been brainwashed with "emancipation" and "woman's lib," and you feel there should be equality of the sexes, and wonder why you are washing dishes — "My husband should be doing the dishes instead of me! I've got a degree!" — then you're never going to love your home.

But if you feel that it's a great challenge to be a woman and a tremendous challenge to be a wife and a mother, and you love your home and your work in it, and you love bringing up the children, then you're going to enjoy homemaking. You'll have a wonderful time because you won't be "wasting" your life, you'll be *living* it!

We sing: "*Ki b'simchah tetzeyu* — you go out with *simchah*." Our Sages explain that happiness *takes you out* of every difficult situation. Others have adopted the wrong attitude, copied from the outside world, which says that only money and material possessions bring happiness. This leads to a never-ending race to acquire more and more. We know, though, that true happiness comes from giving others happiness. When a woman who loves being a wife and mother cooks a meal, she puts her heart and soul into it — just like our grandmothers used to do. If you cooked a beautiful meal which your children enjoyed and they ate it all up, that's a moment of happiness. When they all say, "Mommy, it was wonderful. Thank you," that's a moment of happiness. When you've straightened up the house — even if you know it won't stay that way — you get a feeling of pleasure and satisfaction from a job well done.

If you're doing your job as a wife and mother, love it! Everything you do in your house, as a woman, as a mother, as a wife, is a mitzvah. You are busy with the very first mitzvah of the Torah, populating the world. Whether you're changing a diaper, cooking, washing, ironing, cleaning — it's all a mitzvah. Do it with joy, and your reward will be multiplied many times over.

Bring yourself happiness by learning to see the good in everything. Instead of letting problems make you feel depressed, look at them as a challenge to help you grow spiritually. No matter what, be busy thanking Hashem, from the minute you wake up in the morning until you go to sleep at night, for the gift of life itself.

> *Once there was a couple who were married for ten years and yet had no children. They went to one of the Tannaim and told him they wanted to get a divorce. The Tanna said, "When you got married, it was a joyous occasion. Get divorced the same way. Go home and make a beautiful meal, and then come back to me."*
>
> *The husband and wife went home, and the wife prepared a delicious, elegant meal. She and her husband sat down to eat. They cried together, they drank some wine, and the husband said to his wife, "My dear, you may take the most valuable item in the house and go home to your father."*
>
> *"Thank you," she replied with a smile. She plied him with more wine and he soon fell asleep. Once he was sound asleep, she instructed the servants to place him in his bed and then carry him with the bed to her father's house.*
>
> *In the middle of the night, the man woke up and cried out, "Where am I?"*
>
> *"You're in my father's house."*
>
> *"What am I doing here?"*
>
> *"Didn't you tell me to take the most precious item for myself? Well, you're the most precious item in the whole house."*
>
> *They returned to the Tanna and told him what had happened. "How wonderful" he exclaimed. "Such a couple should not get a divorce — you ought to be blessed with a child!" A year later they were blessed with a child.*

Happiness is understanding that your husband is the most precious thing you have. Do you know how to guard this treasure? Sometimes out of carelessness a wife can be hurtful and cause so much pain. Be careful not to spoil what you have. Nurture your husband, don't break or destroy him — he's the most precious thing in your life.

Happiness is also courage. To live and be happy, you must have the courage to risk anything, and never to be afraid. Fear is unhappiness.

Happiness is also being realistic. A person who lives only in a dream world, never dealing with reality, is a very unhappy person. He is unhealthy mentally because instead of living his life he is escaping from reality. If you're a dreamer, make your dreams into a reality. That takes courage too. The Jewish people wouldn't have crossed the *Yam Suf* if Nachshon ben Aminadav hadn't jumped into the water, so jump into the water. If you do, Hashem will help — your trust in Him creates the reality.

If you want to be happy, make your dreams come true:

> *To laugh is to risk appearing a fool.*
> *To cry is to risk appearing sentimental and soft.*
> *To reach out to another is to risk involvement.*
> *To show and expose your feelings is to risk exposing your inherent self.*
> *To place your ideas, your dreams, your desires, before people, is to risk their laughter.*
> *To love is to risk not being loved in return.*
> *To live is to risk dying.*
> *To show strength is to risk showing weakness.*
> *To do is to risk failure.*
> *The greatest hazard in life is to risk nothing. The person who risks nothing gets nothing, has nothing, is nothing. He may avoid suffering, pain and sorrow, but he does not learn, he does not grow, he does not live, he does not love. He is a slave, chained by safety, locked away by fear. Because only a person who is willing to risk, not knowing the results, is free.*
> — anon.

It is up to us to create our own happiness, to convert each day into a song of happiness. Every day has its moments of happiness. You will be happy **every day** if you work on being happy **every**

minute. Each day, wake up and decide that for the next two hours you're going to be happy. Give thanks to Hashem, and smile at your husband and children and to everyone with whom you come into contact.

Then do it for the next two hours, and the next, all through the day. Give warm smiles — your eyes should be shining. Make other people happy and by the end of the week you'll be much happier too!

14

Appreciation

If you want what you have, you have what you want.
— from the teachings of Novarodok

Avraham Avinu had special coins made. On one side of each coin was written, "I am like dust"; on the other side, "The world was created for me." Always remember that Hashem created the most wonderful creation for you — this beautiful world. Count your blessings all day long.

When you learn to think positively, your life looks different.

Start training yourself to see the kindness in everything. When you make a salad, for instance, you add so many different ingredients. By the time you finish, it looks beautiful. What would have happened if Hashem had made all the vegetables the same color? Or if everything in the world was either gray or black. Imagine: a gray sky, a gray sun — trees and flowers all gray — an entirely gray world. How would you have liked it? It's His lovingkindness that makes such a beautiful world. Take, for instance, the beauty and wonder of a stalactite cave. It's a breathtaking creation. And you don't have to go into a cave to see that Hashem created a wonderful world. Just look at any tree. Notice how many shades of green it has. Thank Hashem for everything.

Be grateful for being able to see this wonderful world. What a gift to be able to open your eyes in the morning and see all the marvels of creation. All too often, we take things for granted. There was a school where one day each year the children walked around with a handkerchief over their eyes so that they would experience how it felt not to see. Or they would wear ear plugs once a year so that they would not hear. All these were meant to teach the children to feel for other people, to learn that "there but for the grace of G-d go I." When you see somebody who doesn't have all the things you have, say to yourself, "If not for Hashem's kindness, I, too, would have to carry that burden. Thank you, Hashem."

What is the difference between a satisfied, content, and happy person, and a dissatisfied, miserable, unhappy person? Attitude! They may be faced with the same challenges, but one is a positive thinker and one is a negative thinker. Do you remember the story of Pollyanna? She was a little orphan girl who lived with her father. Once a year, she would receive a charity parcel. How she prayed they would send her a doll! One year, instead of a doll, the package contained a pair of crutches. Poor Pollyanna started crying. She had wanted a doll so much, and here they sent her crutches instead. Her father then told her he was going to play the happiness game with her: She was going to thank Hashem that she didn't need the crutches! And for the rest of her life she taught people to see the good in even the worst situations . . . because there always **is** something good.

Chizkiyahu, king of Yehudah, should have been the *Mashiach*. During his reign, the entire nation was Torah observant! Even average four-year-olds knew complex *halachic* laws. But because he didn't sing a song of praise and thanks to Hashem, he did not become the *Mashiach* and we are still in exile after 2,000 years. Let's not make the same mistake. Teach yourself to thank Hashem for what you have, because what you have is what you need. Every tool we need for serving Him and fulfilling our mission will be given to us. If another person has something you want and don't have, that means Hashem knows you don't need it — otherwise, He would give it to you. Wanting what the other person has is like wanting to wear his glasses — they're of no use to you.

This may sound like a joke, but it's a suggestion that people who tend to feel miserable have found helpful: Buy yourself a cheap pair of glasses with rose-colored lenses and hang them on the kitchen wall. Every time you think the world's coming to an end, just put them on. Everything will turn rosy, and remind you: Maybe I need to change my attitude. Am I looking at things in the wrong light? A person is as happy as he's made up his mind to be. If you decide you're going to be happy, you'll be happy; if you decide you're going to be miserable, and the world is coming to an end, you're going to be as miserable as possible. So try looking at everything through rose-colored lenses.

Thank Hashem all day long. Turn your life into a song of praise to Hashem. If you're busy thanking, you can't be busy complaining. Even if it's difficult. There's not a single person in the world who doesn't have troubles. But, as the Yiddish saying goes, if everyone would put his bundle of troubles down and be free to pick up any bundle he chose, everyone would take back his own. Coping with problems makes us strong. The most difficult problem in the world can be dealt with if we trust in Hashem. If we see the lovingkindness in even the worst situation, and look at it in a positive light, we will rise to meet the challenge.

15
The Value of Time

Some people complain that life is so hard they can't bear it. If only they would realize that life is the most precious gift there is! King Solomon said that it's better to be a live dog than a dead lion — because as long as you're alive, anything and everything is possible.[1]

Our Sages tells us that evildoers are rewarded here in this world for any good deed they may have done (so that they won't have any credit left for the World to Come). But what kind of a payment can be given here? All the riches in the world would not be payment enough for even a single mitzvah! The gift of life, we are told, is itself the most precious reward there is.

Modern medicine discusses euthanasia, so-called "mercy killing."

---

1. *Koheles* 9:4.

Modern medicine discusses euthanasia, so-called "mercy killing." Some people suggest that if you see a person suffering terribly and having a hard time dying, you should help him die. Our tradition tells us that not only is this not merciful, but terribly cruel. As the Gemara says, "He who shuts the eyes of a dying person is considered a murderer."[1]

A person who is dying is living in a hazy world, suspended between life and death. He may have one second of lucidity and in that second — and it only takes one second — he may think of repentance and thereby gain the World to Come. If we help a person die, we actually take away from him a chance to gain eternal life. Why take away someone's chance for eternal life?

The Ponevezher Rav once commented that he knew no one who lived as long as the Chofetz Chaim. That's a very astounding statement, for although the Chofetz Chaim died when he was ninety-four years old, there are plenty of people nowadays who live beyond that age. What did the Ponevezher Rav mean?

In previous generations when somebody very important or very beloved became ill and his life was in danger, people were asked to donate life. They would say, "I'm giving such and such an amount of the rest of my life to this person so that he will live." We have a tradition from Adam HaRishon that this can be done. When Hashem showed him all the generations from beginning to end, he saw that King David would be born only to die the next minute. Since Adam saw that he had one thousand years allotted to him, he said, "I am prepared to give this person seventy years of my life."[2] We see that Adam did give those years, for King David was born on Shavuos, lived exactly seventy years, and died on Shavuos. Jewish history is filled with many other stories on this topic.

When Rabbi Moshe Londinski, the Rosh Yeshivah of Radin, became very ill, all the yeshivah students went around the town asking people to donate life so the Rosh Yeshivah would not die. Some people gave a day, a week, a month, or half a year. When they came to the Chofetz Chaim, he

---

1. *Shabbos* 151b.
2. *Zohar I* 91b.

thought for quite a while and then said, "I am prepared to donate one minute of my life for the Rosh Yeshivah."

What a shock! What is one minute? To us, not much. But to the Chofetz Chaim, it was enough. He sat with a watch in his hand and calculated how many words of Torah can be learned in a minute. And he saw that if you learn with a certain rhythm, you can learn between 200 and 250 words a minute. Each word of the Torah is a mitzvah, and each mitzvah creates an angel. The Chofetz Chaim wasn't donating a minute, he was donating 200 mitzvos, 200 angels!

This is what the Ponevezher Rav was referring to when he said he'd never met a person who'd lived as long a life as the Chofetz Chaim. All his days were full and perfect, with not a minute lost.

When the Vilna Gaon was about to die, he took his tzitzis in his hand and said that he was very saddened, because in the World to Come he wouldn't have the mitzvah of tzitzis. "Look at the mitzvah of tzitzis,"[1] he said. "It doesn't cost much, but through keeping this mitzvah you can reach the level of seeing the Shechinah. In the World to Come I won't have such a mitzvah."

There is no greater gift than life. Yet we waste it by not realizing how to make use of our precious time, letting it run through our fingers. Once you start becoming more productive, using each moment to the fullest, you'll see that you have much more time than you ever thought, for things you thought you never had time for.

Reb Yisrael Salanter was walking along the street about ten o'clock one night when he came upon a shoemaker sitting in his shop repairing shoes. "Why are you working so late at night?" he asked him. "It's already ten o'clock."

"Rebbe, as long as the candle burns, I can still repair shoes."

When Reb Yisrael heard that, he remembered the verse which says, "Man's soul is Hashem's candle." Our soul is like

---

1. The *gematria* of *tzitzis* is 600. Each *tzitzis* consists of 8 threads and 5 knots. Together they add up to 613 — the equivalent of 613 mitzvos.

a candle! As long as that candle is burning, as long as we are alive, we can still repair. After he left the cobbler, Reb Yisrael repeated the words for hours on end, and eventually it became a famous saying the world over.

From the very beginning — since the creation of the world — until the end of time, each minute has been given a special role, says Rabbi Dessler. All the minutes are like an endless chain, each one having a unique purpose in life. They are like precious jewels on the necklace called Time.

Most people don't know how to make use of this precious gift. They fall into one of two categories: those who live in the past or those who live in the future. The tragedy is that so few people live in the present.

Those who live in the past may have had one outstanding experience which was the crowning point of their life. They may have taken a trip around the world or they may have had a very beautiful wedding attended by many famous people. Then, for the next fifty years, they can't talk about anything else! No matter what the conversation is, they'll always come back to the wedding: who came, how they looked, etc. They spend the rest of their life reliving that one experience instead of creating new experiences every minute of every day. Or a woman may be so busy crying over a difficult youth that she can't even enjoy all the wonderful children and grandchildren she has. A person like that loses out on life. She's not living, she's barely existing. Life for this kind of person is like a desert, with only one point of "life" and the rest a barren wilderness. What a waste!

Every person has within him a small part of that person who waits for tomorrow. People occasionally have the feeling that the day was such a boring, unpleasant one, that they might be tempted to think: "I wish tomorrow were here already. Surely tomorrow will be a better day. Who knows, someone may call, or maybe a letter with good news will arrive. Maybe I'll win a lottery! Something good will surely happen tomorrow. How I wish it were tomorrow right now!"

So you wait for tomorrow. When tomorrow comes, again you wait for tomorrow. And when tomorrow comes, you'll still be waiting for tomorrow. You can spend a whole lifetime waiting for tomorrow! And if the person living in the past loses out on life, so does the person living only in the future, because you can only really *live* in the present. The past is history, it's dead; the future is not yet born. All that you have is today, the present, so make the most of it.

"The days are like scrolls," our Sages tell us.[1] Write in your scrolls the things you wish to be remembered for. Make each day memorable; live it in a way that you won't be ashamed to see later what you have written on the scroll of each day.

Imagine that you woke up in the morning and you'd never seen the world before. You walk outside and see the beauty of nature, the blue sky and the shining sun, the greenery and the flowers — the whole world singing a song of praise to Hashem. You'd feel wonderful, and so grateful to Hashem. If you feel that each day is the first day of your life, that it's a precious gift, you'll do your utmost to make maximum use of it. Take each day as a unit and achieve something: a little bit of happiness here, a smile there, a kiss and a hug to a child, a kind word. Spread happiness. You'll have a glorious day — a day to remember.

The verse, "Who is the man who desires life?" is followed, the Chofetz Chaim teaches, by the answer: "One who loves days . . ."[2] Some people think each day that passes is gone forever. It's not true. We are going to meet all our days again — after 120 years. It will be like watching a movie. Be a lover of your days; do the best that you can with them.

✑ *Don't Worry*

There are two days in every week about which we should not worry. One is yesterday, with its mistakes and cares, its aches and pains. Yesterday has passed forever, beyond our control.

The other day is tomorrow, with its possible adversities and blunders. Until the sun rises, we have no stake in tomorrow, for it is yet unborn.

That leaves only one day: today. Anyone can fight the battle for just one day. One day at a time. It is only with the

---

1. *Pirkei Avos* 2:4.
2. *Tehillim* 34:13.

added burden of those two awful eternities, yesterday and tomorrow, that contentment will escape us.

— Anonymous

Teach yourself to make the most of each day. On a piece of paper, write down all of the things you would like to do in life. Include all of your goals in the list. Then, circle the three most important things you would like to do and copy them onto the second page.

On this second page, make a detailed plan for putting these into practice. Write down plans for getting started and eventually achieving your goal.

The final step is to make the time to achieve your goals. Refer to your list every day and feel yourself focusing on the goals you have written down. Revise your plans if need be. Remember, if you can envision it, you can do it.

16

We Are Forgiven

How is it possible to repent? It is so hard for us to understand what repentance is. We wonder how it is possible that Hashem can forgive something a person did twenty years ago. But we must realize that Hashem is above time and place. Time and place exist only in this world — they are tools for us to work with. To Hashem, everything looks like a huge map laid out on the ground. Events which occurred hundreds of years ago connect with what is happening now; and what we are doing now connects with what will happen in the future. This is how Hashem forgives for something done so many years ago: He takes the deed and the repentance and puts them together and forgives.

The following true story gives a sense of how time connects, how nothing gets lost. If you think about it seriously, it will increase your awe of Heaven.

❧ The Letter of the Dreams

The letter presented here was written over 100 years ago by a famous wonder-worker and scholar, R' Mordechai Oshminer. People from all over the country used to come to him to receive his blessing, and many miracles were attributed to him.

He wrote this letter to a rebbe and friend of his, the Rav of Antipoli, also a very great Torah scholar.[1]

To the friend of Hashem, and to my soul friend, HaRav HaGaon Rabbi Pinchas Michael, Rabbi of Anipoli,

After first inquiring about your health, I would like to tell you a fearful story which I trust that you will tell no one else in the world. Hide this letter where human hands have no access to it, or shred it so that no one else may read it.

On the night before Yom Kippur, while I was studying my regular shiur, I suddenly succumbed to a deep sleep. In my dream, a distinguished man of fine features and a long beard appeared to me, looked at me, grasped my hand, and said, "Why are you sleeping? Awaken, and cry out to your God!"

I drew back in fear, and I woke with the realization that it had been a dream. I dismissed it as insignificant, yet could not help but be afraid. I went to bed and again began dreaming. This time, the same man appeared, accompanied by two other men who informed me that this was a true dream and that I should not despair. I was taken aback.

The saintly man then turned to me and said, "You must examine your deeds, for I have come to you as a messenger from the World to Come." I summoned my courage and asked him to explain. I must have spoken louder than I realized, for suddenly I awoke to find that it had been a dream.

---

1. Quoted in *Beis Avraham* by R' Avraham Danziger.

I did not take this too seriously either, even though my heart beat with fear, and I could not fall back to sleep.

All through Yom Kippur, I wept more than I have ever wept before. I could not understand why, though I thought it had something to do with my dream. I did not dream again until Shemini Atzeres, when I slept in my succah, as is my custom. This time the man appeared again, attired in white. I was deeply moved just by gazing at his noble features and awesome visage. He approached me and informed me that the tears I had shed so profusely on Yom Kippur had helped greatly, but this time, he had been sent to explain how I could mollify a terrible decree which had been issued against me.

I told him that I had no idea what was amiss! He was silent for a long time. I felt uncomfortable and began weeping, repeating that I had no knowledge of the very great sin which was the cause of messengers being sent to me from the World Above. I wept so hard that I awoke. This time, I realized that this was not an idle dream.

On Simchas Torah, I was full of joy, though I did not know why. It was a joy such as I had never felt before. When I went to sleep, I saw that same majestic man once more. His shining countenance was truly radiant, and he was again dressed all in white. He approached me, saying, "How much longer will you bother me for your fate?" I gathered my courage, and asked that in the merit of the Torah and the words of the Sages which I had studied and labored over, he tell me in detail what his mission was, explaining it carefully, so that I would understand everything. He then led me to a magnificent room, the beauty of which could not cease to fascinate the eyes. He told me to sit while he revealed the purpose of his secret mission. He then sat by my side, and began, "I will reveal hidden matters. I am the Mahari ibn Lev (Rav Yosef ibn Lev, one of the prominent Achronim of the mid-16th century).

"While I was still alive, I sat upon the seat of judgment to decide between two people in a beis din. [The Mahari ibn Lev was a dayan in Salonika.] One of them emerged guilty, but, since he was powerful, he refused to adhere to the judgment, and I warned him with the accepted formal warning . . . When I left the courtroom, he approached me on the street and slapped me across my face.

"This action is engraved in his bones to this day. He had no chance of redemption until now. Since you are descended from him, you have been chosen to make amends and give him a chance in the World to Come."

I was speechless for a long time, until the Mahari ibn Lev touched my mouth, asking the reason for my silence. I began weeping, for I did not know how to go about atoning for the sin. The Mahari ibn Lev then told me that I must purchase the volume of responsa which he had written, and study it thoroughly until I was well versed in it. This way, my ancestor would be able to rise higher and higher in the World to Come. I asked what this meant. He told me, gently, not to concern myself with Hashem's matters. How long was I to study the responsa? I asked. Not less than four years, he replied. When I told him that the volume was not in my possession, he said that I must purchase it, but only from the Rabbi of Antipoli. I asked him why, when suddenly I awoke.

I took the dream seriously, but thought that this last bit must be irrelevant. For surely I would be able to find this book somewhere else. Indeed, I asked several people to keep an eye out for the responsa of the Mahari ibn Lev. As time passed and I became involved with communal affairs, I never thought about it — until two weeks later, when again he appeared to me in a dream.

This time, he sternly rebuked me because I had not yet acquired the book. I told him that I had made some efforts to find it, but with no success. He then said to me that he had warned me to buy it from the Rabbi of Antipoli. When I asked him why, he said that since I had assisted him in the past I was being given an opportunity of being an emissary to him now. Besides, the Rabbi (of Antipoli) also had matters to settle with the Heavenly Court. He had begun preparing to print a commentary on a tractate of the

Gemara, but had not finished. The money he would receive for the sale of the Mahari ibn Lev's responsa would enable him to continue with his project . . .

Before the Mahari ibn Lev left, he shouted a warning at me not to disregard even the slightest detail of his instructions this time, for my own as well as for others' benefit. The following day, I was about to send someone to buy the book, but somehow I got caught up in communal problems and was again prevented from doing so. One night, last week, as I went to sleep, I was greatly concerned for my wife who had been taken seriously ill. The Mahari ibn Lev appeared again and sternly told me in my dream that this was his last warning. My wife's illness was due to my own laxity in fulfilling his instructions.

I awoke, my heart pounding with fear. I was about to hire a special messenger to go to you when I learned that the bearer of this letter was traveling to you in any case. Therefore, my Rabbi and Master, have mercy on me and send me this sefer, the responsa of the Mahari ibn Lev, at whatever price you set, for my wife is critically ill. May Hashem have mercy on her. Please pray for her.

Your friend of heart and soul, who writes these lines from the depths of his heart, in tears.

Mordechai of Oshmin

The incident of the face-slapping is historical fact. The man who delivered the slap was Baruch, a wealthy, powerful Portuguese Marrano who lived in Salonika. The incident took place in one of the main streets of that city in public view in the year 5405 — about 350 years ago. Two hundred years later a man was told to settle accounts for an action done by one of his forefathers — and thereby repair his soul. For Hashem, what happened centuries ago in Salonika can be connected with what happened in a little town in Lithuania hundreds of years later.

17

Contentment

ontentment is the secret of happiness, and everyone wants to be happy. If you understand the wisdom that being content with what you have is happiness, then you will not only be "happy in this world" but "fortunate in the World to Come" as well.[1]

When our Sages explain that "envy, desire, and honor-seeking drive a person out of this world," the world they are referring to is the world of happiness. A person who envies others, has many desires, and is proud, destroys his contentment and can never be happy.

---

1. *Pirkei Avos* 6:4.

Envy is wanting something that belongs to someone else, valuing something that isn't yours. We can avoid feelings of envy by understanding that we come to this world for one purpose: to sanctify the Name of Heaven. In order to fulfill our purpose in life, each and every one of us is given the vessels he needs. These vessels — our possessions — are the tools we work with. How can I desire something Hashem has given to someone else? Can I use someone else's glasses? They're of no use to me; they're only good for him, because they are what he needs, not what I need. The same applies to whatever another person has. If something is necessary for our mission, Hashem gives it to us. What the other person has are his vessels to be used for his sanctification of the Holy Name, given to him to fulfill his purpose with them.

Anything and everything we need to fulfill our purpose in life will be given to us by Hashem.

Sometimes we see neighbors or friends with certain possessions we wish we had and we feel envious. "How lucky they are!" we think. We forget that they are being tested with what they possess, and that if they don't pass the test, then that vessel hasn't fulfilled its purpose.

For example, let's say that someone has a white velvet sofa. (Some people dream of having a white velvet sofa!) Although they have the sofa, they're terrified to use it. If someone sits on it, they're afraid there'll be an indentation in it, or that it might become soiled. They would never think of letting anyone sleep on that sofa.

But perhaps Hashem gave that person the velvet sofa so that she *would* let people sleep on it. Perhaps that is the way the sofa fulfills its purpose. Understanding the purpose of our possessions leads us to value them and use them wisely:

> Once Reb Elchanan Wasserman came to the house of a man named Reb Henoch Bengis. Reb Bengis lived in Russia and was very famous for his wealth and his charity. That day it was raining hard. Reb Elchanan didn't want to ruin Reb Henoch's carpet by coming in through the front door, so he went around to the back. When Reb Henoch saw Reb

Elchanan, who was one of the gedolei hador, coming in through the back door, he cried, "Rebbe! What are you doing? Why are you coming in through the back door?!"

"Well," Reb Elchanan explained, "I don't want to spoil your beautiful carpets with my mud."

"But you're spoiling the education of my children," Reb Henoch answered. "I want my children to know that your mud is worth more than my carpets."

Reb Henoch understood the purpose of his carpet. It was more important for him to teach his children a lesson — that the mud a Torah scholar brings in is priceless compared to a carpet, and that a carpet is worthless if it prevents a great person from coming into your house — than it was for him to "protect" his possession.

Not only are we given everything we need, but it is also impossible for anyone to take away something meant for us.[1] As our Sages tell us, "Everything we need for our livelihood is predetermined from one Rosh Hashanah to the next."[2] Feeling envious is foolish, because it's not necessary: What the other person has, he needs; what I need, Hashem gives me. It's all in His hands.

After 120 years, each person will be called by his name in the World to Come; he will be seated on the seat prepared for him, and he will be given what he prepared for himself in this world — nobody can **ever** take anything away from us.

When Moshe Rabbeinu was about to die, he asked to be allowed to continue living. Hashem said to him: "The time has come for Yehoshua to be the leader." Moshe said that he was prepared to live as just an ordinary person while Yehoshua would be king, if only Hashem would extend his (Moshe's) life.

Hashem agreed, and Moshe undertook to treat Yehoshua as his teacher. Moshe and Yehoshua proceeded to

---

1. *Yoma* 38b: "No person can deprive another person of what has been allotted to him, even by a hairsbreadth."

2. With the exception of Tishrei (תשרי): Torah, Shabbos, Rosh Chodesh, and *Yamim Tovim*. If you send your children to learn Torah, Hashem provides that extra, as well as giving extra for whatever is spent on Shabbos, Rosh Chodesh, and *Yamim Tovim*.

the Mishkan, where the Divine cloud separated them, and Hashem spoke only to Yehoshua. Suddenly Moshe felt very jealous of Yehoshua and said, "A hundred deaths and not one jealousy!" [1]

That's how terrible envy is!

✍ *Desire*

Rashi tells us that "whatever the eye sees, the heart desires." [2] Once a person sees something, he starts thinking that he can't live without it. Children will come home from school and say, "Mommy, *everyone* has a watch except me." If you check it out, you'll find there is only one child in the class with a watch!

Alexander of Macedonia, ruler of the known world in his time, set out to conquer Africa, but met with defeat. Alone, he wearily trudged home.

One day, he chanced upon a stream and sat down to refresh himself with the bread and salted fish he had brought along.

Alexander rinsed the fish in the waters of the stream and when he ate them, he felt the taste of Gan Eden.

"This is a remarkable stream!" He drank the water and felt strength flowing right through his body. "This must be a very special stream," he said to himself. "I'm going to bathe myself in its waters."

As he bathed himself in the stream he felt as though he were born anew. "This must be water flowing straight from Gan Eden! I'm going to follow this stream to its source and find out from where it comes."

Alexander followed the stream until he came to the Lower Garden, the Garden of Eden in this world. In front of him stood great golden gates. He knocked, demanding immediate entrance, as befitted a great king.

---

1. *Devarim Rabbah* 9:9.
2. *Bamidbar* 15:39, Rashi.

There was no answer.

He knocked harder.

Still no reply.

He started shouting and pounding on the gates.

No reply.

When Alexander realized he was not going to be answered, he began crying and pleading and begging for mercy. "I have come such a long way!" he cried. "Please open the gates."

No one opened the gates.

Suddenly he heard a voice saying, "This is the Gate of Hashem; only tzaddikim can enter. These gates will open of their own accord for the righteous; they will not open for you."

Alexander begged the voice to give him a souvenir to show that he had been to this place. A hand came out and gave him a human skull.

He took the skull, wrapped it in his handkerchief, put it in his sack, and continued on his journey back to his own country. When he arrived he decided to weigh the skull. He placed it on one side of a scale.

Alexander took out a golden coin from his pocket and put it on the scale, but, much to his surprise, the skull outweighed it. He started putting on more coins, and then more . . . and still the skull outweighed them. He called his servants and told them to bring sacks of gold from the royal treasury and place them on the scale. Still the skull outweighed them.

He called the wise men of the Jewish people to his palace and told them the story. After they had listened intently to the amazing tale, Alexander asked the meaning of the gift he had been given from Gan Eden.

"It's very simple," they replied. "What you received is a human skull, the part of the body which houses the eyes. As long as a person is alive, he is never satisfied — he wants everything he sees. But after his death, when the eye is covered by earth, he no longer desires anything.

"How do I know that what you told me is true?" Alexander asked.

*"Ask your servants to bring in some earth from outside.
It need be only a handful," they replied.*

*The servants rushed to bring in some dirt. They placed
it over the eye, and Alexander was astonished to see that
suddenly the scales tipped to the side of his treasury.*[1]

Learn to control your heart's desires and hold them in check. If
you do, you will find contentment and happiness.

We have to absorb into our subconscious that Hashem alone
supplies whatever we need — it doesn't depend on the mercy of
human beings. Life, livelihood, everything is in His hands except fear
of Hashem, which is up to us. Even when we give to others, we
shouldn't feel that what we are giving is ours. Our Sages tell us,
"Give Him His, because you and yours are His."[2]

Nothing you have is yours, you're only the treasurer. Whatever
you have belongs to Hashem. It's been left in your charge, but it
doesn't belong to you.

With that approach, it becomes easier to part with material possessions. We can say to ourselves, "Perhaps the other person needs
it more than I do." It's easier to give *tzedakah* when you think of it
that way.

✥ When To Look Up Instead of Down

*When Rachel married Rabbi Akiva, her father became very
angry and disinherited her. She went from being very rich
— her father was one of the three richest people in all of
Israel — to being terribly poor. A girl who had once had
hundreds of servants became so poor she had to live in a
haystack. She and her husband were sure there was no one
else in the world as poor as they were.*

*Hashem wanted to show them that there were people
who were in a worse position than they were, so he sent
them Eliyahu in the guise of a very poor man.*

---

1. *Tamid* 32a.
2. *Avos* 3:7.

"My wife has just given birth," Eliyahu pleaded, "and I don't even have any straw to put the baby on. Could you please give me some of yours?"

Now they were content — they had something they could give away. They weren't so poor after all.[1]

There is a profound lesson in this story: When we begin to feel sorry for ourselves because we feel that other people have more, we should remember and take comfort in the fact that there may be others who have less than we do.

Our Sages teach us that in spiritual matters we should always look up, but when it comes to the material world, we should look down.[2] Our problem is that we reverse the order.

If we look around us, there's such a lot to be thankful for — the gift of life, the value of each day. But sometimes we forget, and instead, we waste our days grumbling and complaining.

Once there was a multimillionaire who died and left eighty million dollars in his will to be distributed amongst the various relatives he had named. One of the relatives was so distant it came as a complete surprise to him when he opened the letter from the lawyer. He hadn't even known he was related to this man, and now he was a millionaire! For a few days he was ecstatic and full of gratitude towards this relative who had left him the fortune.

Then one day he found out that the estate had totaled eighty million dollars. All his happiness vanished. "Couldn't he have left me a few more million? All he could leave me was one million out of the whole eighty?!"

This is looking in the wrong direction.

Some people say, "Yes, one really should be content because the Torah tells you to be satisfied with what you've got. But in actual fact, I'd like a _____, and I need more _____. But (sigh) you have to be content, so I'm content." That's not contentment! That's an unhappy person. A contented person has a radiant

---

1. *Nedarim* 50a.
2. Vilna Gaon on *Megillas Rus.*

face. He doesn't feel he lacks a thing because he's busy being happy and satisfied with what he has.

> In the time of Rabbi Chanina ben Dosa a heavenly voice was heard to declare: "In the merit of my son Chanina, I provide for the whole world."[1]
> Rabbi Chanina could ask Hashem for anything, as a son would his father. What was his merit?
> "Chanina, my son, eats a measureful of carobs from Shabbos to Shabbos — yet he is happy with what he has."
> Rabbi Chanina was happy with what he had. He didn't need anything more in life than a measureful of carobs from Shabbos to Shabbos. In this merit he was able to feed the whole world.

To be as content as Rabbi Chanina is a great z'chus. If you have such a z'chus as that, you can provide for the whole world.

Honor-seeking

People who want honor, who feel they have it coming to them, are often unhappy — because they'll never get what they want. This is a fact: The more a person chases after honor, the faster it runs away from him. The minute we are capable of negating the need for honor, the minute we feel we do not need it at all, that's when we start getting it automatically.

What is honor? It's intangible. It's consensus: People agree that so-and-so is on a certain level and should be looked up to.

"Who is honored?" our Sages ask, and provide the answer: "He who honors his fellow man."[2]

In Hebrew, people unthinkingly give credit to others by saying, "Kol hakavod." You know to whom kol hakavod, all the honor in the world, is due? Only to Hashem, because He is the King of the World and to Him is due all the honor.

---

1. *Brachos* 17b.
2. *Pirkei Avos* 4:1.

What Is Contentment in Daily Life?

The secret of achieving contentment in daily life is **moderation**. Clothes, for example, needn't be the latest fashion, but they should always be clean and in good repair. You can't send a child out wearing clothes with buttons missing, a torn hem, or seams ripping apart. In previous generations, they would darn stockings until there was nothing left to darn. Nowadays people think that if something is torn it has to be thrown out.

There is a famous Yiddish story about a man who found a silver button on the sidewalk. "What a beautiful button," he exclaimed as he picked it up. "But it doesn't go with my suit. For such a button, I need a new suit to match." The man went and had a suit made to match. When he saw how beautiful the new suit was, though, he said, "I can't wear this shirt with such a fine suit!" And he bought a new shirt. Then he had to buy a tie and a hat and a pair of shoes. He went bankrupt because of the button!

Let's not be like the simpleton in the story. When you shop, think beforehand and buy what you really need.

The same goes for furnishing your home. A home, as we know, is not the money that's invested in decorating it; it's a reflection of the personality of the woman who lives in it. You don't need to keep up with changing fashions, spending a lot of money in the process. You can create a beautiful home, and also one that's in good taste, by sticking with classic color schemes.

There are houses where no expense has been spared in decorating them, but you can't call them homes. In fact, some of them look more like museums. You sense that there's been a decorator who said, "Put this chair here, buy a rug and put it there, hang that lamp there." There's no warmth or pleasantness. Sometimes the owners themselves feel as if they're really not living in their own home!

A loved home and a lived-in home is created by the warmth of your personality. The more "you" in it, the more beautiful it will be. If you have old copperware, polish it till it shines. Polish your silver candlesticks and enjoy the glow. Furnishings and household items need not be new; old can be lovely when well cared for.

There is no need to rush out and buy everything all at once. Buy items you need gradually and add to them as you go along. You may make a purchase once in six months, or once a year, or maybe even every two years, rather than being busy buying constantly and then needing a bigger house in which to keep it all.

Plan your household purchases just as you plan your shopping for food and clothes. Just because something is "a bargain" is no reason to buy it. It may be a bargain for someone else, but it might not be a bargain for you.

Yaakov asked from Hashem only the undeniable necessities of bread and clothing. Shlomo HaMelech who was the richest man in the world, asked Hashem to give him only what was necessary. "Give me my daily portion of bread," he said. Not poverty, please, because then there is too great a temptation to steal. And not wealth either, because that too is a difficult test, one of faith. He was asking only to have his normal needs fulfilled, and that is what each person should ask for. Let us not set our sights too high.

Shlomo HaMelech also tells us that when a person works hard, his sleep is "sweet," whereas a rich man can't fall asleep.[1] A poor man isn't fussy. He has worked hard all day, and falls asleep easily. A rich man, though, eats heartily and has a hard time falling asleep. The Dubno Maggid explained: What prevents the rich man from falling asleep? It's because he's lying awake thinking that maybe someone else has more than he has. He's too worried about catching up with the other fellow to fall asleep.

If we think about it, we can easily see that Hashem created the world in such a way that what is absolutely necessary is easy to get and relatively inexpensive. Air is still free, and water is still cheap. What takes up the largest part of our budget? It may very well not be the necessities, but the luxuries. It's the little extras that we all want — the latest model car, redecorating the house. The standard of living in the whole world has gone up. Despite the fact that something costs a fortune, people feel they must have it. They are willing to go into debt even if they won't be able to repay their loans, all because they want to keep up with the Joneses. Those who are content to live within their budget are very few and far between.

---

1. *Koheles* 5:11.

Too many women spend more than their income, going into debt and destroying their peace of mind. They spend money without thinking about how much their husband is bringing in — or borrowing — all to maintain a life-style above their means.

How did people manage in the olden days? You can eat well without spending a fortune if you know how to shop. There are families who are quite healthy and have always managed to make ends meet even though they spent very little, because they felt they didn't need much.

Making do develops initiative and creativity. It all depends on your approach. But one thing is clear: Don't buy if you can't pay for it. Otherwise, you'll lose your peace of mind.

In previous generations, people knew they had to live on what they earned. No one thought of eating more than he could afford. People in those days didn't borrow money, because if you borrowed money, you might not be able to pay it back, and that was something to worry about. People were very honest, because they realized how exacting Hashem is in money matters.

> A student of Reb Chaim Volozhiner died suddenly. Two weeks later his image appeared before Reb Chaim and said, "I came before the Heavenly Court and was judged righteous. But they won't let me go into Gan Eden because I didn't pay my rent for the week."

It's better to be content with what you have, than to risk not being allowed into Gan Eden.

❧ A Recipe for Contentment

Take some roots of praise and thanks, plus essence of joy and trust.

Remove from these the kernels of misery and worry.

Take the flower of the pomegranate of wisdom and intelligence, along with roots of patience and contentment.

Pulverize all these ingredients with the mortar of lowliness.

Cook it all in a vessel of humility.

Combine this with sweet words.

Mix all together in the waters of grace and kindness.

Give this to drink to one who is afflicted with the disease of despair, two teaspoonfuls every morning and evening, together with three teaspoonfuls of various explanations and meanings.

Remove all chaff of anger and strictness, and combine with the essence of: patience for the Divine Will, praise, and thanks.

Give to the patient in a vessel of Hashem, May He Be Blessed. Then the patient will rest and relax.

Whoever conducts himself according to these traits will improve himself, heal his soul, and succeed in all his ways and undertakings.

— Attributed to Rambam

18

Emotional Maturity

ome people *never* mature, because they remain shackled to the past. There are people in their fifties who are still busy blaming their kindergarten teacher for the way they turned out. There are those who complain about the second-grade teacher who mistreated them, or a high school teacher who didn't appreciate them enough. There are people — so many of them! — who blame their parents for *everything* that's happened to them.

It's a real secret of life: The minute you stop blaming circumstances or other people, that's the minute you are headed towards maturity and success.

Everyone knows that life isn't easy. There isn't a person in the world who can say that his path has been smooth and problem-free, that he's walked straight through life without a care in the world. We know that life is full of trials, challenges given to us by Hashem. Our job is to face up to them, to cope, and eventually, to overcome.

Emotional maturity is the ability to solve these problems we come up against in daily life; it is the ability to straighten out the differences which invariably arise. True maturity can only be attained when a person decides that his problems are his own, when he stops blaming other people and circumstances for his failures.

If you have been caught up in blaming others, take yourself in hand. Stop blaming your environment, circumstances, and other people. Free yourself from your shackles to the past by starting anew.

Marriage, for instance, has to be worked at day in and day out, *for a lifetime*, because each day brings its own problems to be coped with. Marriage is like a beautiful plant: If you want a plant to flourish you have to give it a tremendous amount of tender loving care; if you want your marriage to flourish and develop into a happy one, you have to realize it will take plenty of hard work. Don't make the mistake of thinking, "Maybe I'll have to work hard at first, but after that it will be smooth sailing."

When couples come for help with problems of *shalom bayis*, they usually are convinced that they have to spend at least two or three hours talking about their problems, to "get it off their chest." But actually, there's a better way: Instead of delving into the past, into who's to blame, for what and when — drop it. Find a point of light, and let go of the past. Start with the present. This method has proven successful because it gives a person *hope*. If he thinks he has to carry the last ten years behind him, he's weighted down. With this approach, he's freed from his shackles. A woman on the verge of divorce who tried this method said, "We've been married for years, but I feel as if we're newlyweds. We let go of the past." As drastic as it sounds, it can save a marriage.

We know that the merit of righteous women has saved every generation, but first you have to *be* a righteous woman! Too many woman are unprepared for their role as a proper wife because they are so busy asking, "Where am I in the picture?" A wise woman — an emotionally mature woman — will solve her problems in the best way possible, without creating discord, and without destroying her *shalom bayis.* She will drop those secular attitudes that are at the root of most marital problems.

Once a girl who had made a fantastic match complained that she was unhappy. After hearing her complaints, I said: "I don't feel sorry for you, I feel sorry for your husband! You're driving him up the wall."

"Me?" she said with surprise. "I've got a B.A. and a M.A., and work at an important job with a lot of responsibility."

"But he was one of the best boys in the yeshivah when you married him!" I told her. "Actually, if you won't change, you should divorce him — because he'd be much better off. Any girl would have thought herself the luckiest girl in the world to marry him. You're unhappy? You're making him miserable!" She wasn't being the right wife for him because she was so busy thinking about her own importance.

We are not only carrying a load from the secular world, but from the non-Jewish world as well. Let's try instead to look at life the way Judaism does. Women in previous generations raised in Torah-observant homes in Lithuania, Poland, and Russia may not have had a secular education, but they had a wisdom that was far richer. They sat with their Tehillim, with their *Tz'enah Ur'enah*, their hearts and lips filled with prayer. And despite poverty, they were content. It's hard to find people nowadays who are as content as they were in generations past.

We are now seeing a generation with many problems, and we have to consider whether there might not be something basically wrong with the education of our girls. Much of what is being presented here should be taught to girls before marriage, even while they are still in high school.

What does everyone want in life? Happiness. **And being a proper wife brings happiness.** Use all your intelligence and emotional maturity to build your home, your masterpiece, to be a proper wife, and make your husband happy. Make him feel on top of the world, not that you always have to be right and he has to listen to you.

Every problem we face up to and overcome strengthens and develops our maturity. **And the basis of this maturity is trust in Hashem.** Without this trust, how could a person ever face up to everyday life? Or cope? Just as a baby nursing at his mother's breast doesn't worry about where his next meal is coming from, so too we should have implicit trust in Hashem.[1] Decide to do the best you can and leave the rest to Hashem.

Rabbi Shlomo Wolbe explains the importance and meaning of such trust:

> A home is entirely founded upon trust in Hashem. It cannot be managed for even one day without that trust. All aspects of livelihood, of family life, pregnancy, birth, child rearing — all of these indicate to the members of the family each day that they have only Hashem to rely upon. Serenity and peace of mind reside in a person's heart only if he is aware of Divine Providence in his home life.
>
> Trust in Hashem calms the fears which gnaw at a person's heart. One who lives with a positive, certain belief in Divine Providence lives in a safe world, for he knows that no chance external event can affect or harm him without Hashem's having brought it upon him as a just retribution, or for his own good. "Even though I walk in the valley of death, I will fear no evil, for You are with me." Evil, in a person's experience, is merely a fall from the world of safety to the depths of happenstance, of thinking that Providence has ceased guiding a man's future, G-d forbid, and that man is relegated to the forces of natural events. This can never happen to a man of firm trust.
>
> Trust does not mean that one may complacently think that everything will turn out for the best. One sullied with sin must not allow himself this false security. Even a completely righteous person who has never sinned may not think that, for the strict rule of justice also reigns in this world. We must know, however, that whatever the Creator brings upon us is done with remarkable exactness, that it is perfectly matched to the truth of our own selves, but only in proportions we can bear, and with great mercy. Nevertheless, one should know in his heart that all is in the hands of Hashem, Who has the power to alter nature and

---

1. *Tehillim* 131:2.

change one's fortune, against which we have no recourse whatever. And even if trouble be nigh, salvation will speedily come, for He is Omnipotent. Nothing is beyond Him.

One should trust in Hashem at all times of trouble and darkness, knowing with certainty that He can deliver us from any danger, that His help is as swift as the blinking of an eye; therefore one should hope and expect His salvation even if the sword is pressed to his very throat. For it is written: "Even if I am about to die, to Him I will look in hope." Trust is the core of fear of Hashem and faith, writes Rabbeinu Yonah. In other words, as long as one has not acquired trust, his fear of Hashem and his faith are only potentially complete. They become real when he lives by his faith. This refers to true trust which one feels in one's heart, and not outward verbal professions of trust which a person's behavior constantly refutes at every minor incident.

Before any venture, whether in business or any other sphere, it is always good to pray for Hashem's help. The following such prayer was written by the Shelah HaKadosh:

"*Ribbono shel Olam*, in Your holy books it is written: 'He who trusts in Hashem is surrounded by lovingkindness,' as it is written, 'You give life to all.' Allot to me out of lovingkindness and bless the work of my hands in this undertaking."

If you want an advocate who will always be there for you, trust in Hashem — He is the best advocate there is.

Trust in Hashem does not mean that you say, "No, right now everything isn't so good, but tomorrow will be better." True trust in Hashem is believing that **it's already good now**. It is realizing that even in what seem to be the most difficult situations there is always something for which to thank Hashem. After all, it could always be worse! So express your trust by saying, "It's good now. It can always be *better*, with Divine compassion and mercy, but it's *good* now." Trust is realizing that Hashem created the world out of love — He had no ulterior motive except to do good to His creatures. The whole world is based on this lovingkindness. Every day we are alive is an expression of His love for us, because Hashem doesn't owe us a thing! We have so much to be thankful for. So even if we think that the situation could be better — even if right now it is painful — we should look for the light within the darkness.

If we have implicit trust in Hashem and look for Divine Providence, we may sometimes merit to see how even difficult situations are to our benefit. It may take days, weeks, months, or years, but we may eventually be able to look back and say, "At the time I thought it was terrible, but now I realize that Hashem did it for my good."

The ability to trust in Hashem can, and should, be constantly strengthened. To increase your ability to trust in Hashem, take verses on trust and **repeat them at least a thousand times** during the week. One simple verse is: "הבוטח בה' חסד יסובבנו — One who trusts in Hashem is surrounded by lovingkindness." [1] Or, if you are having trouble making ends meet, try: "השלך על ה' יהבך והוא יכלכלך — Throw yourself upon Hashem and He will provide for you." [2]

You can find additional verses collected in R' Shmuel Hominer's book *Mitzvas HaBitachon*. He also notes that the Maharal of Prague said in the name of his grandfather that regular repetition of such verses has the power to annul all bad decrees. You and your husband can also strengthen your trust in Hashem by reading the appropriate section of *The Duties of the Heart*. In Hebrew, there is *Emunah U'Bitachon* by the Chazon Ish, as well as a chapter in *HaMaspik L'Ovdei Hashem*, by R' Avraham ben HaRambam.

When the Jewish people left Egypt, the women had such implicit trust in Hashem's promise of redemption that they carried their drums along with them, so that they would have them ready to play and say *shirah*. The men had their doubts, but the women were so fully convinced, so full of faith that Hashem would bring them out of Egypt, that they prepared their drums in advance. In reward, Hashem granted them the privilege of seeing, and actually being able to point to, the Divine Presence.

The Gemara says that rain only falls for those who believe in Hashem. Who are called the believers in Hashem? The farmers.

---

1. *Tehillim* 32:10.
2. Ibid. 55:23.

They plant seeds in the dry ground and trust that Hashem will make the rain fall. Their faith *creates the reality* of the rain coming down. Our trust in Hashem gives Him the power to send us rain. The greater a person's trust in Hashem, the greater will be the amount of influence on him from Above. Trust in Hashem brings things into being. If you have only a minimal trust in Him, that's how much you'll receive — it all depends on you.

Similarly, a woman's trust in her husband empowers him. Our Sages tell us that a man should always eat and drink less than he can afford, and clothe himself with what he has, solely in order not to be ashamed. He should, however, honor his wife and children with *more* than he can afford. Why? Because they rely on him just as he relies on Hashem, the One Who created the world. Reb Chaim Shmulevitz *ztz"l*, the Mirrer Rosh Yeshivah, explains that a family relies on the husband and father to provide for them, and it is this faith and trust which creates in him the ability to do so.

Likewise, if a person believes in himself, he instills in himself tremendous power to do things that are beyond the usual strength of a human being. It's all a matter of self-confidence. Trust in Hashem to help you, then go ahead and do it. You will become greater and greater.

> *About 2,000 years ago, a kohen who served in the Beis HaMikdash said to his wife, "Our poverty has become unbearable. I have decided to travel across the seas to raise money."*
>
> *His wife knew that travel being what it was, if he left the country, she would probably never see him again. She begged him not to leave, but he was insistent. "I can't bear our poverty anymore," he repeated. "I must go."*
>
> *"If you must go, then go," she said. "But how will I provide for myself and the children? What are we going to live on?"*
>
> *"I'll teach you how to identify tzara'as, a leprosy-like condition, and when people come to ask you, you'll know how to answer, and they'll give you a few coins for doing so. That way you'll be able to support yourself and the children."*
>
> *"Speak, for I am listening," was her reply.*

"Let's go over to the light," he began. "If you look at your hands, you'll see that your skin is covered with tiny little hairs, millions of them. Each hair has a fountain which provides it with food. Otherwise it dries up and shrivels, and then that's called a nega."

His wife said, "I wish that your ears would hear what your mouth is saying! You mean to tell me that Hashem is providing for every single hair on your body, and you're going to leave the country to look for money? Where's your trust in Hashem?"

He looked at her and said, "You're right. I won't leave."

When you speak to people who have complete trust in Hashem, like those who administer Torah institutions, you will hear story after story about how they received exactly the sum of money they needed — to the penny — at exactly the moment they needed it.

In a small village near Apta there once lived a simple Jew who ran an inn. To the surprise of local residents, every blessing given by this innkeeper came true. People streamed to his inn from all over, eager to receive a blessing.

Some people, worried that the innkeeper's powers might be coming from evil forces, traveled to the tzaddik of Apta to ask his advice. The tzaddik decided to travel to the inn to see firsthand how the innkeeper conducted himself. He arrived at the inn disguised as a peasant and sat at a corner table to observe the innkeeper. Although he watched him throughout the long day, he could see nothing outstanding about the man's behavior. "He must be one of the hidden tzaddikim," he thought to himself. "Perhaps he stays up all night serving Hashem. I'll watch him tonight and perhaps discover his secret."

But that night the innkeeper simply went to bed and fell into a deep sleep. The next morning, he got up, and after davening, went straight back to work. There didn't seem to be anything special about him at all — except for one thing: He would never let any of his employees handle money transactions.

Finally, the tzaddik of Apta called the innkeeper over to him and demanded to know the source of his power to bless people.

"Who said I've got the power to give out blessings? What are you talking about?"

"I'm the tzaddik of Apta and I order that you tell me your secret!"

"Well," the innkeeper began, "I don't know if I would call it a secret, but I have an enormous amount of trust in Hashem. I've been in dozens of difficult situations, and I always trusted in Him to help me out — and He always did.

"One day, things were especially rough. Business was at a standstill. I had no liquor left to sell here in the inn, I had no money to pay the rent, and my children were starving. I couldn't bear it when they came crying to me for a piece of bread. The family said I should take in a partner, and that with the money I'd get from selling part of the business I'd be able to buy liquor, and business would pick up. Believe me, I didn't want to do it. But I couldn't bear to hear my children crying, so I set out for town.

"On the way, I started talking to Hashem: 'Ribbono shel Olam,' I said, 'You know me. I trust in You and I'm not worried about earning money, because I know You'll provide. You've always provided. I don't want a human being for a partner. If I have to have a partner, I'd rather have You.' And then I said, 'Ribbono shel Olam, how about going into partnership with me? I promise I'll share the profits fifty-fifty with You.'

"The minute I finished, I put my hand into my pocket and found a coin there. I arrived in town and bought liquor and started the business again, but this time with a difference. I kept two accounts: one for Hashem, and one for me. I never let anybody else touch the money, because as soon as I get it, I automatically put half here and half there. Once a month I empty Hashem's box and give the money away to Torah scholars and needy people who deserve help."

After hearing this story, the tzaddik of Apta exclaimed,

"You have such trust in Hashem!" and he too asked the innkeeper for a blessing.

The Alter of Novarodok used to say that if you really trust in Hashem, you are truly rich. But if it's only a rumor, if you only have a reputation of being a person with complete trust in Hashem, then it's like people saying that you're rich when in truth you are poor.

Years ago, a loyal chassid traveled year after year to one of the great chassidic rebbes to ask for a blessing. Not just any blessing, but a blessing to become very rich. Each time, he was disappointed. Once the rebbe blessed him that his children should be well, and another time that his wife should be well. After three or four visits, he came back to the rebbe and cried bitterly: "Rebbe, you always give me the wrong kind of blessing! I want you to bless me that I should be rich, but you tell me to have faith, or that my family should be well!"

The rebbe smiled and said, "You want riches? Go to the nearby village and ask for directions to the house of the richest man living there. Go to his house and ask to stay there for a week. Watch carefully everything he does, and then come back and tell me what you learned."

The poor man rushed expectantly to the nearby village and asked the townspeople where to find the richest man. "He's a wonderful person!" they all said. "You'll have no trouble getting in to see him." And they pointed the way to his house. When he arrived, the door was opened before him and he was invited inside. Once inside, he was treated royally, given a special room and the best food. He walked through the mansion until he found a large room where he saw the owner sitting at a table, surrounded by people. He sat down in a corner to watch.

Throughout the day the rich man saw a constant stream of visitors. Some came to ask for a loan, others handed him money, but for the most part, he gave out money all day long to all who asked. The poor man watched carefully and noticed that from time to time the rich man would excuse himself from his petitioners and turn to open a door behind him and would exit through it, apparently to a private room. He would stay there for half an hour, sometimes an hour, and then return to his chair at the table.

"Aha," thought the poor man. "I've discovered his secret. That must be his treasury, through that locked door. He must go in to get more whenever he runs out of money to give to people."

After a few days, the poor man decided that he had seen all he needed to see, and went to thank his host and say good-bye. "Thank you very much for your hospitality, I'm going home now. I've seen what I came to see."

"What have you seen?"

"Oh, I've seen that people come and go, that you give money and that sometimes people bring you money."

"Why did the rebbe send you here?" his host asked kindly.

"He said I should come and learn something from you."

"You haven't learned a thing!" the rich man exclaimed. "Sit here beside me tomorrow for the entire day, and don't move."

The next morning, after davening and breakfast, the poor man sat down right next to the rich man at the table. The first person to come in was an important manufacturer.

"I own a large factory. I have 600 workers, and I'm in terrible financial trouble. If I can't get a loan, I will have to close down the factory. As for myself, I'll manage, but what's going to happen to 600 families? How will they live? I need a loan of at least 10,000 rubles to keep the factory going."

The rich man listened patiently and then said: "I don't have the money you need, but Hashem will help you. Please wait in the next room. You must have trust in Hashem — He will help you."

The next person came and asked for money. He was followed by another and yet another. The line to the rich man's table was a long one. Each person told his story, and to each the rich man said, "Please wait in the next room."

After listening to tales of woe for some time, the rich man stood up and took out a key. Turning to the poor man at his side he said, "Please come with me."

Overjoyed that at last he would be let in to the secret treasury, the poor man held his breath. The door was unlocked and they entered the room. But instead of a room lined with shelves filled with stacks of money and sacks of gold coins, the tiny room was absolutely bare. In the center stood a small table and a chair, and on the table was a sefer Tehillim. The rich man sat down at the table and began saying Tehillim with heartfelt sincerity, tears streaming down his face. "Ribbono shel Olam," he pleaded afterwards, "You know that I am only Your messenger. I want to help all these people. Please, if You want to help them, let it be done through me." Then they left the room and went back to sit at the table.

Yet another man approached the table, but this time with a different story:

"I've been called up to go into the Russian army. I didn't think I'd ever be drafted. I've been working hard for years, saving up to get married, buy a house, and start a business. Now I have 10,000 saved up and I don't know whether I'm going to come back alive or what's going to happen to me.

"Everyone knows you can be trusted, so I'm going to leave the money with you. I'll pay you 1,000 rubles for your trouble. Keep the rest for me. If I come back, you'll give it back to me. If so-and-so many years go by and I don't come back, it will mean that I'm no longer in this world and you can give the money away to charity, it should bring merit to my poor soul." With that, he left the money on the table and left.

Knowing that it would be years, if ever, before the soldier-to-be would return, the rich man called in the manufacturer who had come earlier and handed him the money. "Here is the 10,000 you need," he said to the astonished manufacturer. In time, the rich man knew, the loan would be repaid or the money would arrive in some other way when the time would come to repay the soldier.

The poor man went back to the rebbe.

"What did you learn from him?" the rebbe asked.

"I learned that if you trust in Hashem, He will truly help."

Our trust creates the reality.

As the Chofetz Chaim said: When it comes to trust in Hashem, you don't have to philosophize about it, you just have to do it.

Of course, a person should never say, "I'll eat and drink and enjoy life without making any effort whatever, for Heaven will have mercy on me." We have been promised that Hashem will bless the "*work* of our hands." This means that we should make some effort. When Hashem sees our efforts, then He helps.[1]

There is a level of faith and trust in Hashem so perfect that effort is not required. But how many people achieve this level?

A man once came to Rabbi Yisrael Salanter and asked for a blessing that the lottery ticket he was going to buy would be the winning number.

"I can't give you a blessing to buy the winning ticket, but I can tell you this: If you have perfect faith that you'll win, then you will win the lottery."

The man didn't hesitate. "I have perfect faith that I'll win the lottery."

"In that case," said Reb Yisrael, "I'd like to become partners with you. Would you sell me half your ticket?"

"Certainly!" the man replied, thinking, If Reb Yisrael buys half a ticket, surely I will win!

No sooner had he said he was prepared to sell half his ticket, than he heard Reb Yisrael say, "Don't buy that lottery ticket — you'll never win! You don't have perfect faith that you'll win, because if you did, you wouldn't want to give away half the winnings to me."

If you have perfect faith (and you have to be honest with yourself!) and put it into practice, you'll see that you don't need anybody — only Hashem.

Trusting in Hashem enables a person to stick to his purpose in

---

1. *Shabbos* 102a.

every situation, despite failure or the opposition of others. His inner sense of security will enable him to achieve far more than others might imagine. He doesn't spend time worrying about what will happen, because he knows Hashem will help.

A woman who is emotionally mature always has a positive approach to life, and sees problems as challenges to be coped with. She has come to the conclusion that her problems are her own, and this leads to self-acceptance. She says, "*Ribbono shel Olam*, I have done my best — now I leave it up to You."

19
Criticism

*A*ny fool can criticize. People don't realize that when they criticize — often with
the best intentions — their negative remarks destroy the other person's self-
esteem. Whether it's a mother trying to edu-
cate a child, or one partner trying to correct the other, the hurt and
damage inflicted by criticism is dangerous.

Often people think to themselves self-righteously, "Well, the
Torah tells us that if we see somebody doing something wrong,
we should point it out to him. I have a duty to rebuke him!" But
criticism is not what is meant by "rebuke." Criticism is negative,
while rebuke is positive. Criticism destroys a person's self-image,
while rebuke enhances it. Criticism shames a person, while rebuke

stems from a deep appreciation of the greatness inherent in each human being.

After 120 years each person will appear before the Heavenly Court to be asked a series of questions. Two questions will head the list: "In the morning and evening *Shema* did you crown your Creator as your King?" And, "Did you also crown your fellowman as your king?" — by treating him considerately. R' Yechezkel Sarne *ztz"l*, Rosh Yeshivah of Hebron Yeshivah, explains that these two questions are placed next to each other because they are one. If a person is lacking in love for his fellowman, he will be lacking in love for his Creator.

Man's kingship and worthiness come directly from Hashem. He was created in the Divine image, and was given dominion over the entire world, which was created especially for him. If we remember this, then honoring other people is not a burden for us, but a privilege, given out of love. Honoring another person means giving him *more* respect than we would give even a flesh-and-blood king. It means honoring him as if we are honoring the King of kings.

> When Avraham was ill on the third day after his bris, Hashem made the day very hot to prevent wayfarers from disturbing Avraham's rest. But Avraham longed for the mitzvah of receiving guests, and sat at the entrance to his tent waiting.
>
> Hashem came to visit him, and, seeing his distress, sent him three "guests" — angels in the guise of ordinary Arabs.
>
> Avraham said to himself, "I'll ask Hashem to wait while I greet the guests. If He agrees, it will be a sign that these travelers are very important people." Hashem indicated his willingness to wait.
>
> "And if I see them honoring each other, I'll run to meet them." [1]

Just imagine: Avraham saw that Hashem was prepared to wait while he greeted the guests, so he knew that they must be extraordinarily important people. But that wasn't enough for him. He wanted to see how they treated each other. If the three travelers

---

1. *Bereishis Rabbah* 48:9.

treated each other with respect, Avraham was ready to run to greet them!

Every human being deserves respect because *every* human being is created in Hashem's likeness. The answer to "Who is honored?" is "He who honors his *fellowman*,"[1] not he who honors only the rich, the powerful, and the famous. When we give other people the honor and respect they deserve, we too automatically gain in stature, as we understand from Rabbi Pinchas ben Yair's answer in this story:

> *Once Rabbi Pinchas ben Yair, the father-in-law of Rabbi Shimon bar Yochai, traveled with his students. They came to a very famous river called Ginai. As they prepared to cross to the other side, the water of the river became stormy. Rabbi Pinchas then said, "Ginai! You prevent me from going to the Beis Midrash?" And the river parted for him.*
>
> *The students waiting to cross the river asked Rabbi Pinchas: "Can we go along with you?"*
>
> *Rabbi Pinchas ben Yair answered: "He who knows in his heart that he has never in his life offended or insulted another person can cross safely."*[2]

How many people would be able to cross that river?

Our Sages point out that we can see the extent to which we should go to avoid shaming another person from the story of Bilaam and his donkey. When Bilaam went to Moav to curse the Jewish people, Hashem sent an angel to block his path. Bilaam did not see the angel — but his donkey did. Three times the angel blocked the narrow path, and three times the donkey balked. Bilaam, furious when his foot was pressed up against the stone wall, struck his donkey for causing him to be hurt. At that moment, the donkey opened its mouth and began talking like a human being! It was a miracle, created by Hashem on the sixth day of creation.

We are told that the angel then killed the donkey. Why?

Let us imagine that there existed in our time a donkey that could talk like a human being. If you were to hear that this donkey was

1. *Pirkei Avos* 4:1.
2. *Yerushalmi Demai* 1:3.

due to appear in the city where you live, how much would you be willing to pay to go and see it? Now multiply that amount by thousands of people in every city in the world and you can begin to imagine how much a person owning that donkey would earn. It would be in the billions!

Not only would such a donkey earn a fortune for its owner, but its very existence would be a tremendous influence on people to believe in Hashem. They would say, "Look at the kind of creature Hashem created, a donkey that speaks like a human being!" and they would stand in awe. Millions of people would start serving Hashem! Why kill such a marvel?

Our Sages teach us that the reason the donkey was killed was to spare Bilaam shame.[1] That donkey had been Bilaam's trusted beast of burden for years and knew all his secrets. Bilaam, while being the greatest non-Jewish prophet who ever lived, was also one of the lowliest human beings who ever lived. When we mention his name we automatically call him "Bilaam the evil one." Even a person such as this — a person whose personal code of behavior was degenerate, a person who was prepared to curse the Jewish people — must be spared shame. Hashem was willing to forgo whatever gain might be had from allowing the donkey to live, in order not to shame such an evildoer.

How much more so should we be careful with the honor of every human being.

We also learn that even stones — the stones of the Altar — deserve respect. The purpose of the *Mizbe'ach* was to bring peace. Its stones were not cut with an iron implement, because metal is used for instruments of war. In approaching the *Mizbe'ach*, a ramp was used instead of steps, because even putting one foot higher than the other to climb steps might be an affront to the dignity of the *Mizbe'ach*. "Those stones neither hear nor speak — they don't care whether or not you shame them. But because of the importance of the *Mizbe'ach*, because it makes peace between the Jewish people and their Father in Heaven, you must be careful with the honor of those stones."[2] How much more so should you not shame your

---

1. *Bamidbar* 23:33, Rashi.
2. *Shemos* 20:23, Rashi.

friend who is in the form of your Creator, and who cares whether or not you shame him.

It is a fact that many prominent people who have suffered public shame did not live long afterwards. Their lives were shortened by the anguish.

Not everyone can give rebuke. It has to come from love.

We can learn much from the way Moshe Rabbeinu spoke to the Jewish people just before his death. Although he spoke words of reproof, he never directly mentioned any wrongdoing, but instead only alluded to it by mentioning the places associated with the incidents.[1] Yet we might think: For forty years Moshe had done so much for the Jewish people — couldn't he have allowed himself to give them one good telling off? How many times had he stood before Hashem and begged forgiveness for them, how many times had he saved them after they angered Hashem? And when, after they made the golden calf, Hashem wanted to destroy the entire nation, wasn't it Moshe who had begged for mercy and said, "If you want to harm the Jewish people, then please don't mention my name in the Torah"? What hadn't he done for the Jewish people! Yet Moshe Rabbeinu was so careful not to offend that he spoke only in allusions.

Shlomo HaMelech said: "Don't rebuke a scoffer, he'll hate you for it. But if you rebuke a wise man, he'll love you for it."[2] If you rebuke the other person by telling him he's a fool and giving him a long list of his faults, he'll hate you. But if you approach him with love and tell him how intelligent he is, and how unbecoming it is for him to act in a certain way, and how far above such behavior he is, then he'll love you for it because he'll feel that you appreciate him and are only pointing out something for his own good.

You can tell whether or not the rebuke you give is done out of love by seeing whether or not you're getting enjoyment out of telling off the other person. Criticism given just for the pleasure of criticizing the other person indicates a terrible character flaw. If you don't appreciate the other person, then don't start listing his faults

---

1. *Devarim* 1:1, Rashi.
2. *Mishlei* 9:8.

because you're not going to do it properly. Instead, come to a full stop and say to yourself: "I'm going about this in the wrong way. Let me try a more positive approach."

Many people are unaware that their critical remarks, which often come automatically, are really an attempt to make themselves look better at the expense of another. By destroying the other person's self-esteem and making him feel small, we hope to gain importance. It is an offense our Sages say is one of the very worst.

Criticism does not make people change their behavior. People who are criticized do not accept the fact that what is being told to them is true. Let's say you work in an office and have been given a project to complete. When you present it to your boss, he isn't satisfied with it and starts criticizing you and your work. Will you accept the criticism in silence? No — you'll argue with him about each point he brings up. It's a rule: People don't like criticism. When faced with it, they'll insist they are not to blame. A worker will tell the boss, "I did exactly what you told me to do." It's natural for people who have been criticized to defend themselves. They'll argue every point and try to explain everything away. For best results, it's better not to criticize.

So we ask ourselves: How can we rebuke another person? First of all, if you want to point out certain things that need to be corrected you must first think of the other person in a positive way. Note all his good points. You must feel a tremendous appreciation and love for the other person before you can even begin to point out any faults.

Not everyone can point out faults. Done in the wrong way, it can hurt the other person so deeply that he'll never forgive you.

One of the gedolim was a guest in the home of a family of modest means. The lady of the house felt her home was too plain for such distinguished company. She would have liked to have been able to offer him fancier meals served on a more elegantly laid table and wished she had a larger home in which to host him.

One day she apologized to her esteemed guest for the smallness of the house: "I wish it could be more comfortable here for you — there's hardly room to move."

He said with a smile: "We say in Yiddish, 'Nisht vi gericht vigezicht — it's not what you intend, its the way you do it.' "

With rebuke too, it all depends on how it's done. As Shlomo HaMelech said, "The tongue can be like a sword . . ."[1] Of the twenty-four hours in a day, we can spend about sixteen of them talking to other people. Sometimes — whether it's to family, friends, or others we meet — we make remarks we shouldn't. We forget. We're tense or we're in a hurry, and in our rush to get things done, we say what we shouldn't.

Because people are apt to lose patience and make negative remarks, it's a good idea to learn to speak with honey in your voice. There are some people who have such a sweet way of talking that it's a pleasure to listen to them. As a reminder, buy a jar of honey and put it in a very conspicuous place in the kitchen where you can always see it. Every time you open your mouth to speak, imagine you're putting in a spoonful of honey first. Imagine that the words coming out are covered with honey — smooth and sweet. Put honey into every word you say!

In the beginning it will be a bit hard, but later you will become accustomed to speaking sweetly and it will be a pleasure. Children are especially receptive when they are spoken to with a sweet voice. Experienced teachers know that the best way to teach children is by keeping calm and talking quietly. When spoken to in this way, children listen and absorb. I have never yet heard of success in education accomplished by screaming. A child who is screamed at becomes stone deaf. He retreats to a different world to protect himself from all the noise coming at him. Talking sweetly, but firmly, is the best method.

When we speak sweetly, it usually comes from a heart full of love and appreciation. The words of such a person are more readily heard and accepted.

At the time of the British mandate, Reb Aryeh Levine would regularly go to visit the young members of the underground resistance who were imprisoned in Yerushalayim. Reb Aryeh was loved and respected by all. Even the British guards never searched him when he came to the jail.

---

1. *Mishlei* 12:18, Rashi.

At the same time that Reb Aryeh paid these visits there was a priest who came to visit the non-Jewish prisoners. One day the priest decided to ask Reb Aryeh a question that had been bothering him for some time: "I don't understand it. When you come, your prisoners are full of joy. My prisoners are never glad to see me. What's your secret?"

"I'll tell you the difference," said Reb Aryeh. "When you come to visit your prisoners, you feel yourself to be a very important man, the priest, who is doing a favor for those criminals he's going to visit. You're doing your duty. So the prisoners don't feel that they have a friend in you.

"When I come to visit my Jewish prisoners, I come like a brother. I suffer along with them, and they feel it — so they're very happy to see me. That's the difference."

If you rebuke another person because you are somewhere up there and the other person is somewhere down there, it will not work. He will not accept what you say. But if you talk to him with love, as if you are talking to your best friend, that makes all the difference. That was the difference between Reb Aryeh and the priest.

Everyone wants to put the world right, but it's a very difficult undertaking. Where should we start? Actually, the easiest place to start is with ourselves. But people usually think it's easier to start somewhere else, and that's the problem. Our Sages tell us that the minute we start with ourselves, we are going to do very well indeed: "Adorn yourself first, and then adorn others."[1] The battle of life starts with ourselves. If we begin by working on the personalities of other people, it can become a very dangerous undertaking. Only after you have worked on yourself and reached a certain level of development can you then begin to help others.

Criticism can take many forms. Nagging is one of them.

Most couples who divorce, it could be said even 99% of them, divorce not because of major problems, but because they argue over trivial matters. Tension over little things can come into the home and ruin the marriage. Some wives, for instance, nag constantly. It's very hard to live with a person like that. Let's say there

---

1. *Bava Metzia* 107b.

is a certain chair in the house which needs repair. What will a nagging wife do? She begins one day by saying to her husband, "Would you mind fixing this chair? It's falling apart. Do you think you could put a screw in or glue it together?" Her husband answers: "All right," and leaves for work. Later, when he comes home for supper, tired and worn out after a hard day, she says, "What about that chair?" He doesn't answer.

The following morning, her husband has fifteen minutes for breakfast before he rushes out. When he sits down to eat, she starts in again: "What about the chair? I told you yesterday the chair's falling apart." Whenever she sees him, instead of saying hello with a bit of honey in her voice and asking him how his day was, she talks about the chair! It gets to the point where he's built up a wall to block out her remarks because he knows he's going to hear about that chair. Some husbands give in. They'll come in late for work or miss out on learning just in order to have peace and quiet. A smart wife will either learn to repair the chair herself, or call an upholsterer. Is it worth destroying your marriage over a chair?

Once a woman became very jealous of her next-door neighbor. She saw that her neighbor had plenty of food to feed the family, and that they were all beautifully dressed, while her own family was dressed in rags and often went hungry. So she began to nag her husband constantly.

One day her husband had had enough. "Do you know what our next-door neighbor does for a living?" he asked her. "He's a thief! That's why he's rich. He can afford to buy his wife and children beautiful clothes and to feed them very well. Do you want me to become a robber too?"

His wife answered, "Yes I do. I, too, want to have beautiful clothes and plenty of food."

The husband went to the next-door neighbor and said, "I want to join your gang."

"Okay. Tonight we're going out and we'll take you along."

That night he joined the gang of thieves, and that very night was the night the king decided to send his soldiers out to look for them.

Whom do you think they caught? The newcomer. And they hung him.

When King Solomon said that a bad wife is more bitter than death,[1] he was discussing this type of wife.

Another type of wife criticizes her husband because she is disappointed in him. He's not an angel, he's only human, and like everyone, he has his shortcomings. So she decides: "He is not exactly what I had in mind. I wanted a husband with qualities A, B, and C, and he has X, Y, and Z. Maybe I'll make something out of him." She thinks that she's bought some flour and he's going to be the dough she'll knead. But a human being is not dough, and generally does not allow himself to be changed. This thought does not occur to this type of woman. She has decided that if her husband isn't quite up to what she wants, she'll turn him into what she wants. "It is all right," she says to herself, "I am going to work at it." By the age of eighty she is still trying!

Once you decide that you're going to accept the other person — with his faults — you're going to have marital harmony always. It's when we're trying to change the other person into what we want him to be that we lose. Sometimes — in a moment of annoyance, thoughtlessness, or carelessness — you say an unkind word and inflict a lasting wound.

We see what can happen when a wife is not careful, when she is too demanding, when she wants to change the other person too much. But how can we point out what needs to be corrected to someone we love very much?

We should start off by telling him all his virtues. First of all, tell him what a wonderful person he is. Go on to enumerate all his good points. Then say, with a lot of affection, that you would like to point out one little thing. You would like to say that in your opinion, and you very much hope that he won't mind at all and would he please excuse you for even mentioning it, but would he please allow you to point out (and here you can lower your voice) that it is just not fitting for him to be doing such a thing. Don't come with a long list of the other person's faults! Remember, you're not quite perfect yet yourself.

---

1. *Koheles* 7:26.

If you give this kind of rebuke, spoken from a loving heart, the other person won't be offended; he will sense your sincerity. You are crowning him as your king. You are feeling positively about him and seeing him in a good light. "Hatred awakens strife and argument, but love covers all transgressions."[1] When you love someone, you don't even see their faults.

The best way to influence another person to change is through praise and encouragement. One woman was disappointed that her husband never remembered their anniversary. He never brought her flowers or other little surprises. She decided that instead of complaining about it, criticizing him, or nagging, she would get what she wanted in a positive way. She casually mentioned a new bestseller she had heard about, and said she would love to have it. That's all she said that day on that topic. The next day, she mentioned the book enthusiastically. After a few days, her husband came with the book. He had absorbed her message without her nagging him.

When he gave her the book, she showed him how thrilled she was. She thanked him as much as if he had given her a diamond necklace: "Oh thank you! How did you think of it? It was wonderful of you." It was as if he had thought of it himself, not that she'd planted it in his mind. When he saw how such a small thing brought her so much pleasure, he felt it was worth trying to give her more pleasure. From then on, he would occasionally bring her flowers and a little surprise here and there. After all, if it makes his wife happy . . .

The recipe for happiness is not to criticize, not to nag, not to torment, not to provoke, not to tease. And not to try to change the people around us. Success in marriage depends not only on finding the right person, but being the right person yourself.

Yes, you can change the person you married, but it can only be done gradually. Give yourself at least ten or twenty years. Rabbi Yisrael Salanter said that to break one *middah*, to change one character trait, is harder than learning all of *Shas*. Think of it — by learning *daf yomi*, one *daf* a day, it takes over seven years to finish

---

1. *Mishlei* 10:12.

Shas. At seven years for each *middah*, if you have twenty *middos* to improve, you need one hundred and forty years! How can you expect to change all twenty at once?

We have to be very careful and make sure to rebuke by being positive. If we think with love about all the other person's virtues, we can have a tremendous influence. But if we're stingy with compliments, as we sometimes are, we won't see results. Often we know the other person, whether it's our husband or child, is wonderful, but when do we comment? When they do something we don't like. It's better to be generous with praise, and look for opportunities to say a few words of appreciation.

A *tzaddik* never looks down at other people. When people come to him for a blessing, his shining countenance and sparkling eyes radiate love — because he loves every Jew.

> *Reb Leib Chassid, the grandfather of Reb Yehoshua Leib Diskin, lived in Lithuania and was considered the greatest sage in his generation. Once when he came to shul he saw a group of children running around and making a lot of noise. Instead of shouting at them and telling them to get out, he went over to them and said:*
>
> *"Children, if we make any noise, we'll be sent out of shul."*

By including himself with the children, Reb Leib made himself part of them. Rather than talking down to them, he was talking to them from their level. Even a child deserves respect.

If you want one of your children to do something, always preface your request with a "please." Never command a child. You're not living in an army barracks — it's a home. And when the child does what you've asked him to do, make sure to say "thank you." Even if you're under a lot of stress and have a million things to do, make the effort to show your appreciation. In the long run, it's more important than the other things you're busy with.

People always fulfill expectations. If we fulfill our own expectations of ourselves, our husband will fulfill our expectations of him. Children are no exceptions to this rule. Take, for example, a child playing with a ball and stick. If his mother says to him, "Yankele, you're a big boy and I know you're going to be very careful not to break that window," Yankele is going to feel so big and important that he will make sure to keep away from that window. But when his mother expects him to break it and shouts tensely, "Yankele! Don't go near that window! You're going to break it!" it's certain that Yankele will break that window.

If a child constantly hears, "You're a bad boy!" or "You're a naughty little girl!" he gives up. Why should he try to be good when he's already been given a bad name? But if you always call him your little *tzaddik*, he'll try to live up to it. Explain to him that sometimes the *yetzer hara* convinces a person to do wrong, but you know he's really a *tzaddik*. Even the smallest child can understand this concept. Talk to him about throwing the *yetzer hara* out. Say, "You're a really good little boy, but when you let the *yetzer hara* in, it makes trouble for you."

The prohibition against shaming another person applies to a two-year-old as well as an adult. Sometimes a visitor will be very critical of a child, and the parents, correctly, feel they want to protect the child from the barrage of criticism. The best way to handle the situation is to say to the adult, "I love you very much and I'm very happy you came. May I ask you a big favor? My children are not used to hearing things like this, so could we change the subject?" Or do it with a joke, in a very nice way, and go off in a different direction. **But stop them.**

And how should we react if someone offends *us*? What we really need at those moments is self-control. We need to be strong of character and forgive the other person. If you feel too angry to forgive the other person right away, work on yourself. Write down your feelings and get it out of your system. Otherwise, the hurt and anger will eat you up and damage your health. Decide you're going to forgive him because it's good for you and good for him.

When someone has hurt our feelings and we forgive them and do not offend them in return, we are immediately forgiven all our transgressions. Hashem will treat us the way we treat others: If we treat *them* better than they deserve, He will forgive *us* — even if we don't deserve it.

20
Mother-In-Law and Daughter-In-Law

Our obligation to honor our parents is so great as to be almost beyond our comprehension. If we think about what our parents have done for us, the sleepless nights they endured, the worries and anxieties they had while raising us, the hours and sometimes days at a time they must have spent carrying a crying baby in their arms, we can only begin to appreciate the extent of their endless devotion. We owe them a tremendous debt of gratitude!

One of our great Sages, Rabbi Tarfon, is noted for the exemplary manner in which he honored his mother. The following incident illustrates the degree of respect he accorded her:

Once, when R' Tarfon's mother was outside in the garden, her slipper fell off. To spare his mother's feet the pain she might have from walking on the rocky ground, Rabbi Tarfon put his hands on the ground for her to use as stepping stones, and thus she was able to walk back into the house.

This is surely showing tremendous respect for a parent. But there is more to the story:

When Rabbi Tarfon became ill, his mother went to the Sages and asked them to pray for his recovery in the merit of the outstanding honor he gave her. The Sages then asked her, "What exactly does he do for you that you consider him to be such a wonderful son?" and she told them the example mentioned above. They replied: "What he does for you is well and good, but you should know that he has not reached even one-ten-thousandth of a percent of what the Torah expects of a Jew when it comes to honoring his parents!" [1]

The debt of gratitude we owe our parents is endless.

For a woman, though, there is something which overrides this obligation — her obligation to her husband. When a woman is married, her first priority is her husband, and her duty to honor her parents is subject to his approval. If he doesn't like his in-laws and doesn't approve of her having contact with them, she has to go along with his wishes. But if he is kind, he will allow her to honor her parents as much as he wants her to honor his own, and she will be able to do everything possible for them. Husbands, in turn, should strive to emulate King David, who called Shaul "my father," even though he was his father-in-law, and accorded him the honor and respect due a father. [2]

If you look at the Ten Commandments, you will see that the commandment to honor parents is immediately followed by the admonition not to steal. There is a connection between the two: If children don't see their father and mother honoring their own parents, it's as if the parents are stealing the grandparents from the

---

1. *Yerushalmi Kiddushin* 1:7.

2. *Chayei Adam* 27:24.

children![1] By denying the grandparents the respect due them, the parents are in effect making them worthless in the eyes of the grandchildren. Instead of giving them grandparents to look up to, they are making them almost nonexistent, in effect "stealing" them from the grandchildren. Such parents are also denying their own children the opportunity to learn how to honor parents, and will pay the price in the future when their own children fail to honor them.

When we say the word "mother-in-law" or *shvigger*, there is an immediate derogatory connotation. But think for a minute: The woman the whole world calls your mother-in-law is actually the person who brought up the husband you love. She raised and educated the very person you chose to marry, the one in whom you found everything you were looking for. She must have done quite a good job, and deserves a great deal of gratitude for her accomplishment. Once you begin thinking of it that way, the picture changes. As one new bride said, "During that first week I thought a lot about how much I owed my mother-in-law for raising such a wonderful son. I wanted to show her how much it meant to me, so I went over to her and hugged her and said, 'Thanks for giving me such a wonderful husband.' "

Every daughter-in-law can do so much for her relationship with mother-in-law if she treats her in the right way. The first step is to study her, to see what makes her tick, just as you study your husband and each child. If your mother-in-law is a very warm, non-interfering person, then you can create a relationship with her like that of mother and daughter. Remember, though, that once you create such a relationship, you can't complain if she acts like a real mother and gives you advice!

On the other hand, if you have the kind of mother-in-law who has negative comments to make about everything, then the best approach is to be very respectful but keep your distance. With this type of person, if you ask for favors you are giving her an opening to expect something from you in return. Accepting her favors — whether it involves constant baby-sitting, financial support, or buying the children's clothes — will make you indebted. She will then feel, and justifiably so, that she has a right to voice her opinion. If you sense

---

1. *Tanna d'Vei Eliyahu* 26:26.

that she's the kind of person who has something to say about everything, be very nice, treat her with great respect, but be wary of spoiling the relationship by accepting too many gifts. And if you want to maintain your privacy and independence, don't ask for favors.

With every mother-in-law, the first step in developing a good relationship is to give her a lot of respect. Try your best to bring her happiness. You can ask her for the recipes of your husband's favorite foods. It's a rule that every son loves his mother's cooking. No matter how bad a cook she may be, even if she burns the food, for him his own mother's cooking is the taste of home, and he'll never forget it. You may be a better cook, but it doesn't matter. Ask your mother-in-law which dishes he likes, and don't be too embarrassed to accept her help in making them. If she wants to send over the food already made, accept it — it makes her feel wanted and needed. She may want to teach you how to make it, or she may continue to bring it already prepared. Even if you'd rather make it yourself, let her bring it several times before suggesting that she teach you how to make it. In showing her that you appreciate her cooking, you are increasing her sense of self-worth.

Whenever we ask a person for advice, it builds his self-esteem and gives him a sense of closeness to us, so do ask your mother-in-law for advice. But **never ask her for her advice on matters between you and your husband** — this area should remain private. In other areas, give your mother-in-law the feeling that her advice is valuable and appreciated. She'll feel that she is still important and hasn't been discarded. She'll feel wanted, needed, and loved — and love makes a person want to live. If she is an older person, she will need even more love, affection, and warmth.

Another point for enhancing your relationship with your mother-in-law: When you come to visit, don't act as if you've come for a vacation. There are daughters-in-law who work very hard, so they think that when come to their mother-in-law's house they're entitled to five-star-hotel treatment. The minute they arrive they sit themselves down and don't budge from the chair. They may offer to help, but they do it in such a way that no self-respecting mother-in-law would ever accept. "Do you need my help?" they say. When someone says that, the automatic response is, "No, thank you, I can manage," because the implication is that they cannot manage without your help. When a mother-in-law has worked so hard to prepare a beautiful meal or Shabbos for the family, implying that she can not manage and needs help is an insult. Of course she'll say "No, thank you."

Instead, think of yourself as a daughter, not a daughter-in-law. We say that when a child gets married, you don't lose one child, you gain another. When your son gets married, you gain a daughter; when your daughter gets married, you gain a son. So when you, as a daughter-in-law, come to your mother-in-law's home, come as a daughter. Do you go to your mother's home and sit down in a chair without moving? Or do you care about your mother so much that you get up to help without asking? Do you ask your mother if she "needs help" or do you go straight into the kitchen to help serve? Behave the same way when you visit your mother-in-law, unless you sense that she is decidedly uncomfortable when you do.

For harmonious family relationships, remember: A mother accepts things from her son that would hurt her if they came from her daughter-in-law. Let's say your mother-in-law invited you for Shabbos and you accepted. Then in the middle of the week you found out you made a mistake with the dates and you can't come. What should you do? Don't call to cancel. You should **never be the one** to pick up the phone and say, "I'm sorry, we can't come." Instead, ask your husband to make the call. Your mother-in-law will accept the disappointment much more easily if it comes from her son.

Another important rule for a daughter-in-law is: **Never interfere in quarrels**. If your husband is having an argument with his parents, don't side with him — because afterwards he won't forgive you. Later, he may even feel that he was in the wrong. Stay out of family arguments and do not interfere — it's not your business, unless he asks you to get involved. Often women destroy their marriage because they never learned one simple secret of family harmony: **Never criticize your in-laws.** Never. Under any circumstances. Even if they give you trouble. Your husband will never forgive unfavorable remarks made about his parents. If you want to achieve the most out of life with your husband, use a positive approach to everything — your in-laws included — even if they're difficult people. You can always find something good to say about everyone. If, for instance, they don't have the same religious standards as you, you can focus on the fact that they are people of good character, devoted parents, that they're kind, and that they love you.

If your mother-in-law is the possessive type and you value your privacy and independence, keep a distance. It's preferable to move into a tiny little apartment of your own, rather than into a luxurious house together with or right next to your in-laws if you want to remain independent.

If your husband is the youngest child in his family, your mother-in-law may be experiencing the "empty-nest" syndrome. She is at a turning point in her life and doesn't know what to do with herself. She may often make constant demands on your time that you find hard to fulfill. A solution is to find ways of keeping her occupied. Work behind the scenes to see that friends invite her to come with them to classes or join them in volunteer work. Make sure she becomes involved, that she's called to participate in various outings and activities. She will be happier, and you will be too, because she will not be pulling at you to fill her time.

Often women want to know what they should do about a mother-in-law, or other parent, who doesn't know much about Judaism yet offers lots of advice on child raising. Such a parent may be told, "I very much appreciate hearing this and I know it's a psychological approach, but Judaism sees it this way." Psychology is just beginning to discover what Judaism has been teaching for thousands of years. There is nothing wrong with using some of the methods it offers, as long as you do it in the Jewish way. Instead of looking at such advice in a negative way, you can say, "You're right, that's a very good idea" — but do it your own way. If they suggest, as one woman's parents did, that the home be run democratically, and that everyone vote on major issues, you can just say, "That's a very good idea and I'm going to adapt it into my scheme of things." Whether you choose to use their ideas or not is up to you. But always say thank-you for the idea, because it's very disrespectful to argue. Even if you're not going to follow their advice, thank them for it. Avoiding arguments and side-stepping fights will leave both sides feeling good about themselves and each other.

Being a mother-in-law is apparently just as difficult as being a daughter-in-law. In some families, you hear a mother-in-law saying,

"My daughter-in-law? She's got a mother, let *her* buy her presents. I buy presents for my daughters." This attitude can only cause jealousy in the family and bad feelings. Once your son is married, you've gained a daughter, so treat her like one.

There's a saying in Yiddish: *A shvigger darf shenken, shlingen, un shviegen* — A mother-in-law should "give presents, swallow whatever she's got to say, and keep quiet." They also say that when a mother-in-law comes to visit her daughter-in-law she should have *a shmeck, a leck, and aveck* — she should take a deep breath, have a bite to eat, and then leave, i.e., make it short and sweet.

As a mother-in-law, before visiting your daughter-in-law always ask what to bring. The idea is to bring what *she* likes, not what you like. Some daughters-in-law hate their mother-in-law's presents. Even the most beautiful, expensive garment bought for a grandchild will sit in the closet if it's not her taste. If you have such a daughter-in-law, don't buy her presents; give her money instead. Let her buy the children what she wants; it doesn't have to be your taste, it has to be *her* taste. She is the one who has to live with it, so she is the one who has to like it, even if you may have better taste. If you want what is good for the family, you'll be happy to give her the money and let her spend it as she sees fit. You will be giving her two presents in one: the present itself, and the pleasure of buying it.

When you go to visit, don't bring candy for your grandchildren if your daughter-in-law prefers that they not eat sweets. Ask her what you can bring for them. And always find out when it would be convenient to stop by. Some mothers-in-law drop in at the most inconvenient times. When their daughter-in-law has at last managed to give the children supper and get them into bed and feels that she's somehow made it through a long, tiring day, they appear. The children jump out of bed in excitement and the evening starts all over again. Her daughter-in-law feels like fainting right on the spot. Such a mother-in-law is behaving in a tactless way, thoughtlessly ruining her daughter-in-law's evening and making life difficult for her. If she wants to visit, let her come at the beginning of the evening and help make supper, give the children their baths, and put them to bed. That's true consideration.

As a mother-in-law, don't go into your daughter-in-law's kitchen unless you're invited. It is none of your business whether or not the dirty dishes are piled sky high. And don't go around opening cupboards and doors — that's being nosy. If your daughter-in-law wants to treat you like a guest, act like one: Sit down, drink a cup of coffee, play with the children, and then leave. Don't interfere, and avoid all criticizing!

The parents of a young couple can often find themselves in a tug-of-war over "rights and privileges" if they're not careful. If the young couple lives in the same town as both sets of parents, arguments can arise over how much time they spend at his parents and how much time they spend at hers, who they go to for the holidays, or whom the baby is named after. Often the halachah gives clear guidelines, yet people tend to make an issue out of the very events that should bring families closer together. A word to the wise: If you're a mother-in-law, **always give in to the other side**. If you do, the children will love coming to you. It's usually the demanding people who are hard to tolerate. The young couple may give in to their demands, but they won't like it. The more independence you give your children, the more they come back to you. The more independence you give them, the more they love and respect you and love coming home. The more a mother ties the children to her apron strings, the more they want to get away and never come back. To avoid this negative reaction, let the other side be first.

Work at making the relationship between you and your daughter-in-law's parents a friendly one. You may be a marvelous parent and you may have the means to be very good to the young couple as well. You may have even bought them an apartment, or furnished their home with little or no help from the other side. Sometimes children come with nothing into a family. They may have left their parents' home with barely the basics, and you bring them into your family and give them everything. Many parents mistakenly make an issue out of this, saying: "We have given you everything and they have not given a thing!" Remember, when you give, you are actually doing it for yourself. By giving, you are getting a lot of pleasure. You experience the fun of giving, plus the enjoyment of helping your children. If the other side is not giving, don't mention it. Never say, "Look what I am giving you — what has the other side given?" Couples have eventually wound up in *beis din* to end their marriage because there have been so many arguments about such things. Stay away from this dangerous issue. It will only jeopardize the marital harmony of the young couple.

For wonderful family relationships, everyone should be busy praising everyone else. Praise your daughter-in-law so that your son appreciates her more, and the same applies to your son-in-law. Praise him. When your daughter sees your positive opinion of him, she will find more and more to admire in him. A mother should say to her daughter, "You have the most fantastic husband and wonderful in-laws." A mother-in-law should say to her son, "What a wonderful wife you have! What marvelous in-laws you have." With this approach, the relationship flourishes as people begin to appreciate each other more and more. They look at each other in a different light when they're praised. On the other hand, if a son hears derogatory remarks from his mother about his wife he will go home and look at his wife through his mother's eyes. Instead of seeing her good points, he will see her in a negative light. His mother's comments can ruin his marriage. How dare she! It's none of her business — she should be happy he's married! So remember: **Never say anything bad about your daughter-in-law to your son.** Never. After all, you want him to have a happy life — why destroy their marriage?

The points mentioned here provide a basic outline, a starting point to add to from your own experience in life. As a daughter-in-law, think of how hard it must be for your mother-in-law to spend her life bringing up a son and then feel that she's losing him. On the other hand, if she feels she's gaining, she won't be jealous and demanding. As a mother-in-law, love your daughter-in-law, for you've gained a daughter without the hard work. It all depends on you having a positive approach.

21

Stay Close to Hashem

When we're worried about something, our prayers are more intense. When someone in the family is not well, the tears stream down. When we have it hard, we remember to turn to Hashem. It's when we are too comfortable and life seems easy that we're liable to forget Him.

Sin causes us to fall asleep and forget why we are here. We forget that Hashem expects something from us, that our whole purpose in this world is to sanctify His Name. When that happens, suffering wakes us up. Even the smallest discomfort, the most minor inconvenience is considered suffering. If a person reaches into his pocket to take out three coins and pulls out only two, his distress is real and considered a type of suffering. If he wants to put his coat on and the sleeve is turned inside out and he has to turn it right-side out, that too is a form of hardship. If he enters the kitchen to get something but forgets what he came for, if he looks for something and can't find it, that's suffering too. From the minor troubles in life to the major miseries — it's all considered suffering.

Although it pains Hashem to cause us even the smallest amount of suffering, He does it out of love, to save our lives. He wants to awaken us to give us a chance to perfect what needs to be rectified, to complete our mission in life. When something happens to cause us distress, we should view it like a red traffic light, warning us to stop and take a good look at the road we are traveling — and how we're driving.

The minute we realize the purpose of life's trials and tribulations, we look at all suffering in a different way. Instead of seeing it as "punishment," we feel tremendous love of Hashem for saving our life. We look at each stop as a "red light," as an opportunity to improve ourselves and our situation. When Shlomo HaMelech wrote, "The voice of my Beloved is knocking,"[1] he was referring to Hashem's call in every generation. Hashem knocks. It's up to us to answer.

> Rabbi Eliezer ben Hyrcanus, the great Torah scholar, was so esteemed that Rabbi Akiva kissed the stone he sat on, comparing it to Mt. Sinai, because he gave forth such an abundance of Torah while sitting on that stone.
>
> One day, when Rabbi Eliezer became ill, four of his students, Rabbi Tarfon, Rabbi Yehoshua ben Chananyah, Rabbi Elazar ben Azaryah, and Rabbi Akiva, who were already venerable sages themselves, came to visit him. Seeing his suffering, each one in turn offered words of encouragement. One said, Rebbe is like rain to the world — without rain, the world can't exist. A second said, He is like a sun. When Rabbi Akiva spoke, though, he said, "Suffering is a very good thing."
>
> Upon hearing this, Rabbi Eliezer said: "Prop me up so that I can hear the words of my pupil Rabbi Akiva who says that suffering is a very good thing."
>
> He then turned to Rabbi Akiva and asked: "Akiva, why

---

1. *Shir HaShirim* 5:2.

do you say it's good to have pain and suffering? Where did you hear that?"

And then Rabbi Akiva told him this story.

Menashe, the son of Chizkiyahu, became king when he was twelve years old. He ruled the Jewish people for fifty-five years, and for those fifty-five years all he did was wrong in the eyes of Hashem and caused the Jewish people to sin.

How could Chizkiyahu, under whose reign even little children three or four years old knew the complex laws of ritual purity, under whose kingship the entire nation knew Torah, have a son so evil?! When Menashe became king, he led the entire nation into idol worship, going so far as to put an idol into the Kodesh Kodashim and making everyone bow down before it! For fifty-five years, he misled the nation entrusted into his rulership. They were fifty-five long years of collective sin. Is it possible that Chizkiyahu, king of Yehudah (who taught Torah to all the Jewish people and was worthy of being the Mashiach), did not teach his own son Torah?

Certainly not! He taught Menasheh the entire Torah. Yet all the effort he put into teaching him Torah had no effect. Although Chizkiyahu was leader of the nation, he was not successful in helping his own son.

After Menashe had ruled the Jewish people for fifty-five years, however, Hashem sent the king of Ashur to wage war against the Jewish people. Menashe fell into the hands of the Assyrian army and was taken captive. They decided to kill him by roasting him alive.

They made a huge copper kettle full of holes, like a giant sieve, and put Menashe inside. Then they put him over the fire to roast him. As the copper heated up and Menashe began to feel uncomfortable, he started praying. But not to Hashem. He prayed to every idol that existed in the world, beseeching each one in turn to come to his aid. As the heat intensified, and he received no answer, he suddenly remembered: "When my father carried me on his shoulders to cheder he used to repeat a certain verse all the time: 'When you will be in trouble and all these things will come to pass, *(everything the prophet had promised), then you will return to Hashem your L-rd, . . . for He is compassionate . . .'[1] I will pray to Hashem, and if He answers, fine. If not, then He is like all the idols."*

When the angels heard that Menashe had started praying to Hashem, they closed all the gates of Heaven. "Such an evil person! For fifty-five years he caused the Jewish people to sin and worship idols and now he wants Hashem to save him?! We won't let his prayer go up to the Heavenly Throne," they declared.

But Hashem said to the angels, "Menashe wants to return to Me. If I don't accept his prayers and repentance, it will close the door to all future ba'alei teshuvah for all generations. I have to show the Jewish people that teshuvah exists even in the worst case. I must accept the teshuvah of Menashe." Hashem then made a special opening under His Heavenly Throne, and the prayers of Menashe entered through that opening.

A miracle occurred, and Menashe was brought back to Yerushalayim and lived in true repentance until the end of his life.[2]

"Sometimes," Rabbi Akiva said to Rabbi Eliezer, "nothing helps except suffering."

Suffering reminds us of Hashem. Even a person who is on the right track can be prompted to aspire to and attain an even higher level of righteousness through suffering. Out of deep love, Hashem will give such a person a chance to earn greater reward by facing trials and tribulations with *acceptance*, instead of resistance. Praying for betterment of the situation is part of acceptance. Sarah, Rivkah, and Rachel were all barren, and each one became closer to Hashem through prayer. We should always consider that perhaps Hashem awaits our prayers. By accepting suffering with love, a person becomes imbued with tremendous spiritual power.

Acknowledging our pain can be part of acceptance. Once a very great *tzaddik* lay ill and dying. Visitors asked him, "How are you

---

1. *Devarim* 4:30-31.
2. Based on *Sanhedrin 94b*, 101b; *Yerushalmi Sanhedrin* 10:9.

feeling?" to which he answered, "*Baruch Hashem*, worse." That's accepting suffering with love. He told the truth — that he felt worse. But he said *baruch Hashem*. Even pain gets a *baruch Hashem*, because it shows acceptance of Hashem's judgment. If you find someone like this, beset by suffering yet accepting the judgment, go and ask him for a blessing, because his blessings will come true.

We can't comprehend why suffering befalls a person. Often a person is so wonderful, so filled with Torah and good deeds that when people see him suffering they wonder, "Why should he suffer like that?!" But how can we know what Hashem wants from a person? Can we fathom the complexity of Hashem's way of running the world? Who are we to ask questions? "Hide yourself a little while until the time of trouble passes," we are advised.[1] It's not our business to argue, it's our business to accept whatever Hashem sends.

Even if it's hard to come to terms with what is happening — and sometimes it's *very* hard — it's better not to allow our lack of knowledge to overwhelm us. Many who expressed doubts in the concentration camps lost everything — their faith, their belief, and trust in Hashem — never to regain it.

We only know one thing, and of this we must be 100% certain: It's all *chesed* and *rachamim*; it's all given with great love.

So feel deep gratitude to Hashem, and count on His help. Pray endlessly, for His mercy can annul the decree.

In addition to repentance and prayer, there is another response to suffering: giving charity. The following true contemporary story shows just how effective this can be.

> A well-known Torah scholar was told that his situation was one of life or death, and that without major surgery, he would not have long to live. The surgery they recommended, though, was itself a dangerous life-threatening procedure. Faced with such a serious decision, he traveled overseas to Bnei Brak to seek the advice of the Chazon Ish.
>
> The Chazon Ish greeted his guest warmly, and began a Torah discussion with him. The pair spent the next five hours together, talking in learning, but every time the visitor tried to ask the sage's advice about his operation, the

---

1. *Yeshayahu* 26:20.

Chazon Ish would put him off. Instead, he invited him to return the next day.

The visitor from abroad returned day after day, yet the time he spent together with the Chazon Ish was devoted solely to delving into the Gemara. Every time he tried to bring up his medical dilemma, he was met with silence. Not having received an answer to his pressing problem, and left with only one day before his scheduled return home, he felt compelled to try to broach the subject once more. "I must return home tomorrow morning," he began. "Please advise me. What should I do? Should I undergo the operation or not?"

The Chazon Ish then asked him, "Do you have any ma'aser money with you? Give it to me and I'll give it away to tzedakah."

Naturally, his visitor hastened to comply, and gave him the sum he had set aside for charity.

"Oh no," the Chazon Ish said, "we'll need more." A few more bills were removed from the wallet and placed on the table, but the Chazon Ish indicated that they weren't sufficient. The esteemed guest took out most of the cash he had, until the Chazon Ish asked, "How much do you have left?" There was just about enough to get to the airport. "You can keep that — give the rest to me."

After the Chazon Ish had taken all the money, he told him, "You can go ahead with the operation. It will be all right."

The scholar flew home, underwent the dangerous surgery, and had a complete recovery.

He lived for another twenty-five years.

This is known as *kopher nefesh*. In addition to its lifesaving aspect, it is also an effective way to deal with suffering.

Sometimes, after 120 years, a *tzaddik* comes before the Heavenly Court, where his merits and debts are put on the spiritual scale, only to find that some part of his soul remains unperfected. He is then told: "You have a choice. You can go to Gehinnom for twelve months, or you can return to the lower world to correct what must be corrected."

The suffering of Gehinnom is beyond our imagination. Rabbi Dessler once said that if a person were to pass his finger through a burning candle, no matter how painful it might be, it wouldn't be even a millionth of the pain of Gehinnom. Gehinnom is burning shame. In the World to Come, there are no physical boundaries and we are able to see everything in a clear light. We'll be faced with all our deeds of a lifetime and our shame will be overwhelming. We'll cry out, "How could I have done such a thing!?" Many people faced with the choice of twelve months in Gehinnom or a return to earth in a different body, choose the latter alternative. They want another chance to rectify what must be corrected. Sometimes, they need only arrive again in this world as a newborn baby. Just the fact of being born, of the soul coming down again, gives them a z'chus. Sometimes a soul lives for a few years, sometimes it has to live for eighteen years. And some people need a hundred years. We become very attached to this world, to everything physical, to people and our feelings for them, but we should remember that the overall plan is a big one. We can't see it or understand it, but everything is connected.

The root of some people's *neshamah* goes back generations. It's a very profound subject that is beyond our comprehension. The famous story of the childless couple who went to the Ba'al Shem Tov to ask him for a blessing for children has become a classic illustration:

> *After years of painful childlessness, a couple sought the blessing of the Ba'al Shem Tov. Time after time they begged him, only to be refused. One day, as the woman cried and pleaded with special intensity, the Ba'al Shem Tov sat deep in thought. Finally he said, "Yes. You will have a baby."*
>
> *The couple returned home and within a year, they became parents of a wonderful, exceptionally beautiful baby. Their joy was unbounded.*
>
> *At the age of two, though, the child died. Hearts full of sorrow, they returned to the Ba'al Shem Tov. "What kind of a blessing did you give us? The baby only lived for two years!" they complained.*

The Ba'al Shem Tov then related the following incident: There was once a powerful king who ruled over a vast kingdom. He ruled justly and peacefully, and had no enemies. Yet, the king and his queen were extremely sad, for they didn't have children. They went to doctors, visited spas, attempted remedies of all sorts, but to no avail. As each effort failed, the king grew more depressed.

One day he confided in an advisor, who suggested that he had just the right plan — the king should present the Jews in his kingdom with an ultimatum: If his wife did not bear a son within a year, the Jews would be expelled from the countries under his dominion. Desperate for a child, the king agreed with the idea, and issued the decree.

The Jews of the kingdom were in shock. They attempted to persuade the king to rescind his edict but they did not succeed. Throughout the kingdom, in every city, town, and village, every Jewish man, woman, and child came to shul each day to pray for salvation. Tehillim was recited, special supplications were inserted, fast days were declared — the populace stormed the gates of Heaven.

In Heaven a debate raged. Some angels maintained that the king had been destined to remain childless, and that he had done nothing to warrant a change of fate. Other angels pointed to the unending stream of tears and prayers of the Jews of the kingdom — were those supplications to go unanswered? Hashem issued His decree: If a neshamah was willing to descend and save the Jews, the king would have a child. If there was no neshamah that would agree to go, the Jews would be banished from the kingdom.

The malachim made a plea to the neshamos, and one neshamah agreed to be sacrificed. The Jews of the kingdom would be spared.

The day the child was born was a festive one throughout the kingdom, but especially for the Jews. They were overjoyed, and they expressed their gratitude to Hashem for His help.

At the palace, the baby boy proved to be a precocious child. He began to speak at several months and was reading *by a year. When he was eighteen months old, the king was compelled to hire a noted pedagogue to instruct the brilliant and inquisitive prince.*

Each day after their morning lessons, the prince's teacher retired to his private chambers for several hours, locking the door behind him. One day the young prince followed him, watching through the keyhole as the man donned black boxes on his arm and head and began to study from a large tome. The boy was intrigued, but the door was locked. He dared not breathe a word to anyone, but he decided that he would follow his teacher each day — maybe then he would understand.

Day after day, the prince stood at the keyhole, as if transfixed. But he still did not understand: What were those boxes? What was that book? He bided his time.

One day the teacher neglected to lock the door. This was the chance the child had been waiting for. As soon as the instructor sat down, the prince opened the door and entered, catching him unaware.

"What are you doing here?" the teacher demanded.

"What am I doing here? What are you doing?" the prince responded. "I've been watching you each day for weeks. You must explain all this to me."

The teacher swore the prince to secrecy and explained that he was a Jew, and as such he wore tefillin, davened, and studied each day. The student had many questions, but the teacher tried to put him off. "What is in the boxes? What does it mean to be a Jew? In what ways are you different from my parents? To Whom do you pray? What do you study? Who wrote the book?" The teacher brushed him off, and the child left the room.

When the time came for their afternoon study sessions, the prince was more tenacious. He demanded answers — complete, in-depth explanations — or, he threatened, he would betray the teacher's secret. The teacher had no choice but to comply.

The prince was impressed with what he learned. He wanted to know more, and as the years passed he sought to emulate his instructor as much as possible. Then, after several years, he approached him with a more difficult request: "I would like to become a Jew."

The words struck like a bolt of lightening. The teacher explained to the prince the difficulties of being a Jew, that he was sacrificing his chances of ever becoming king, and he highlighted the dangers involved — the dangers to the prince, to the instructor himself, and to the Jews under the king's rule — but the prince remained resolute. He was committed to conversion to Judaism.

"If that is the case," the instructor said, "I have an idea. When you reach the age of twelve or thirteen tell your father that as part of your training as the future king you feel that it is necessary to go and see how the people destined to live under your dominion live. Explain that you have always been sheltered and that now you want to see the common folk and their way of life. If you are still bent on becoming a Jew, once you are out of the palace, escape to another country and convert there."

The young man agreed to the plan. And this is in fact what he did, living the rest of his life as an outstanding tzaddik.

When he passed away, his neshamah was remarkable in its brilliance, it was almost flawless. The only minor imperfection it had was that it had suckled from a non-Jewess for the first two years of its life. The Heavenly tribunal decided to send the neshamah back to this world for two years. It is this lofty neshamah that you were chosen to receive for safekeeping.

This is not to deny the parents' sorrow. There is no doubt, though, that the experience brought them closer to Hashem. We have many stories of Eliyahu HaNavi seeing the plight of the poor and suffering and begging Hashem to let him intervene to improve their lot. In each story, the newfound wealth or comfort becomes a barrier, distancing the recipient from Hashem. In these stories Hashem always says, "I'll let you help him, but see that because of your help, I don't lose him." Yet time after time, the poor man who becomes rich becomes so busy with his property that he forgets all about Hashem, Who then says to Eliyahu, "What did you do to him? He was one of My dearest people. You lost him for Me. Now take the money away from him."

Even in our time, people find that human understanding of what is good for a person is limited. Several generations ago, two men came before the Rabbi of Cracow with this dispute:

"I have been blessed with great wealth," one began. "Several years ago I was walking through the marketplace in Cracow when I saw a man selling baked goods," he continued, with a nod to the other party to the dispute. "I went up to his stand to make a purchase and he offered a novel Torah thought.

"Naturally, I was quite surprised to hear this from the mouth of what seemed to be a simple baker. Curious, I began talking with him about Torah subjects and was astonished to see the depth and breadth of his scholarship. 'You're wasting your time standing here and selling bread and cake!' I said to him. 'You are a great Torah scholar. Let's make a deal: I'll provide you with all your needs and you'll sit and learn. It will be a Yissachar and Zevulun partnership, and I'll have a share in your Torah.' Then I asked him, 'How much do you need to live comfortably? Just tell me, and I'll make sure you get it every week.'

"He agreed, and I made sure to give him the money every week. He and his family lacked for nothing, isn't that so?" he concluded, turning to face the former baker.

"Yes, esteemed Rabbi, what my friend has said is true," the Torah scholar spoke for the first time. "He kept up his part of the bargain. But after two years, I felt compelled to go to him and ask him to annul our agreement. I told him I wanted to go back to baking for a portion of the day. 'What's the matter?' he asked me in alarm. 'Is the money I'm giving you insufficient?'

" 'Oh, no,' I assured him, 'it's already more than we need. But I must tell you this: Since you began supporting me, I feel that I have lost a certain closeness to Hashem. When I had to provide for myself, I would pray to Hashem

for money to buy flour, then I would pray to Hashem that the flour be clean, and when I kneaded the flour, I prayed to Hashem that the bread and cakes would turn out well. I prayed to Hashem when I was baking and then I prayed to Hashem again when I was selling, asking that He send customers — I was praying to Hashem all day long! And I felt so close to Him.

" 'Now that you fully provide for me,' I told him then, 'I feel that I've lost that aspect of the relationship. I'm too comfortable!'

"I prefer to suffer and feel near to Hashem!" the baker exclaimed passionately to the Rabbi of Cracow.

"But I want the z'chus of your Torah!" the rich man countered. "I am not prepared to annul the agreement."

The baker's only concern was his closeness to Hashem, not material comfort. He understood that possessions are worthless, and that only spiritual attainments have any value.

There are times when, in our suffering, we feel that Hashem has turned away from us. This only adds to our distress. The minute we realize that Hashem loves us and wants only our good, that it is He Who saves us from harm and watches over us, then we begin to feel tremendous love for Him, and become increasing grateful. Learn to see only the *chesed* that Hashem does every day, every minute, every second. Feel and know that Hashem wants only your good.

And if suffering does come, realize that it could have been much worse. It is more like a loving, caring father's discipline of his child, intended to correct his behavior and help him become a *mensch*. In other words, any suffering given is given with great mercy and is much less than what a person truly deserves.

There are two mitzvos in particular which shield a person from suffering, and every woman should be involved with them: charity (*tzedakah*) and acts of lovingkindness (*gemilus chesed*).

22
Modesty — Our Crown

A woman should be attractive, but not attracting. Judaism is a way of life, not just a religion. The Torah guides us through every detail of life, from the minute we open our eyes in the morning until we go to bed at night. We are taught, for example, that there is a special way to get dressed and undressed.[1] When getting dressed, attention should be paid to which shoe and which sleeve is put on first, and when getting undressed, each article of clothing should be taken off separately, rather than all at once. Why should this be important? What difference can it possibly make? And why can't we just say to

---

1. *Kitzur Shulchan Aruch*, siman 3, sif 4.

ourselves, "There's nobody home right now — my husband's left already and the children have all gone to school — I think I'll just walk around the way I want"? We can, but it would be a mistake. We are *never* alone. As practicing Jews we know that Hashem's glory fills the world. Even if the door is locked, we are always in His presence. This is why even when we are alone, we should always conduct ourselves with modesty.

Many people automatically think of clothing when modesty is mentioned. They think, "Oh, those religious people — they cover their hair, wear long sleeves and stockings." They are under the mistaken impression that modesty is nothing more than that, but in fact, dress is only one aspect of modesty. What the Torah calls *tznius*, modesty, is all embracing. It covers every aspect of life. There is modesty in wisdom, in *yiras shamayim*, in behavior, in character, in the way we talk and the way we think. If we believe ourselves to be more important than the next person, it shows a lack of modesty in our thinking. Feeling superior to another person when we speak with them is also immodest. There is such a thing as modesty in deed, as when a person refrains from telling others about good deeds he has done. "Only in that which is hidden from the eye is a blessing found,"[1] say our Sages. The less you talk about what you do and the less people know about it, the more good will come from it.

> *Ruth was exemplary in her modesty.*
>
> *All the other women in the fields would bend over when they picked up the fallen grain, while Ruth would crouch to do so. They used to raise their skirts to carry the sheaves, while she didn't. The other women would joke with the harvesters, but she remained apart. They would glean from among the bundled sheaves, while she only gleaned from what was abandoned and ownerless.*
>
> *And when Naomi said to her, "Wash and anoint yourself with oil; put on your clothing and go down to the threshing place," Ruth went as she was, taking her clothes with her to change later, for she did not want to walk outside all dressed up.*

---

1. *Taanis* 8b.

When Ruth ate, she was not gluttonous, and this too made a deep impression on Boaz. Noting all these expressions of her modesty, Boaz recognized that Ruth must surely be fit for royalty.[1]

What is the reward for modesty? Worthy children. Boaz chose Ruth for his wife because of her modesty, and she became a mother of royalty, ancestress to kings and prophets.

Our Sages tell us that Rachel's modesty was rewarded in that among her offspring was Shaul HaMelech, whose modesty was in turn rewarded in having Esther descend from him. A woman must always bear in mind that the more modestly she behaves, the greater the possibility of having sons who are Torah scholars who will enlighten the world with their Torah and righteousness. The verse, "A princess's greatest honor is within — it is more noteworthy than her golden embroidered garments,"[2] means that a modest woman is worthy of producing high priests who are clothed in gold-embroidered garments. Modesty benefits a woman in this world, while securing her a place of glory and majesty and palaces in the world to come.

Modesty is a guarantee of holy, righteous children.[3]

The beauty of a woman is within. She makes herself beautiful for her husband, not for the public.

When Bilaam wanted to curse the Jewish people, he noticed that the doorways to their tents did not face opposite each other, and no one could look into his neighbor's house. There were three million people in tents, yet not even one tent faced the doorway of the other! So great is the modesty of the Jewish people that the blessing Bilaam gave become famous: "How good are your dwelling places, your tents. . ."[4]

Hashem is called the "Guardian" of the Jewish people. The Chofetz Chaim asks, though, what kind of guardian is He. Is He paid for guarding us, or is He doing it for free? In Jewish law, there is a difference between the two. If you ask someone to watch your valuables and you pay him for it, he is held strictly accountable for their

---

1. *Rus* 1:3-8, Rashi in the name of the *Midrash*.
2. *Tehillim* 45:14.
3. *Chofetz Chaim, Mishnah Berurah* 1.
4. *Bamidbar* 24:5, see Rashi.

safety. On the other hand, if he is not paid, his work is considered voluntary, and his accountability is less.

Since we don't pay Hashem for guarding over us, then His guardianship is conditional. Hashem will watch over us only if there will not be seen among the Jewish people something unseemly.[1] That's the condition. If Hashem sees something immodest, He won't want to watch over us, says the Chofetz Chaim, and then we are in great danger. That's why so many terrible things happen. He says that one of the reasons Hashem watches and guards over the Jewish people is because of modesty, and he warned against the great danger for his generation because they were not careful with it.

In the days of the Chofetz Chaim, three generations ago, even nonreligious women dressed more conservatively than they do now. How much more so should *we* be concerned that the Guardian of Israel not take away His guardianship. Our entire existence would be endangered!

A nonreligious woman will wear something whether it's comfortable or not — if it's in fashion. But we are princesses and must conduct ourselves accordingly. Modesty is our crown. Can you imagine a princess complaining about a ten-million-dollar diamond tiara on her head? Would any woman say, "Oh, I'm hot, and it's so heavy," and take off her jeweled crown? Would she throw such a precious crown on the ground because it's uncomfortable? The answer is no. Her crown is so priceless, so precious, and of such great value to her that she'll keep it on her head no matter how heavy it is, or how hot and uncomfortable she may feel. The same applies to each and every Jewish woman: Modesty is your crown — it's too precious to throw away. Until you get used to it, you may be hot, it may feel heavy and uncomfortable, but recognizing its worth, you will never discard your precious crown.

Hashem is very exacting with *tznius*, as the following well-known historical incident illustrates:

> *The daughter of Rabbi Chaninah ben Tradyon walked very beautifully. One day, she overheard several Roman generals remark on the beautiful way she walked. When she heard*

1. *Devarim* 23:15.

the compliment, she began to walk even more beautifully. For this lack of tznius, that very minute her punishment was decreed in heaven: Upon the execution of her parents, she would be taken into captivity.

When the events came to pass, the girl's sister, Bruria, who was the wife of Rabbi Meir, was naturally distraught. "Please," she begged her husband, Rabbi Meir, "please save her from such a terrible fate." Despite the great danger involved, Rabbi Meir decided to try to redeem his sister-in-law.

Disguised, and carrying a large purse of gold coins with which to bribe the watchman at the gate, Rabbi Meir traveled to where the girl was being held.

"I'll give you all this money," he whispered to the guard at the gate, "if you give me a certain girl being held captive inside."

"Are you crazy?" the watchman answered. "They'll kill me if she's missing."

"Take the money," Rabbi Meir said, placing the sack full of gold coins in the guard's hand. "You can keep half for yourself and use the rest for bribes."

"What will I do if all this money isn't enough? They'll pursue me wherever I run."

"Just say: 'G-d of Meir, answer me.' Don't worry; nothing will happen to you — you'll be saved."

The guard agreed, and Rabbi Meir took his sister-in-law home, much to the relief and happiness of everyone concerned.

Meanwhile, the Romans had discovered her escape. "Where is the girl?" they demanded of the watchman.

"A man came, gave me money, and took her away," he answered fearfully, begging for mercy. The Romans ignored his pleas and dragged him out to be hung. As they placed the noose around his neck, the watchman remembered what Rabbi Meir had said to him, and he cried out, "G-d of Meir, answer me!" They were unable to hang him.

They tried again. Again he cried out, and was saved. Determined to punish him, the Romans tried once more to hang him. Again the watchman cried out as Rabbi Meir had told him *to, and again they did not succeed. The Romans then asked him: "What are you saying just before the rope breaks?"*

"A man told me that if you would try to kill me I should say this verse and I would be saved."

The Roman authorities had a picture made of Rabbi Meir and set it up over the gates of Rome, promising a bounty to whoever would bring Rabbi Meir to them.

To avoid capture, Rabbi Meir was forced to escape to Babylon, and lived the rest of his life in exile.[1]

A family tragedy — and all because of what some people might call a "slight" lack of modesty.

Famous fashion designers were once asked why they bring out their collections twice a year, instead of once a year, or even once every two years. Their answer should give us pause: "With each new style, we try to attract the eye to a different part of the woman's body." The entire purpose of fashion in the non-Jewish and secular world is to attract attention. Such styles awaken the wrong kind of thinking in men. Only if fashion is within the bounds of modesty do we go along with it.

If you want to dress fashionably, fine. But be modest about it. Don't wear clothing that attracts undue attention. Fashion has to suit our ideas of modesty — otherwise, it's not for us. One of the Ten Commandments is: "Do not covet." When does a person come to covet somebody else's wife? When she attracts too much attention. A woman should be very careful not to attract attention. She should learn the art of being tastefully well dressed without attracting attention.

We think we've made new discoveries, but our Sages tell us that the first Beis HaMikdash was destroyed because of three sins: bloodshed, adultery, and idolatry.[2] They explain that the "adultery" referred to here was lack of modesty: "The daughters of Zion are haughty. They walk with outstretched necks, with painted eyes they take careful steps, and they make noise with their heels."[3] To attract attention

---

1. *Avodah Zarah* 17b-18b; *Me'am Loez* on *Vayeishev* 4.
2. *Yoma* 9b.
3. *Yeshayahu* 3:16. See Rashi on *Yoma* 9b.

in those days, a tall girl would walk alongside a short girl. Another technique used by girls then was to take a long wig and add it to their own hair, so that it would seem that their hair was thicker. They would also paint their eyelids with color — like eye-shadow. And then they did something we haven't caught on to yet: They would fill the hollowed-out heels of their shoes with perfume. They would go out walking all painted up and when a young man passed by, they would knock their heels on the pavement to release the fragrance of the perfume. Our Sages tell us that the perfume was like poison to the men, for it brought them to thoughts of sin. In Judaism, thoughts of sin and bringing a man to express himself in an improper manner is a great sin and that's exactly what they did. It was this absolute lack of *tznius* that brought about the destruction of the first Beis HaMikdash.

What is modesty? It is true beauty. We say, "A beautiful home and a beautiful wife enhance a man's greatness." What is meant by a beautiful wife? "Grace is false, and beauty is vain, but a woman who fears G-d, she shall be praised."[1] In Judaism we talk about inner beauty, which is true beauty. No matter how lovely the shape of the eyes or the curls of the hair, such beauty is not lasting. Even a person born beautiful can turn ugly if his soul is not beautiful. Beautify your soul through beautiful deeds and you will become more and more beautiful as time goes on.

A woman should always find favor in her husband's eyes. She should be attractive and well groomed (this includes personal hygiene) — because otherwise her husband will lose interest in her. That moment when your husband arrives home after a hard day at *kollel* or work is a special time. Make the effort to be especially beautiful for him then. Let him come home to a queen, and feel himself a king in paradise.

Your goal is that your husband should never be able to make an unfavorable comparison between his home and his wife, and that of another. One woman was very upset when her husband came home and said, "Why is it when I go to my friend's house it's always clean and ours is always a mess?" It's terrible when a husband feels this way. You want your husband to see beauty in you, and he *will*, if he can admire you.

---

1. *Mishlei* 31:30.

Beauty is the special favor, *chen*, seen in Yosef. His purity of soul expressed itself in a modesty that was beautiful. True beauty could be found in our Matriarchs, Sarah, Rivkah, Rachel, and Leah. Sarah was exceptionally beautiful, yet Avraham did not realize it until they crossed a river and he saw her reflection in the water. Sarah's beauty was so outstanding that she prayed every day to Hashem that she should not be "attracting" to others because of it. True beauty like this is a reflection of the special inner refinement seen in a king's daughter — a Jewish woman.

Once we understand the secret of a woman's true beauty, and the tremendous power a woman's modest behavior has in controlling her own personal destiny as well as the destiny of the Jewish people, we can use our common sense to put it into practice. Even though most women know these things, it pays to stop and think about the subject again.

One aspect of modesty that is of utmost importance is for a woman to cover her hair in accordance with halachah.

> *Kimchis had seven sons. Each one, at one time or another, served as High Priest. Even more remarkable is that this came about without any of her sons dying in order for this to happen. In each case, there was a special reason why the brother currently serving as High Priest needed a temporary replacement. Since in Judaism nothing just "happens," it's all Divine Providence, the Sages went to ask Kimchis in what merit she had the privilege of seeing each of her seven sons serve as High Priest. Her answer became legendary: "The walls of my house have never seen the hair of my head."* [1]

There is no doubt about it. The Zohar says that a woman who is very particular with covering her hair, allowing no hair at all to show, is promised that her children will be endowed with graciousness and will be among the most important people of their generation. She is also promised that her children will be like an olive tree, which stands above all other trees for its leaves never fall and always stay green. In the same way, a modest woman's children will be more important than all other people in the

---

1. *Yerushalmi Yoma* 1:1.

world, and her husband will be granted blessings from above and below: riches, children and grandchildren, and will be blessed from Zion and merit to see the good of Yerushalayim and peace. It's a promise.

In all areas of our dress and appearance, modesty must be a steadfast role. For example, even though you may have a nicely styled wig, you must take care that your intention is to make yourself attractive for your husband, not for anyone else. In the same vein (being attractive to your husband), a woman must take care of her skin using moisterizer and make-up in such a way that it looks natural.

A woman's clothing, while it may certainly be pretty, may not call undue attention to her. It pays to think before buying; with a little creativity, clothes can be altered to fit your needs. In choosing jewelry you should not be ostentatious as this, too, is immodest.

Some men don't care about the house, and they're not interested in the food, but they do want a wife they can be proud of. A good wife will take this into consideration and try to always look her best for her husband, while making sure to remember that she is the King's daughter.

Modesty is making yourself beautiful for your husband.

23

Children

here are two kinds of houses: one that is like a hotel, and one that is a home. Unfortunately, far too many people find that their house is more like the former. What's the difference between the two? In a hotel, strangers come from all over to stay for a few days in a numbered room; they might meet in the corridor or the lobby and say good-morning, but that is their only connection — they live side by side without knowing each other. In a home, people live *with* each other.

If your house is a place where people live side by side and have no time for each other, where they just come in to eat and then run out again, then it's a hotel, not a home.

It's the woman's job to turn her house into a home.

Your home should be a veritable ship — with you, captain at the helm. It's your job to build the character of your children. It's you who has to equip them for life and give them the ability to cope. Otherwise, what will they have to take with them when they leave?

Take a look at the secular world . . . and then compare the faces you see there with the faces of your religious friends. You'll see that they look entirely different. Look at their children, and then look at your children and compare the faces — they're worlds apart. A person who keeps Torah and mitzvos is different. He has an inner security which comes from trust in Hashem, and this serenity is reflected outward. His every act and expression are a credit to his Creator. Other people, seeing him, feel drawn closer to this Source of holiness.

> *It happened after a week-long seminar for people interested in becoming religious. The program had been rich and varied: lectures, discussion groups, learning sessions. Many teachers had brought their families along with them to enjoy the vacation opportunity at a well-appointed hotel.*
>
> *By the end of the week, many of the participants felt they had learned enough to convince them to begin mitzvah observance. One man, though, surprised the organizers with his comments about the week:*
>
> *"None of the lectures here convinced me of anything. If that's all there is to Judaism, I'll stay the way I am."*
>
> *Startled, his listeners nonetheless responded politely. "We're very sorry you feel that way," they said, and, thinking he was about to leave, wished him well. But they were in for another surprise.*
>
> *"Don't misunderstand — now that I've said that, I want to tell you a story. I am an importer of candies. Kids go crazy over one particular brand, so when I knew I was coming here for the week, I decided to bring along a carton of the candies to give out to any children who might be here.*
>
> *"After one lecture, I brought out some of the candy. The children's eyes popped when they saw it. One of the lecturers had his children here, and a son of his was in this*

group. When I handed out the candy, this child, who must have been about four or five years old, said to me, 'Is this kosher?'

"I nearly fainted. I knew the children loved these candies. I could only answer, 'I don't know.' He said, 'I'll take it and ask my mommy. If it's not kosher, I'll bring it back.'

"A little while later he came back and said, 'My mommy said it's not kosher.' He handed the candy back to me and said, 'Thank you very much, but I don't want it.' "

The businessman paused and looked at his by now rapt listeners. "I want you all to know that nothing in the whole conference impressed me more than this child. Children love this candy, but that little boy had been brought up to know he could control himself. He wouldn't eat it if it wasn't kosher, no matter how much he wanted it. That little boy convinced me more than anything else in this seminar what Judaism is all about. I'm going to come back and bring my whole family along with me."

What convinces others? Us. The way we live. Our homes. Our children. Let's make ourselves a fortress, our homes a fortress, and each child so strong in Yiddishkeit that he is a fortress. With so many problems nowadays, it's not enough to say, "This is allowed and this is not allowed." A mother has to be single minded about educating her children. We have always had such women and it is due to these mothers that we have a generation of Torah-observant Jews.

The woman sitting next to me on the flight from London to Toronto said she had been living in Canada for thirty years and had just come back from a high-school-class reunion in England. The now middle-aged graduates had gotten together for ten hours and each one had told her classmates what she had done with the last thirty years of her life.

"Most of us were just ordinary women. We got married and set up homes. The only person who really succeeded," she confided, "was one of us who never got married. She became a television star."

"Excuse me," I said, "but are you sure your friend has succeeded? She's already nearing her fifties. How long will *she be able to continue to be a star? In a year or two, people will forget her and she'll be left alone. She'll have nothing left in life. Do you know who has succeeded? You! You showed me the pictures of your grandchildren. You've built a masterpiece. She hasn't done anything with her life. What's being a television star?"*

Not only is the woman the foundation of the Jewish home, but she is the prime educator of the children. Rabbi Samson Raphael Hirsch put it very beautifully:

On the women of the House of Israel, the mothers of the Jewish people, rests the obligation to take upon themselves this role of education. It is the mother who saves and encourages the spirit and soul of Israel and provides the spiritual preparation for its continuing existence. Righteous women throughout the generations have rescued the spiritual and moral future of our people many times. Today, too, the eyes of the house of Jacob are turned to them.

"Who will bring the man in Israel to sanctity? Who will remove from his environment all that is false? Who will purify his heart and his spirit? Who will educate him to loathe lowly and sensual pleasures? Who will educate him to be a person of pure character who strives for sanctity? Who will educate him when he is still small, by means of speech and deeds, habits and teaching?

"The Jewish mother. The mother of the house of Jacob, whose whole being and whose every deed is imbued with purity. It is she who overcomes all negative outside influences, while raising the banner of family purity. It is she who educates her sons and daughters to the great and important role common to us all: to be a perfectly faithful Jew."[1]

At the time of the *Beis HaMikdash*, over 2,000 years ago when even the "civilized" world was sunk in ignorance, a *Kohen Gadol* named Rabbi Yehoshua ben Gamla established schools for children. Why would schools be necessary? After all, it says in the *Shema*:

---

1. R' Samson Raphael Hirsch, *The Jewish Woman*, translated from the German.

"You should teach it to your children" — and *you* means the parents! They should be the main educators of the children. Rabbi Yehoshua ben Gamla saw a need and persisted, saying that he was worried about the orphans. The first schools were established only in Yerushalayim; many children attended and benefitted greatly. Nevertheless, he found that it was difficult for most orphans to undertake the trip, so R' Yehoshua ben Gamla established schools everywhere. In every town and village, schools for all Jewish children were established, and we are told that it is in his merit that Torah was not forgotten by the Jewish people.[1]

Nevertheless, it remains true that the main obligation for teaching the next generation rests with the parent, not the school.

We live in strange times. Parents think their obligation is to see to their children's material needs, to feed them, give them a home, clothe them, buy them toys, and in general, spoil them a little bit — and they think education is the job of the schools. They are making a horrendous mistake. Of the twenty-four hours in a day, a child spends at most eight or ten hours in school. The rest of the time he is in your care, and it's you who gives him *everything*. The most outstanding people are children of parents who have invested themselves in their children. It's the children whose parents have time for them, time to sit and learn with them, that turn out the best.

"You open for him," says the Haggadah. *You* means the mother. *You* are the one who *opens* everything up before your child by talking to him. Our Sages say that even when she is expecting, a mother is educating her child. The unborn baby experiences and absorbs the world through hearing his mother's voice — her proper speech, her prayer, her singing. Modern research confirms that a baby in the womb responds when the mother talks, and already recognizes her voice when he comes into the world. When he cries, it is this familiar voice of his mother which can calm him more readily than any other. A mother knowing this will begin even while expecting to talk and sing to her unborn baby. How unfortunate that some people need ultrasound and tape recorders to prove this to them when our Sages told us this fact over 2,000 years ago!

Every mother must realize that education is a gradual

---

1. *Bava Basra* 21a.

process. Her job doesn't begin and end by her saying to the child, "This is what I want you to do and that's that." She has to work at educating her children. If we have great Torah personalities, it's because we have women who raised them. And without such women, we would be bereft of such leaders. The mothers of *Klal Yisrael* **are** *Klal Yisrael*.

If you want to build a great house, you have to become a great woman — great in acceptance, love, and education.

A mother must be a living example. This is the secret of the true educator. Our Sages teach us that the character traits we aspire to and attain through self-sacrifice, those *middos* we acquire with *mesiras nefesh*, are passed on for generations. Rachel, for example, took for herself the attribute of "silence." On her wedding night, she did not reveal that Leah had been sent in her stead. Imagine what it meant for Rachel to keep quiet — she gave away her happiness! Think of it — to have another woman in the house for a lifetime! All in order not to shame her sister. Rachel's son Binyamin inherited this painfully acquired trait. His stone in the *choshen* was called "*yashpeh*," and Rashi explains: "*yashpeh* — he has a mouth, and doesn't say." Although Binyamin knew the secret of Yosef being sold to Egypt, he told no one. "The *Shechinah* kept quiet," he said, "so I will also remain silent and not reveal the secret." From Binyamin came Shaul HaMelech, who never revealed that he became king. From Shaul HaMelech came Esther, who did not reveal her people and her homeland. A character trait can thus be passed on through the generations for thousands of years!

Leah acquired the attribute of "praise." When her son Yehudah was born she said, "I praise and thank Hashem." The Hebrew root of praise (*hoda'ah*) also means "to admit." Her son Yehudah was a person who admitted the truth. He could have denied the incident with Tamar, but he revealed the truth in order to save her. From Yehudah descended David HaMelech who sang praises to Hashem all his life. From David descended Daniel who gave praise to Hashem even in the lion's pit.

By aspiring to greatness and choosing to act with nobility of thought and deed, a woman develops her character. The greater the self-sacrifice entailed, the more strongly a character trait will be passed down to her children and all the generations to follow. This is how a woman creates the masterpiece we spoke of earlier. What she passes on to her children gains her immortality.

There is a well-known story told about the Chofetz Chaim that bears repeating here because it so beautifully illustrates what should be a basic approach to education:

> The Chofetz Chaim once came to the village of Radin, and went to immerse himself in the local mikveh. To his surprise, the water was ice cold.
>
> "Why is the water so bitterly cold?" he asked the man in charge.
>
> "Rebbe, honestly," the man replied, "I put all the water that was in the hot-water tank into the mikveh. I don't know why the mikveh should be cold."
>
> The Chofetz Chaim went up to check the hot-water tank. When his fingers touched it, he realized that the hot water tank had never been heated in the first place — no wonder the water in the mikveh was cold!

Education works the same way: If your input is cold, the other person gains nothing from it. But if what you give to your children comes from your heart, it will warm them and stay with them forever.

When the Torah teaches us about the rebellious son and his punishment, it says that he became that way because "he didn't listen to his father's voice and his mother's voice." Since no word in the Torah is superfluous and each letter and every dot is precious, why didn't it say "his parents' voices"? The Kotzker Rebbe offers an explanation which should inspire every parent. A child becomes rebellious because he does not hear his father's voice: He never hears his father learning Torah, he never hears his father saying *brachos* aloud, *bentching* aloud, or saying *Shema* aloud. What can you expect from him? Such a child never heard his mother's voice either: He didn't see his mother lighting Shabbos candles, he didn't hear his mother saying *Tehillim*, he didn't hear her praying, and he never heard her voice teaching him to say blessings out loud. That is why he became a rebellious son — he heard neither his father's voice nor his mother's voice.[1]

---

1. *Devarim* 21:18.

Children need to see a living example.

Educating a child must always be done in a natural way, though, and should never be heavy handed. For instance, if you want your children to become *bnei Torah*, you have to make them love the Torah. In the olden days mothers would sit and rock the cradle and sing songs about their child growing up to learn Torah — starting when the baby was just a day old! That's what the mother of one Torah luminary did. Even while expecting she began going from one *beis midrash* to another, asking the sages to bless her, that her baby grow up to be a great Torah scholar. After the baby was born, she put his cradle in the *beis midrash* so that from the very first minute his ears would absorb Torah. Her prayers were fulfilled. The child grew up to become the famous Rabbi Yehoshua ben Chananyah, about whom our Sages said: "Blessed is the woman who bore him."[1]

How does a mother teach her children even abstract concepts like *yiras shamayim*, reverence for Hashem? This question was once asked of Reb Yechezkel Levenstein, the Mirrer *mashgiach*, who answered: "It's like a glass of water. If it's poured so full that it overflows, then whatever overflows, the other person gets." If the mother is so full of *yiras shamayim* that it spills over, her children will be filled with it too.

If you are filled with happiness, it will spill over to your children. If the mitzvos are a joy for you, they will be a joy for your children too.

---

1. *Avos* 2:8, see Rashi and *Yerushalmi Yevamos* 1:6.

24

Educating for Torah

When one sun sets, another rises; when one *tzaddik* dies, another is immediately born. Yet where are all the new "suns" — the great Torah scholars and leaders — to replace those whose loss we mourn? Do we delude ourselves into thinking that today's children are endowed with less capability than in previous generations? On the contrary, today we have young children who are brilliant and have unbelievable potential. The question is: Why don't they turn into *gedolim*? What happened? The reason is: Their education is at fault. They are not encouraged to be industrious. In previous generations, everyone understood that you have to toil in order to achieve something. From the earliest age, children were accustomed to working. As they grew older, those who learned

Torah studied eighteen hours a day. They didn't become bored or give up in the middle. They persevered and became Torah giants. It's not enough to have a brilliant mind, you have to utilize it.

And you need the encouragement of the parents, especially the mother.

Everyday we ask Hashem to "make the Torah sweet for us."[1] Who makes the Torah sweet for the husband and children? The wife, the mother. If, when a child comes home from school and says, "Guess what? I scored the winning goal today!" his mother gets all excited about it and says, "Oh, that's wonderful! Come here and I'll give you a kiss," what message does the child get? That his mother likes him to kick balls. A child is prepared to do anything to get a kiss from his mother and gain her appreciation! If he sees that she is so happy when he kicks a goal, he will practice day and night kicking goals in order to be a good football player. But if he comes home and tells her he kicked a goal, and she doesn't relate to it; and then when he tells her what he learned in *Mishnah*, in *Chumash*, in *Dinim*, and she calls all the children together and says, "Children, come and hear what Yankele learned today in yeshivah! How beautiful it is — let's all listen!" what then does Yankele feel? That his mother likes him to learn Torah, that it's the best thing there is. Or if, at the Shabbos table, the children are encouraged to say *divrei Torah* and no one is allowed to disturb the one who is speaking — the parents are appreciative, each child has his time, and nobody leaves the table — then each child knows that Torah is very important to his parents. And the husband knows the Torah is important to his wife, because she shows him in a thousand ways that his learning gives her the greatest joy in life.

There is a wonderful family where the mother brought up a large family in a small one-and-a-half-room apartment. All of her children became *gedolei Yisrael*. She was once asked how she did it. Her answer: "I never disturbed anybody, neither my husband nor my sons, when they were learning. But whenever they picked up a newspaper, I would say, 'Now you can help me.' " Her family knew that learning was the most important thing in life for her. This is the proper way to teach children.

---

1. *Birkas HaShachar.*

An example which perhaps is more telling than any other is that of the wealthy family who lived in a large industrial town in pre-war Europe where the community was decidedly nonreligious. Although they were practically the only religious people in the town, this mother was determined that her children become *bnei Torah*. When her son reached the age of learning *Mishnah* there was no one in the town to teach him. Her solution? She taught him herself. Her son grew to become a *ben Torah* in a town where he was the only religious boy! This woman made their home into a fortress: Not only did her son become a *ben Torah*, but all of her daughters married *bnei Torah*, quite an accomplishment for a woman who did not have even a single religious friend. That is the power of the education a mother can give to her children.

Another mother used to wait up for her sons so that when they came home from yeshivah late at night, she was ready with a hot glass of milk. She wanted them to feel that she was so happy they were learning that she waited up for them. This gave her children the feeling that their learning was important and that their mother appreciated it.

The aristocracy of the Jewish people belongs to those who learn Torah. The crown of priesthood is inherited, as is the crown of kingship, but the crown of Torah knowledge can be had by every Jew. Everyone can wear the crown of Torah by learning Torah. Our royal families, and there are not many of them, are those who have produced generation after generation of great Torah scholars. Yet unlike the other crowns, the crown of Torah is not inherited — there is no guarantee that each succeeding generation will follow in its father's footsteps. When they do, it is often because the parents had time for their children. They gave of themselves; they sat and learned with their children. A mother may be able to review the *Chumash* and *Mishnah* with her son, but a boy needs a father-figure who will learn *Gemara* with him. Great families come to be because those raising the children have devoted themselves to the education of those children.

You can't fool a child. If you seek to compromise, the child will be less than you are. Let's say there's a family that likes the traditions of Judaism. They enjoy singing around a Shabbos table, but when morning comes, the father gets up and says to his ten-year-old, "It's good for you to go to *shul*." Then he takes the car and drives to the beach. A child won't see any truth in this — he'll be laughing at his parents. If you want your child to go to *shul*, you have to go with him. If you want to have a Shabbos table, you have to make a Shabbos table.

The Shabbos table is one of the major places of education in the Jewish home. Parents should prepare stories of *Chazal* during the week. While children should be expected to sit at the table, don't make it a long drawn out agony for them. They should be given the chance to share the prepared material they bring home from school. If you have a large family, you can let some of the children speak in the evening, and some in the morning. Ask them questions about what they've learned. Teach them *zemiros*. Tell them stories of *Chazal* and *gedolei Yisrael*. If the family eats together during the week, that, too, is an opportune time to hear either a halachah or a story of *gedolei Yisrael*. Encourage the children to discuss and ask questions — that's the way to develop a child's mind. Make the table an unforgettable experience so that your children will carry the experience with them their whole life.

You can invite guests, but the guests should know that they're coming to see you at your table, not that they take over while the children go crazy. Parents can often get so involved with the guests that the children start climbing the walls! If you feel your children are too young for the Shabbos table to be a long affair, make it short and sweet. *Bentch*, send the children away to their games, and sit down with your guests. Don't drag it out. The same applies to the *seder* table. The mitzvah of Pesach is to tell the story of Pesach to your children! If you have guests, they should hear you devoting yourself to your children. Nowhere is there a commandment in the Torah to tell the story of Pesach to your guests. There are people who on principle do not invite guests because they want to devote the entire *seder* to the children. Children can spend weeks anticipating the *seder*, each one preparing a notebook with *perushim* to say. Give the children a chance. It's part of their education and will be a tremendous experience for them. In addition, you are developing their minds and their ability. When we tell a child, "Say a *dvar* Torah," he will learn to express himself. Children are capable of standing up and giving a speech at a very young age if they're given the encouragement to do so. Later, they'll have the ability to speak in public.

Make the mitzvos sweet for your children. Tell them that our Sages say every mitzvah we do creates a guardian angel. One grandmother overheard her grandson mumbling his *brachos* at lightning speed. She said to him, "You have an angel from that *brachah*, but he's so small and weak. If you say your *brachah* carefully, word for word, you're going to make such a wonderful strong angel." After that, his *brachos* were a pleasure to listen to.

If we're gentle and loving with a child, we can instill in him all the beautiful character traits which will last him for a lifetime. Before he even begins to talk, begin teaching him to say, "Thank you." When you give him some raisins or a fruit, smile and say, "Say 'thank you' to mommy," and he'll learn to say, "Thank you," for everything he gets. And if he gives you something, always say, "Thank you." Make a game out of it. The same goes for apologies. Sometimes you may have punished a child unnecessarily. Tell him you're sorry and he'll appreciate it. He'll also learn that people are not angels, that they can make mistakes.

Teach your children appreciation. Your husband should say to the children: "The house looks so clean and nice — what do we say to Mommy? 'Thank you' "; "Mommy did the laundry for us and now we have nice clean clothing to put on. What do we say to Mommy? 'Thank you.' " You should do the same with regard to your husband's involvement. This will teach them to appreciate and respect other people.

And when you ask your children to do something, always say, "Please." One woman complained that her fourteen-year-old daughter is willing to baby-sit for all the neighbors but refuses to watch her own younger brothers and sisters. A little discussion revealed that this mother never said, "Please" or "Thank you" when asking her daughter for the baby-sitting. Never command children; ask them nicely. If you do so, you'll never have to remind them because it will come automatically.

Teach your children consideration for others by being an understanding mother. Show them how to feel for other people and how to help others carry their burden. Be considerate of your children. Always try to think: How is my child feeling in this situation? Don't be cold, hard, and unfeeling. Don't say to a child who has just fallen and whose knees are smarting and burning, "There's nothing the matter with you. Get up!" A child who hears that from his mother will feel that she doesn't understand anything. But if you say, "Come, I'll wash your knees and put a Band-Aid on," you're being an understanding mother. Your child will feel that his mother knows how much his knees are stinging. The minute he feels his mother understands his pain, half the pain is gone.

The saying "Charity begins at home" comes from the Torah. The halachah tells us the priorities: Relatives come first, then neighbors, then residents of your town, then people of other towns, etc. A woman, especially, has to know where her priorites lie. If you're giving to others at the expense of your husband and children, you should ask a rabbi whether it is true *chesed*. A woman can do a lot of *chesed* during the day, but she cannot sacrifice her home or let herself be taken advantage of. If you agree to watch your neighbor's children for five hours while she goes out to a play and because of that your own children won't be able to go to bed and all the children are running around out of control, something is wrong!

If your home is one of love for your children at the same time that it is a home of *chesed*, your children will automatically learn to do *chesed*. They will see you busy with guests, serving them, and they will give you a helping hand. You can send them to help other people, and you can send them to baby-sit, but everything has to be within a certain limit. You need to make rules: Until what time are they allowed to stay out? How many times a week can they help out? For good health, a growing child needs proper meals and enough sleep. Unless you make firm rules, your child can be taken advantage of, and it might not be *chesed* at all in the end. If a neighbor asks your child to babysit your answer will depend on the circumstances: If she's simply disorganized and wants to go shopping at your chldren's expense, it's not right. On the other hand, if she really needs it, you will want to do whatever you can to help. If a neighbor has to go to the hospital and she has no one to stay with her children, it's even worth getting a child out of bed to help out.

Teach your children from the start: When they pass a poor person with an outstretched hand, they should always give *tzedakah*. When someone comes to the door asking for a donation, teach them to give. It's part of their education. At the same time, keep in mind that the biggest *chesed* your children can do is to give you a help-ing hand. Sometimes people find it easy to run to do for others while neglecting to do what they have to do at home. *Chesed* should not be done at the expense of the major priorities of the home. If you manage your home well and most of the things are done, then if somebody needs you, it's wonderful to run to help. But don't let your children go without a meal while you take on a different "case" every day. If you don't know your priorities, I can promise you that you can be out of the house twenty-four hours a day — because there is plenty to do.

Each and every child should be doing something to help out around the home. The real test of *chesed* is doing that which is hard. True *chesed* is staying home and missing a wedding you really want-ed to go to — if the *Ba'alei Simchah* will not be hurt — so that two people, who have no other evening available, can meet each other in your home and hopefully find their partner for life. It's being willing to forgo your own pleasure for the happiness of others.

25
To Be a Good Mother

The relationship between parents and children is essentially based on teaching, not love. Many people have never learned this, and of those who have, many have forgotten. You can give a child endless love without educating him, without forming his character, without disciplining him. You can give him nothing but love — and he'll turn into a spoiled brat.

Other parents think their relationship with their children should be based on control. They are wrong too.

Parenting is based on **teaching**. To be a good parent you have to be a very good teacher. If you're not one by nature, learn to become one.

It goes without saying that *siyata d'shmaya* (Heavenly assistance) is a prerequisite for every success in raising children. Even so, we must put forth our best effort.

Here are some basics for success in education:

1. **Invest in your children.** Give it everything you've got. It may mean sacrifice on your part. Let's say there is something you would enjoy reading that doesn't fit in with the standard in your home. If you have children who can already read, you can't have such material in your house. It would ruin your children's *neshamos*. So, although you feel you wouldn't be affected by such reading matter, you give it up for the sake of your children's education.

   As a parent, you can't impose standards on a child that you do not demand of yourself. Let us say that there is a mother who, when she is outside the home, is dressed just as she should be. She covers her hair and even in the greatest heat of summer wears stockings and clothing with proper sleeve lengths. But when she comes home, it's a different story. She's melting from the heat, so she "makes herself comfortable." What will happen is that her children will "make themselves comfortable" in their dress *outside* the home as well as inside, because they see that their mother has a double standard. She is one person for the outside world, and another for the house. Any mother who is concerned about the education of her children will make sure to get dressed the way she should be dressed the minute she gets up in the morning: sleeves, stockings, and hair covered. The children will then know that Mommy is the same, **always** — that there are no two standards of behavior. A child who sees conflicting standards grows up to be a very confused person. He doesn't know what is true and right, and he doesn't know how to act around other people. Consequently, he is unhappy and insecure.

   It is important to realize: You may have to give up things you want to do in order to be a good educator of your children.

2. **Never stop praying** — prayer can change everything.

   > The story is told of a kohen who was exiled to Babylonia after the Beis HaMikdash had been destroyed by Nebuchadnezzar. This kohen had ten children, six sons

and four daughters, and he was very worried about what would happen to his children living in Babylonia. He would pour out endless tears daily, asking Hashem that his children should not stumble and come to sin from living in exile. He never let a day go by without praying for his children.

Hashem heard his heartfelt prayers and added fifty years to his life. He merited to return to Jerusalem with Ezra and Nechemiah, and to see his children, his children's children, and his great-grandchildren serving in the rebuilt Beis HaMikdash.[1]

Your children should see that you pray for them daily. To the Chofetz Chaim, his mother's *Tehillim*, soaked through with her tears, was the most precious *sefer* he had. When you light the Shabbos candles, have your children gather around you. Together, everyone should pray for the well-being of the parents and the whole family. Teach them how. And even from a very young age, a child should be taught how to ask Hashem to send a speedy recovery to someone needing it.

Children should also feel your concern and caring for them, and should see that you pray for their success. It gives a child a sense of security to know his parents care about him so much. It can save a child's life.

One wonderful family had nine children, five girls and four boys. All the children were outstanding, the pride of their parents and a credit to their community.

The family was heartbroken when one of the boys fell in with bad company and began to slide. Even though the father was no longer young, he fasted for forty days. Day and night he sat in shul and prayed . . . and his son returned and became a true ben Yisrael.

3) **Never fight with your children.** This is a major point in successful education. Parents who fight with their children destroy both the home and the child. The secret of not reaching the stage where you are at odds with your children is to be a little smarter than

---

1. *Taana d'Vei Eliyahu* 18.

they are. Be creative in thinking up ingenious ways of handling them, new ways of dealing with them so that they comply with what is expected. Always try to stay one step ahead of them.

And never fight with your partner. When parents create a warm and loving atmosphere of mutual respect, it feeds the child's soul. Parents may have differing opinions, but children don't have to know about it. Parents should present a united front. A child brought up in such a home will feel the security that comes from standing on firm ground and will develop a healthy personality. He will grow up to become an emotionally, physically, and spiritually healthy adult.

In a home where the parents' respect for each other is mutual, the child sees that each parent considers the other's opinion. Daddy has a very high regard for Mommy's opinion and Mommy has deep respect for Daddy. When you present a united front to your children, when your children feel you and your husband are a unit, you will succeed. Parents may have different personalities but they're united by a common goal: the good of their children. They can work out their differences together, but not in the presence of the child.

Letting the child see that the parents have differing opinions is not only destructive to the personality of the child, but it will undermine the marriage as well. Children are smart: If they sense that their parents have differences of opinion, they'll try to play one against the other in order to get what they want. Some children know they can get more out of one parent than the other. But for the parents who talk things over, there will be no such thing as "I say" when the other parent says otherwise, because they'll both say the same thing. Never allow the children to come between you and destroy your marriage.

4. **Look after your health.** A mother who is healthy enjoys her children. A child whose mother looked after herself during pregnancy is born calm and quiet, and isn't sensitive to every change in the weather, needing one antibiotic after another. A healthy mother has healthy children. If you take care of yourself, you'll be able to enjoy your children.

As surprising as it may sound to some people, good food is

an integral part of education. A good mother tries to always have meals ready on time.

Plan ahead and always have food in the house. When the children come home, there should be a tasty meal — all ready for them. Children should feel satisfied and happy after the meal. A child may be nervous and irritable when he comes home from school, but after you give him a good meal, he'll be a different child. It was only hunger that was making him act that way. Good food makes everyone calm, so make sure the food is ready and that your children don't have to wait. This means not waiting to start cooking when they come home, but having the meal on the table when they arrive.

The same approach applies to babies as well. It's best to keep a baby happy and quiet. When he wakes up hungry, feed him. Some young mothers make the mistake of making their baby wait for his meal. They let him cry until he can't bear it anymore. Don't wait. Don't feed a baby by the clock, feed him the minute he's hungry. And don't let him scream for his meals. Doing so will make for a tense and nervous baby. In general, it's not good for a baby to be left to cry unnecessarily. It only trains him to be a screamer. Then later on, he'll scream for everything he wants.

5. **Break unhealthy patterns.** Too often we educate our children based not on our principles, but on certain patterns we saw in our parents' home. These patterns may not be positive, so it's essential to remember: Patterns can be broken. We may have absorbed these patterns when we were very young and impressionable, and although it's not easy, it's sometimes very important to break them. In one instance, a woman came to a counselor complaining that her daughter was a problem child. "I have five young children," she began, "and the oldest, a girl, is six." As she described her house, it turned out that she was demanding of this child what one normally asks of a fifteen or sixteen-year-old! Her way of demanding was to spank the girl constantly. The child became stubborn and a "problem child." When asked, "Why do you hit the child so much?" she said, "My mother used to do that to me." It's a fact: Mothers who hit their children are usually children who were hit. This is the type of pattern that should be broken.

You can break patterns. You don't have to hit your children if you were hit. There's a better way. You have to think: Was the pattern I saw good enough? Or should it be changed? Ask yourself: Can I create a new pattern? And decide that you can. You don't have to live according to a pattern. There can be a better way. If you know a better way — one your parents didn't — you don't have to follow their pattern. The trouble with patterns is that since they have been instilled into us, we react automatically at times of stress. One way to break negative patterns is to rehearse positive reactions. When you're alone, practice how you're going to react in a more positive way the next time such a situation occurs. If you rehearse your new positive reaction often, the next time an incident arises, your response will be this new positive reaction instead of the old negative one.

Let's say you automatically hit because you were hit. You decide that you don't like this method of educating your children. You decide how you're going to react the next time your little boy breaks or destroys something, or misbehaves. You repeat to yourself endlessly: "The next time Yankele does that, I'm going to react like this." Then when the "next time" comes, the new pattern automatically takes over.

6. **Good parents plan room in their lives for their children.** If a woman is very active socially, if she's busy organizing the whole neighborhood and has very little time for her children, then she's not really being a mother to them. She may be a very good social worker, and it's very nice that she's so active outside the home, but what are her children gaining from this? The same applies to a father. Is he so busy earning money or studying that he has no time for his children? If so, there's something wrong.

Educating children takes time. Parents must be prepared to give their time and their attention to their children.

Parents often wonder: How much time should a father give to the children? An hour a day, an hour a week? The answer is that it all depends on the family. In one family, every Shabbos is devoted to the children. Each and every child has an hour or so with the father when he reviews with him what he learned during the week. In another home, it may be that during the week, the father, either at dinner time or in the evening when the children come home, keeps an eye on the children as they prepare their homework. Both parents interest themselves and ask questions and make sure the child knows what he has to learn, and that he has prepared his homework. Usually every *cheder* gives the children a sheet on Friday covering what was learned that week, and it is the father's responsibility to review it with the child.

Children look forward to seeing their father. Each child, even a two-year-old, should have a chance to be with him for at least ten minutes every day.

Everyone wants attention. If a child hasn't seen his father all day, let him have a few minutes of his time and he will calm down. (This doesn't mean that a father can't have a little peace after he walks in the door. Children should be taught to give their father a wonderful welcome, and that he needs to sit and relax when he comes home.) But a father who is unwilling to make time for his child, who can give him everything materially but nothing of himself, is not a father — he's a bank.

When we spoke about priorities earlier, we mentioned the woman who is so house proud that there's no room for her children in her spotless home. A mother like this would rather see her children out in the street all day than have them inside, "spoiling" the house. Such children have no home and no mother — and they are certainly not getting an education at home. A home is neither a showplace nor a museum. It has to be planned with children in mind. There should be plenty of room for them to grow in, and they should feel good in their home.

7. **Don't live through your children.** Any discussion of being a good mother would not be complete without mention of the following point which is so important that it bears consideration by every mother.

Some women have had a hard life. They may look back and say that they didn't have the kind of childhood they would have liked, or that their teenage years were difficult, or they may have an unhappy marriage. And they want to make up now for everything they missed in life. How can they do it? Through their children.

The child becomes a possession, instead of an independent

being, a soul to be raise and educated. These mothers think the child has to fill up all the emptiness in their lives. This is a very serious problem, because the child is going to be a very unhappy child. He will never get the education he deserves, or the love. Do you know who such a mother loves? Herself. She loves herself so much that the child becomes just an extension, a chance for her to get everything she missed in life.

A possessive mother doesn't allow her child to go and play with his friends; she keeps him with her all the time. A possessive mother makes her children feel helpless and incapable of managing for themselves. She does everything for them, saying, "You can't do that — you're too little. Let Mommy do it." Although she enjoys her role, she's destroying her children. They become helpless and very attached to her. They feel that they can't make a move without her. That's a possessive mother.

Raise your children to be independent. Don't be like those mothers who tie their children to them hand and foot. Children raised this way find it hard to leave their mother to get married — they can't visualize living away from home!

> *As she sat beside the open window, she saw a cocoon on the windowsill. While she was watching, the cocoon broke and a butterfly struggled to get out. Minutes passed as she watched the butterfly try to free himself from the cocoon. She felt sorry for the butterfly and decided to help it gain its freedom. She reached out and opened the cocoon fully. The butterfly emerged — but it was never able to fly.*
>
> *Only by struggling to open the cocoon do the wings of the butterfly become developed enough to fly.*

Just as the struggles of the butterfly actually train it to use its wings, so do the efforts of our children develop their independence.

Make it a rule: Don't live through your children. Don't expect your children to provide everything you've missed in life. You don't live *through* your children or *for* your children — you live *with* your children. It's like husband and wife: You don't live side by side, you live *with* each other. Side by side is a hotel. Being part of each other is a home.

26

The Nature of the Child

*T*o a child, his parents are the greatest, smartest people in the world. He is sure they see and know everything. They are the best people in the world . . . or, *chas v'shalom*, the worst people in the world. To a child, his parents are king and queen, the most important people in his life. They fill his world. He listens to them, he adapts himself to fulfill their desires, he observes their actions in order to copy them, and very often, without realizing it, he turns out to be just like them . . . or sometimes, the exact opposite. Either way, the results are an outcome of the parents' influence.

Just as a woman has to study her husband, she must also study her children. It's an amazing fact that every human being is so individual. Not only are their faces and fingerprints unique, but all the internal organs differ from person to person as well. Each person's heart, stomach, and lungs differ from those of another individual. A mother may have twelve children, yet each one of them will be a unique individual in his own right, with a different nature which she must study. A mother must be able to deal with each child according to his own nature, and should never use one cut-and-dried approach for all children. She needs to know how to cope with each child separately as well as all of the children collectively. In a family of twelve, there should be twelve "only children." Each child should know that he has a special place in his mother's heart. He should feel that his mother has time for him as an individual, and not only time for all the children as a group. Rabbi Dessler once said that every human being is 100 percent, but everyone's 100 percent is different. One person's character may be 30 percent altruistic, another person's 50 percent, while in yet another person, altruism may make up only 10 percent of his character. Every character trait exists, but the proportions in each individual differ. That's why it's important to study your child and find out what makes him tick.

Good parents should be more concerned with the development and welfare of their child than with whether or not they are satisfied with him. Instead of asking herself, "What's good for me?" every mother should be busy asking herself, "What is good for my child?"

Caring and concern for a child can only be based on a thorough understanding of the nature of children in general, and the nature of each child in particular. To reach this understanding of her children, a mother must study each child and, even more, bring herself down to his level of thinking. Rabbi Yisrael Salanter was especially emphatic about this point: "Going down to the level of the child," he stressed, "means realizing that for a child, his paper boat floating in a puddle of water is a big ship sailing the seas. When a grownup comes and callously treads on that little paper boat, the tragedy is as great for the child as if an ocean liner had just sunk."

One of parents' biggest mistakes is to make demands of their children according to their adult thinking, instead of according to their child's four-year-old, six-year-old or ten-year-old thinking. We tend to forget that **children are not on our level**. Your two-year-old cannot function according to your way of thinking. It's impossible because his mind hasn't developed to that point. In order to teach him, you have to go down to his level. Some parents demand the impossible of their small children while the child for his part may not even have the slightest idea of what's being asked of him. When he doesn't respond the way his parents want him to, they start shouting and punishing. Even then the child may still not do what they want him to because his level of thinking is not developed enough to understand their demand.

Avoid this pitfall. Instead, try to see the world through your child's eyes. A baby, for example, finds walking a major achievement. He will set out to proudly explore his new world — your house. When your baby begins walking, get down on the floor and see what's interesting from his point of view. Go through the whole house and put all potentially dangerous or breakable items out of his reach. Constant warnings not to touch and explore will make a child feel like he is in prison, so don't turn the whole house into one big "No." You can, though, decide to work on two or three things that you don't allow him to touch. You may, for instance, choose to leave your plants where they are. Then, when your toddler goes over to them (and it is very interesting to touch them and dig in the earth!), you'll take him away and say, "Yankele, you're not allowed to play with the plants. Mommy doesn't let." After ten times, he'll get the point, and he won't even go near the plants. It's like showing him that something is hot. If your toddler was about to touch a hot oven, would you start screaming, or would you jump up and catch him before he touches it? If each time he heads for the stove you gently stop him, show him it's hot, and say, "Hot!" he'll stay away from it. It takes patience. Every time you feel yourself about to lose your patience and begin shouting, remember Rav Preda, who was willing to teach his student 400-800 times when necessary[1] — and that will stop you (*Eruvin* 54b). After all, why should you lose patience with a child when every child is a child of Hashem?

A mother who "solves the problem" by keeping her baby constantly in a playpen, never giving him the freedom to explore, may

---

1. *Eruvin* 54b.

have a seemingly well-behaved "good" child, but chances are that he has simply accepted his lot. The child may appear happy, but he is paying a price for it. He is being what his mother wants him to be and sadly, not himself. In a few more years, if he has good teachers and plays with other children, he may be able to free himself of this restraint, but we can never be sure.

A child begins life knowing nothing. He observes carefully everything that surrounds him, especially people, to see how they conduct themselves. And the people who occupy his thoughts, and whose deeds have the main authority for the child, are his parents. Children look up to their parents. They look to them for ideas, for ways of thinking and feeling. They learn from them a standard on which to base their future decisions. Often without even being aware of it, parents are teaching and educating their children as much as if they were sitting and teaching them in a classroom.

There is, for example, the typical oldest child in a family. He is usually a very responsible child who willingly carries the burden and responsibility of the home. Parents tend to confide in such a child, for he can keep secrets. Sometimes these children are even more responsible than their parents. They want to help their mother so much that they are the first ones to wake up when the baby cries and often call out, "Mommy, can't you hear the baby crying?" They also tend to be worriers. Parents need to make sure a child like this doesn't become old before his time, overworried and overburdened.

Then there is the "sandwich" child, who is usually a more difficult child to raise. These are often the second and sixth child, sandwiched in between the rest. They're a different make of child, usually tougher than the rest, yet equally good children. If you have a lot of patience, you can turn them into fantastic personalities. Such children need a lot of attention, and even when they get it, they often feel they're being deprived. Whatever you do for them is never quite enough. Parents must realize that although the sandwich child may seem problematic, he is probably very gifted. It only takes patience on the part of his parents to bring out the best in him.

There is a type of child who hears what you say to him the first time you say it; you tell him once, and he's there. On the other hand, every family has a child who the parents think of as difficult because they sometimes have to repeat what they say to him twenty times before he understands what they want. It's a mistake to think of this child as problematic. It's simply not true. It's not that he's a bad child; it's just that Hashem created him that way. Although this type of child only understands what you're saying after the twentieth time, it may be that after the twentieth time he hears the message better than anybody else! And once he's heard it, it will stick with him for the rest of his life.

Never lose patience with this type of child, and certainly never scream or hit. If, for instance, you've called your three-year-old several times and he still hasn't come, take him by the hand gently, talking to him calmly as you lead him through supper, bath, and bedtime. Shouting and screaming will accomplish nothing, because it's in his nature to be the way he is. In school, these children are often the ones to ask questions because they want to really understand the material being taught. Unfortunately, teachers easily lose patience with them. It's a tragic mistake, because these children are usually gifted and have within them the ability to become great people — if only we have the patience for it. With such a child, a mother has to show up regularly at school because the teacher's attitude will be more positive when she knows the parents take an interest.

In every home, especially in large families, there is usually one child who is like an angel. This child never asks for anything, and never complains about what she gets or doesn't get, even though she may feel hurt. It is especially important for the parents to see that this child's needs are not neglected. She too should get a new dress and not only hand-me-downs, even if she is the fourth child in the family. Unlike other children who are constantly demanding, this one never demands. It's up to you to see that she receives her fair share of rights and privileges. When it's time for a special treat, like being taken out shopping, she too should have her chance, even if she's always prepared to give in and give up her turn for someone else. It's also important to make sure that such a child isn't overworked. Look out for her needs, and see to it that her rights are not overlooked.

With children of all types, experts say the biggest mistake parents make is ignoring problems, thinking they will pass. Part of a mother's job is to pay constant attention to her child's behavior, always asking herself, "Is it like him? Is this how he usually acts?" For instance, if a child who was usually a very positive, friendly, outgoing child suddenly becomes afraid of people, his mother should ask herself why. She should wonder: What could have happened to cause the change? Is he being pressured, or under some kind of tension? Has he had a shock? Has something happened in the family to bring about such a state? Then she should watch to see whether the problem is just a minor one that is likely to pass with caring and reassurance, or if it is a problem that is growing and developing into a more major one.

Certain problems are more common than others. Between the ages of about three to eight, children go through stages where they're very much afraid of certain things. And we have to be on the lookout to see whether these fears and their expression, the problems that can be connected to them, are not becoming exaggerated.

Until the age of about eight, children may have sleeping problems. The child wakes up in the middle of the night crying. Leaving a small light on in the children's bedroom often solves the problem. If you've done everything and the child is still afraid to go back to sleep, it's most likely because he's had a nightmare. Even though it's hard for you, put on your robe and sit beside the child until he falls asleep again. You might have to sleep in the children's room but try to avoid taking the child into your bed. Children should not become accustomed to getting into your bed. If they do, you won't get any rest at all. Very rarely, as a special treat, you can take them in to your bed. It may be on Shabbos morning that you let all the little ones come in with you. You tell them a story and they have a wonderful time. This too is an expression of love. But in general, it's better for the child if you help him get over his sleeping problem by getting him used to falling back to sleep in his own bed.

Another common fear of young children is a fear of cats and dogs. Don't think it's a joke — it's not. Such a child is capable of walking off the sidewalk into the road under the wheels of a car when it sees an animal because he's so terrified. Whether or not a child will be afraid often depends on whether or not his parent is afraid. There is no reason to be afraid of animals; animals are afraid of us. Teach your children the verse people say when passing a dog: "*u'le'chol Bnei Yisrael lo yecharatz kelev l'shono*."[1] Tell him that dogs can smell fear, but won't do him any harm if he stays calm. As for cats, they are usually more afraid of people than we are of them. Be creative in handling your child's fears. My grandmother in Slobodka had a cat, and as much as we children loved going to her home, my sister was very afraid of the cat and didn't want to go. My father thought of a solution to the problem: He wrote a letter to the cat! He told my sister that he was writing to tell the cat not to do her any harm, and gave her the letter to bring to our grandmother to give to the cat. My sister brought the letter and she wasn't afraid of the cat ever again.

Some children are afraid of noise. You have to know what exactly is bothering them. With many small children, it's the vacuum cleaner. They start screaming the minute you put it on. Other children suddenly become afraid to go out of the house, and almost everyone has children who go through a stage of being afraid to go to school. They won't tell you they're afraid to go to school, but they'll get a stomach ache before a test, waking up so sick they can't move! You have to calm them down. Actually, what is the child terrified of? Your reaction. He may be afraid he won't get good grades, especially if you — his parents — demand the impossible of him. If your expectations are in line with the child's ability, and you know that he is trying his best, reassure him. Tell him, "It's enough that you studied hard for the test and will give it your best effort," and send him off with a kiss.

What should you do if a child tells you he's afraid to walk home from school by himself? Should you go and pick him up every day, or should you encourage him to walk home alone? If the walk is a short one and there are other people on the street, help him to become accustomed to walking home by himself. Begin by walking with him a few times to show him that there's nothing to be afraid

1. *Shemos* 11:7.

of. Then, let him walk part of the way himself, but stand watching him where he can see you. Let him go ahead and then you follow him. In this way, you'll teach him gradually not to be afraid. Never try to *force* a child to overcome a fear, but instead find creative ways to help him overcome it.

Some children are excessively timid. These are children who when you put them in a swing are afraid of swinging, or the ones who don't want to go down a slide. A child like this lets other children push him around in the kindergarten. When another child takes his toy away, he's helpless. He'll stand around crying, but he won't do a thing to help himself.

A child may have social problems. He may be afraid to play with other children. You see him always standing on the side. Another child is too independent, a loner. He likes to have other children around, they fill up the space, but he doesn't need them, and doesn't want to play with them.

Children need help with their problems. A mother has to be aware of her child's problems when they first begin. If she sees that they are only a phase that passes in a week or so, fine. If she sees that the problem is continuing, she has to begin analyzing it and looking for a solution.

Some children are natural-born leaders. When they are young, they don't know how to channel this ability and often appear bossy and controlling instead. They aren't capable of letting other people take over — they have to lead all the time. This is not good. Such a child has to be told that everyone needs a turn at being the leader. A dominant child like this has to learn to give in to others.

Sometimes you find a child who is never happy. No matter what you do, no matter how good you are to him, he's never satisfied. You can give him a lot of attention, you can indulge him, but nothing is good enough. This is a child who is extremely negative.

There may be a problem with a child who clings to his mother. Even after she sits with him in kindergarten for a month or more to get him used to it, when she leaves, he'll attach himself to the teacher and cling to her. He'll follow her around everywhere, never playing with the other children or getting involved in any of the activities. Or there may be a problem with a child who refuses to stay with a baby-sitter. He doesn't want to let his mother out of his sight. Often this happens to children whose parents have left them without telling them that they're going out. The child then becomes afraid of being deserted and makes sure to watch his parents' every move. Parents should be honest with their children. If you are going out to work, say to your child, "Mommy has to go to work now." Tell them, "Daddy and Mommy are going to a wedding." Their baby-sitter should be someone they know and like, not a stranger. Let them know who is going to be staying with them before you leave. That way the child will not wake up in the middle of the night and feel deserted, like the little girl in this story:

> Sarale was three years old. When her parents went to a wedding one evening, they decided to take Sarale's older brothers and sisters with them, but to leave her home. Sarale didn't know her parents were going out and she was sleeping when the baby-sitter came.
>
> After a few hours, Sarale woke up. She was surprised and upset to find her parents gone and began crying. Before the baby-sitter was able to comfort her, she "had an accident" which upset her greatly since she had been clean and dry for quite some time.
>
> Two weeks later, Sarale told her parents this story: "Once upon a time, there was a little girl. And this little girl's mommy and daddy went to a wedding and they left her alone with the baby-sitter . . . and the little girl woke up and all the beds were empty!" She told them the whole story and finished by saying: "Next time you have to take Sarale to the wedding. . ."

This child had been hurt, and it's a good thing she was able to express it. Not every child can express their hurt. Some children carry the hurt inside, which is very detrimental for the child.

Never run away from a child. It's the worst thing you can do. It destroys the child's trust in you, his sense of security, as well as his self-confidence. If you are going out, make sure your children know the baby-sitter. Tell them you're leaving, give them a kiss, and tell them to be good.

And never, ever leave a child alone. There are grown women who have still not forgotten the time their parents left them alone when they were small. They were terrified, and the fear still stays with them. Nor should children under the age of twelve be given the responsibility of watching their younger brothers and sisters. They will be too afraid to go to sleep, and will be worn out the next morning.

If you see your child regressing, moving backwards into behavior he already gave up months ago, pay attention. There may be a reason why a child who has been already clean and dry starts wetting again; or why a child who stopped sucking his finger or a pacifier starts all over again; or why a child who slept the whole night through starts waking up screaming in the middle of the night. Find out what is causing the problem and look for a solution.

Don't assume that your child is afraid of what you think he's afraid of. People often think that a child is afraid of another baby coming into the house, but he can usually cope with that. He can even cope with going to the hospital for an operation. But he can't cope with being shamed in front of other people. Don't send him to school dressed in a way that will cause the other children to make fun of him. Don't subject him to their ridicule. Children are terrified of other children laughing at them. For that reason, they're afraid of being left back in school, of getting a bad grade, or of being punished in front of other children. If your child comes home in a terrible mood, find out what's bothering him. Maybe he had a hard time in the classroom or on the playground.

Ask your children open-ended questions. If, for instance, your son comes home and says he's angry at another boy, discuss it with him. The worst thing to do is to start lecturing him. Say to him, "Yankele, you've had a hard time at the playground and you've come back in a very bad mood." If he says he's so mad he wants to beat the other boy up, listen. He is trying to tell you that this person has not been very nice to him. You can say, "Yankele, I hear that you want to beat this person up. The Torah is not in favor of beating other people up." Then hand him a pillow or a ball and say, "If you want to beat somebody up, give this ball about ten good hits and let's see if you feel better." Then ask him, "Why did you want to give that friend of yours a beating? What did he do to you?" You can already assume that the other child did something, so you can say, "Was Avremele mean to you today in the playground?" By leaving the question open ended, he'll continue the conversation. And because you are listening, he will tell you what happened.

Some mothers are worried that asking their child what happened will encourage him to speak *lashon hara* (give a negative report about another person). But a parent **must** ask his child. It's part of education. Otherwise, the child will have problems. Afterwards, explain that he should judge the other boy positively. Tell him that he should be nice to this boy, and that if he is, in the end he'll win him over. Once you explain it to him, he won't talk *lashon hara*. But if you start out by saying to him, "Don't say any *lashon hara*," he's going to burst. He's got so much to tell you — such a lot of things worrying him, troubling him, hurting him, and destroying him — yet he won't be able to say anything because it's all *lashon hara*. First let him see that you understand.

Parents should talk things over together. If they think the child is having a problem, if he's coming home from school or *cheder* unhappy, you must call the teacher to find out what's going on. Always keep your finger on the pulse; otherwise children suffer. Why leave a wound and a scar? Sometimes it's good for a child when things are a bit hard for him, but we don't have to make suffering part of it. If your child is suffering — if the teacher is bearing down on him unnecessarily without understanding what the background is, or if he's having a hard time with his friends — don't ignore the problem.

Often, time and your reassurance will help the child while he is growing out of one of these phases. So while you shouldn't become a nervous wreck about it, remain aware. You needn't run for help immediately, but if a problem doesn't solve itself within two or three weeks, or even a month, you have to do something about it. A child may need help, and why not give it to him? He may need special education. Why not? If you can help him, why not? Don't demand of a child what he's not capable of doing. That's one of the major problems today. We try to live up to the Joneses physically as well as materially. If they have the latest model car, we must have one too; if their house has just been redecorated, so must ours be. Who says so? And who says your children have to compete with other people? They have to compete with themselves, to the best of their ability. Don't ask a child to bring home 90's or 100's when he's only capable of bringing home 50's. His 50 is worth more than somebody else's 100 because he's making the effort for it. A child should do the best he can, and it's your responsibility to help him to make the most of himself. He doesn't have to compete with anybody. He doesn't have to bring home top grades. As a teacher for over thirty years, I can tell you that grades are not that important. Once the entire staff of the school where I taught sat down to discuss the two generations — mothers and daughters — who had gone to our school. We found out that it wasn't always the most brilliant pupils who had turned out most successful and brought up the best families. In fact, many of the brilliant pupils didn't turn out well at all; they had a lot of problems in life. It was the average girls, even some of the scholastically weaker ones, who made the best wives and mothers, and raised the most wonderful families. When a girl goes for a *shidduch*, she doesn't bring her report card along, she brings herself! It's her character and personality that are important.

27

Behavior in the Home

ome should be a place a child runs *to*, not away from. Children hate a home where they are ordered around — it arouses their resentment and opposition. A child may refuse to help when he is ordered, yet in homes where children are brought up to feel they are part of the home, when the mother says, "Yankele, please take the garbage when you go out," the child will be only too happy to do so.

Everyone in the house, including children, should have duties. Everyone should know what his duties are, and no one should get paid for doing them. We have reached a stage where children expect to be paid for helping out around the home. It's part of their job, not something you have to pay for. Do you get paid for cooking and washing and cleaning? No! Because the home is a partnership in which everyone has a share.

Arrange to hold a family conference. You can even post an official-looking announcement: "Tonight at seven o'clock there will be a family meeting. Please be there." Discuss the chores that need to be done around the home, and make a chart to hang on the wall. There will be no complaining about whose turn it is to do the dishes or arguing about who should put away the wash when it's written in black and white each day. In designating the tasks, take into consideration how many hours a day the child spends in school and how much homework there will be. There will be pleas to be excused from chores because of tests, but don't give in. Children's lives are full and busy with school and extracurricular activities, but they have to learn to set aside that half hour a day or more for fulfilling their responsibilities to the home. It's part of their basic training and will stand them in good stead when they become adults with their own homes.

With younger children especially, it helps to make it like a game. Give them points for helping you clean the house or for putting all the toys away. Keep them busy. Children can learn to help from a very early age and they'll have a tremendous thrill from it. Even young children can have a turn at making breakfast or lunch, and the smallest can help set the table. All you need is patience. The best time to start getting your children involved in helping carry the burden of the house is when they're young, even if it may seem easier for you to do everything yourself. The mothers who have patience with their young children who want to help will be the ones who have an easier life when their children grow up.

Two-year-olds love to help, and if you let them when they're two, they'll help you as they grow by doing even more, and they'll enjoy it as well. Tell them how wonderful they are for helping Mommy, and give them a big kiss. Praise them for always being ready to help Mommy. Fourth graders enjoy trying to cook and bake. So what if they make a mess? It doesn't matter. If your nine-year-old wants to bake a cake, let her. At first, you can help her clean up afterwards; later, she'll learn to do it herself. Don't spoil it for her. Some mothers make their children feel very little and stupid, like the mother who said about her ten- and twelve-year-old daughters, "I can't have them helping me around the house — they don't know how." By the age of ten or twelve a child should be cleaning the whole house! Let them learn from their mistakes. When a child starts walking he falls down, but he picks himself up and tries again, and eventually he does learn to walk. Let your children get started. In the end, you are going to get a great deal of help from them.

Make it easy for your children to succeed and be good. If you put up a mitzvah chart and one child seems to be doing everything so exceptionally well that the others just give up, don't let them get discouraged. The high achiever can compete against himself, and the others can compete amongst themselves. If you give rewards for *improvement*, not just achievement, they'll try even harder.

Learning to respect other people and their property begins in childhood and is taught in the home. Well-brought-up children will play quietly while their mother sleeps late on Shabbos morning. Their father gets up in the morning and gives them a drink if they are quite small, or makes *kiddush* for them before he goes to *shul*, and then tells them to play quietly, to let Mommy sleep a little longer. Even after he leaves, the children are very careful not to wake up their mother. They'll walk around on tiptoe so that she can catch up on her sleep. This is teaching them respect.

Parents should set an example. If you have neighbors in close proximity, don't use a washing machine or dryer, late at night, that sounds like a tractor. You may be guilty of stealing a neighbor's sleep, and there's no way to pay it back — you can only ask their forgiveness. Teach your children to respect your neighbors. Don't send your children out to play when it will disturb others. If you live above other people, don't allow your children to jump and run around too much or play ball in the house. Your downstairs neighbor may be old or sick, or may have high blood pressure or not be feeling well.

In many homes you find that the children nag: "Mommy, what can we do now? There's nothing to do." They're bored to tears and annoy their mother constantly until she can feel her temperature rising. Keep your children occupied. You can buy them a million games, a million toys, but if you don't teach them how to play with them, you'll have closets full of games that the children don't know what to do with. You have to sit down and teach your children to play; afterwards, they'll know how to play by themselves.

When you were a little girl, you probably didn't have Lego or as many Fisher-Price toys as your children have now. A generation or two ago children had fewer bought toys, so they developed creativity. They played with pots and pans, matchboxes, etc. They would cut up paper and make up games. Now they have so much that they're bored. Teach your children to think, to be creative and to occupy themselves.

If you don't work outside the home, try to get an hour's rest before the children come home so that you can be around when they're there. Make yourself available to them. If they need help with their homework, you'll be there. If they fight, as occasionally all normal children do, you'll be there. The children need your proximity. It gives them warmth, comfort, and confidence. Even though they'll run off to play somewhere else, they'll come back to see if you're still there . . . if you're around.

Just as communication is essential between husbands and wives, so too it is essential to communicate with your children. It begins when they are babies and, with care, will continue for life. Tragically, some parents lose communication with their children as they get older. Never cut the lines of communication with your children. Be a mother who can discuss everything with her child. Adolescence, for instance, is a very unpredictable age. Even the best children can have questions on faith. If they've lost communication with you, they'll have no one to talk to. If your fourteen- or fifteen-year-old comes and asks you about Hashem, if he's troubled, don't start screaming, "I don't want to hear questions like that." If you can't answer his questions yourself, go to one of the experts in the *ba'al teshuvah* movement — they have appropriate answers to every question. Help your child cope and solve his problems. Keep your lines of communication open for those very difficult times children go through, like *shidduchim*. Help your children grow by letting them discuss things with you. When a child has a problem, some parents send him away in the hopes that somebody else will solve the problem for them. Usually, if you don't face up to problems they continue to grow. Problems have to be faced up to, and solved.

There are three times in a day when a mother really has communication with her children: 1) in the morning, when she sends them off to school; 2) in the afternoon, when they come home from school; and 3) in the evening, at bedtime. You have to plan your day in such a way that you utilize these times of communication to the fullest. Let's say you have a family of eight to ten children and you don't work outside the home. Plan to have supper ready an hour before the children are due, so that you can rest before they come home. If it will take you two hours to bake a cake and you can afford to buy one instead, even if it's smaller and everyone will get less, weigh the choice carefully. Maybe it's better for the children to have two hours of your time than a freshly baked cake. Your presence is essential so that whoever needs help can get it. Leave everything else for the time being — it will get done in the end. This is one of your priorities: to be around, to see that everything is calm, that nobody fights. If a mother works, she can't come home and expect to rest while the children run around the house unsupervised. She can only rest if she has someone to watch them or take them out to play.

Bedtime is a very important hour for children. Don't send children to bed as punishment, with spankings and crying. It's a very ineffective way of educating. Let them go to bed happy, and they'll have a happy, relaxed, and restful sleep.

Siblings inevitably do fight, but if parents respond in the right manner, it can be over in just a few minutes. You have to be very firm and say, "In our house, we don't behave like that."

On the other hand, in a home where the parents — especially the mother — make comparisons between the children, the child will feel a lack of love, and fights can become an everyday occurrence. If one of your children has not behaved well or done well enough in school and the mother comments, "What's the matter with you, Yankele? Look at your brother Moshe — he's such a good boy," automatically, Yankele will go over and start a fight with his brother. Who caused it? The mother. Never compare children; never tell one child that the other one is better than he is. You'll only make them dislike each other. Each child has his virtues, and each one has to have a different approach because Hashem made him different. Tell them both how good they are and keep them busy with constructive activities.

And although you want to encourage responsibility, your expectations from your children should be realistic. It's always a mistake to demand too much of a child. A mother, for instance, who sends her five- or a six-year-old out to walk a six-month-old baby in his carriage on a main road is not teaching her child responsibility — she's being foolhardy and risking the life of the baby. That five- or six-year-old can meet some friends, join their game of jump rope or hopscotch, and forget all about the baby. It has happened more than once that younger children left in the care of their not-that-much-older siblings have wandered into the middle of the road or gotten into other dangerous situations. Never rely on the judgment of a young child. What a child can think up is beyond your wildest imagination.

We can thwart them — or encourage them. If you take your children to the playground and one of them climbs up a huge ladder and starts crying, "Mommy, I can't get down," don't panic. He needs to understand that if he managed to get up, he can most probably get down. Say calmly, "You managed to get up there. I'm waiting for you and I'll help you climb down." You're training your child to realize that if he got himself into it, he can find a way out of it — that's independence. You're not punishing the child, you're training him to cope. The message is: Yes, it takes more effort to get down, but you *can* do it.

Have a positive attitude to all the little falls and scraped knees of childhood. It's part of play. Stay calm and loving. If you get hysterical about every little thing, your children will turn into fearful children, terrified of moving normally. Learn how to comfort a child: Tell them that you too fell when you were a little girl, but that nothing happened and you got up again. Encourage them to keep on playing.

Mothers sometimes wonder how they should react if their child gets hurt doing something he knows he shouldn't do. First, calm him down. Then talk it over with him. Ask him how he feels about it. Don't say, "I told you so." As we said, it's not a good idea in a marriage to want to always be right, and it's not a good idea in childraising either. Later though, after the hurt has passed, you can say, "Yankele, why did you get hurt? What happened? You jumped. That was your responsibility. Do you remember what I said?" Ask him what you said beforehand. Discuss it with him. Sympathize.

He'll come to the conclusion himself that it was his own fault. Just as your husband shouldn't feel that you're blaming him or trying to show up his faults, so too your child should never be subject to this kind of negative attitude. When you destroy another person's self-image, it will boomerang back to you in the end. So never, ever say, "I told you so."

We have to teach a child not to cause damage, yet we should not punish him when he does. We teach him to take care of possessions because they are the tools Hashem gave us to fulfill our mission.

Even with the best education, things do get broken. In every home children cause damage, break, and destroy. Instead of shouting and screaming, what should our attitude to this be? We should keep three things in mind: 1) If a vessel broke, that means it had finished its service and it's a sign that you don't need it anymore. Therefore, there is nothing to be upset about. 2) We say, "The vessel broke and *we* were saved." Always remember that it's better for something to happen to wood, stone, or glass rather than to a human being. Be grateful to Hashem that it was only that, and nothing more. 3) Translate your loss into money. Let's say the child broke a crystal vase. How much is it worth? $50 or $60? Are you going to lose your temper for $60? It's not worth losing your temper for a million dollars! A person who loses control loses his Divine countenance; he's no longer a human being, he's an animal. Is it worth it for $60? If a child breaks a $3 glass are you going to get angry? Is it worth it? Never punish children for things that break. Your approach should be to teach them that everything Hashem gives us is for His service and we should take care of what we have because we use it to serve Hashem.

28

Disciplining the Child

Education is patience, it's love, it's affection, it's warmth, it's encouragement. It's the mother. You'll find that you are the heart of the home. Whether it's problems at home or school, problems at work or in society, your husband, your children, and your friends will always pivot to you. With a good word, a smile, encouragement, you are the shining light. It's all up to you.

Children fulfill our expectations. Show them that you expect them to be fantastic . . . and they will be. The Gemara gives us this glimpse into how to build a child's self-image:

> *There was once an extremely brilliant, but very lazy student named Yossi. Although he was the son of R' Elazar ben R'*

Shimon (bar Yochai), instead of wanting to sit and learn, he wasted his time in idleness.

When Rebbi came to visit the town after R' Elazar's passing he found out about Yossi. Being the great educator that all of our Sages were, Rebbe came up with the right approach: He gave Yossi semichah.

In those days, it was not an easy thing to join the exalted company of those scholars who were granted semichah, and anyone who did so was entitled to wear golden robes.

Before leaving the town, Rebbi entrusted Yossi's education to R' Shimon ben Isi ben Lekunia (Rebbe's uncle). Every day the young man would tell R' Shimon, "I want to leave." But R' Shimon told him, "Here they treat you like a scholar — they dress you in a golden robe and call You Rabbi. It's better for you to sit and learn." And R' Shimon devoted himself to helping his reluctant student grow to fit his golden robes.

Ultimately, he became one of the great scholars of the generation.[1]

To motivate a child, give him something to aspire to. Never say, "You can't." Say, "Yes, you can. Try a little harder and you'll do better." If you tell a child he's a no-good failure, he'll be so discouraged, he'll give up on life. He'll say to himself, "Why should I try or even care?" But if you tell a child he's a wonderful person, he will become that wonderful person.

Rabbi Yitzchak Elchanan was the Rabbi of Kovno about 100 years ago. He stood head and shoulders above most men in his vast Torah knowledge as well as sterling character, and was looked up to by all as one of the leading rabbis of his era.

One day, a young man came to him and asked him to ordain him as a rabbi. In those days, rabbinical authority was granted only after a grueling two-week-long test. An aspirant had to know all four sections of the Shulchan Aruch by heart.

---

1. *Bava Metzia* 85a.

Rabbi Elchanan began asking the young man some questions and soon discovered that the applicant lacked the knowledge necessary to pass the test. When he realized this, instead of saying, "You didn't pass the test," Rabbi Yitzchak Elchanan sat down and wrote him a semichah any scholar would be proud to have. Then he told him, "This is the semichah I want to give you. But you're not ready for it yet. I shall leave it here in this drawer, where it will wait for you, until you are ready.

"In the meantime, go home with this list of what you need to know. Learn it very thoroughly, and come back in two years' time. If you know everything on the list, the semichah is yours."

Encouragement builds self-confidence.

Your confidence in your child proves to him that he is capable of achieving. Your appreciation — a kind word and a smile — will build his ladder of success. A child is prepared to do somersaults in the air to get a smile and a good word from his parents. That's what he's hungry for, a kind word, a hug, a kiss — it's food for the soul.

Don't be like mothers who only enjoy their children when they're asleep. It's very important to enjoy your children. The years when the children are young pass so quickly. They are a precious gift. When you're so busy with the diapers, the cooking, the cleaning, the washing, and the children crying at night, don't feel that it's drudgery, that you can't take it anymore. Remember that these children entrusted to your care are Hashem's children, and give them your utmost. It will turn your house into a Gan Eden that your children will love. They will thrive in the warmth and happiness in the home.

Keep a photo album, and write down your children's clever sayings along with the photos so that you'll be able to share them with your grandchildren years hence. Sit down every once in a while to relax for ten minutes or so with this wonderful living chronicle. Look at your children when they were babies; remember all the happy moments — it's a pleasure.

When a child comes home from school complaining that the homework is too hard for him and that he'll never be able to do it, his mother should help him with it *unobtrusively*. She can sit near-by to answer questions and help him finish, without doing it for him. Do you think all outstanding students accomplish their task on their own? Many of them have devoted parents who help them along. When it's homework time, they're around. There are parents, even those with big families, who care. They build up their child's self-image and prove to him that he's capable.

Baruch Hashem we have a generation of *bnei Torah* because of such mothers.

Pushing a child to achieve — the opposite of giving encourage-ment — has negative consequences. Children, in order to save their lives, can turn into dreamers. They may take hours to finish their homework. One thing is certain: A child is not born a dreamer. He's either bored, or he feels pressure and has found a way of escaping from reality. I once taught a little girl whose mother drove her, ex-pecting from her what was appropriate for girls twice her age. She wanted her daughter to *daven* three times a day and be tops in every subject. In order to escape this pressure, the girl lived in a dream world. Although she was a brilliant child, in class, when everyone else was writing, she was busy looking around the room. When the class had finished, she would "wake up" and find she hadn't written a word.

There is no need to drive children. Saying, "You can do it your-self; I won't help you," is not the way to solve problems. You can gradually help a child and show him that he can do it himself; then he will become convinced that he *can* do it himself. But you can't force him to do something himself by calling him lazy or accusing him of dreaming. The best way to help a child achieve is to awaken motivation. Especially if a child feels picked on — and every family has such a child — shower him with praise.

Why did Rav Preda, who repeated the same thing to his student 800 times, have such patience? Because he knew he was teaching a son of the king, a child of Hashem. His whole approach to teaching, along with his attitude to his student, was elevated by this realiza-tion. A teacher of the king's son or daughter is devoted to the task. He can't fall asleep at night because his mind is churning, thinking, How can I better present the material so that the child will under-stand it? Or wondering, How can I help my student solve his problem? If the Alter of Slobodka had a student who wasn't doing well in his studies, he would fast and pray for him to improve. He was capable of fasting forty days for a student!

> One Shabbos, Rabbi Yaakov Neiman, later Rosh Yeshivah of Ohr Yisroel, visited the famous mashgiach of Lomza Yeshivah in Lithuania, Rabbi Moshe Rosenstein. He saw the mashgiach sitting with a little boy, asking him questions and testing him on that week's parashah. Rabbi Neiman was quite surprised that the great mashgiach found time to sit with such a young child, asking him questions and learning with him! He whispered in his ear, "Whose little boy is that?" The mashgiach whispered back, "HaKadosh Baruch Hu's."
>
> Later, after the child had left, the mashgiach turned to Rabbi Neiman and said, "Why were you so surprised when I said that the child is HaKadosh Baruch Hu's? If I had told you that he's Yankel's or Berel's or Zev's child, would he not have been HaKadosh Baruch Hu's child? Every Jewish child is a child of HaKadosh Baruch Hu."

Children are precious to Hashem. They cleave to Him, and their prayers are beloved by Him. We love little children for this closeness, for their purity of soul. Yet we are taught that each child is born with an evil inclination (*yetzer hara*), and that it is our job to teach him to overcome it. This is the basis of education. Unlike some theories which encourage parents to let children follow their instincts, Judaism teaches that the human being has to be shaped. You have to teach a child to control his bad traits, his *yetzer hara*, and to work on improving all his inborn characteristics.

Rabbi Dessler said that perhaps the most important component of education is consistency. If you want to educate, you have to give encouragement and show appreciation, approval, and consideration. Most of all, if you want to succeed, you have to be consistent in your demands and responses.

Good education means that the children know that "in our house we behave in a certain way." They know that there are certain basic rules in your home, that when you get up in the morning, you wash *negel vasser*, you say *modeh ani*, you dress yourself, and you speak nicely to people. There is a certain standard of conduct in the home. But it's not enough to have rules, they must be explained. Good parents communicate their feelings to their children. Some parents become annoyed and spank their children for not obeying, yet their children have no idea why they are being spanked. They can't understand what they did wrong, or what their parents want from them or why they are shouting — because the parents never clearly explained what they expected. Tell your children: "This is the way we speak in our house. . ." "This is the way we do things in our home..." "This is what has to be done now. . ."

If a child complies with what is expected of him, the parents must show their approval. If the child does not comply, then they must express their dissatisfaction and displeasure. Children need to know in advance what their parents' reaction will be if they intentionally go against the rules of the home. And they have to know equally clearly that if they do obey the rules, their father and mother are going to show approval. Good parents make sure that the saying, "When I'm bad, nobody forgets; when I'm good, nobody remembers," is not the norm in their home. You have to tell a child when he's good, not only when he's bad. If he has not conformed to the rules, he knows in advance that you're not going to be very pleased. If a child is willfully disobedient, he has to know that he's going to be punished. That is **consistency**.

Any punishment given has to fit the crime. Let's say, for example, that you gave your daughter permission to go play at her friend's house and you told her to be home by 7:30. A smart thing to do would be to phone her at 7:15 to remind her of the time and give her a chance to start preparing to come home. That would give her a chance to finish a game and collect her things. But let's say you haven't reminded her and you're looking at the clock. Seven-thirty comes and she's not home, 8:30 passes and she's still not back. By 9:30 when she turns up, you're just about raving mad. It's hard to say who is more to blame, the child or you. The punishment could be that for the next week or so, she won't be allowed to go anywhere after school. She will realize that if she goes out, she must come home on time, and that any time she comes home late, she won't be allowed to go out to play for a week. The punishment fits the crime.

While discipline means being consistent, it doesn't mean being dogmatic. Children need routine. They become confused by mixed messages — if you behave one day like this and the next day like that. They need consistency — sameness — but sometimes you should break the routine. On school nights bedtime may be seven o'clock, but the world won't stop if occasionally it's later. When you want to take them all out, when you have a wedding in the family, they don't have to be in bed at seven o'clock! Vacation time, Chanukah, Pesach — give them a chance to enjoy it. They will know that you are firm and that there is a routine, but that the routine can be broken occasionally. Then when you ask them to take a nap in the afternoon so that they can go out with the family that night, they'll be happy to comply. Flexibility is part of consistency.

There are parents who are terrified of their children. Whatever the children want is done. It's almost as if the children are running the home, not the parents. Don't let your children run the home. Sometimes, it's much easier at the moment to indulge the child rather than to discipline him. Disciplining a child takes a lot of mental and emotional effort. Sometimes you may want to just give up. Don't. You have to be strong, because ultimately it's for your child's good.

If you have pity on your children, you'll cripple them. If you feel sorry for your daughter when she is at the age when she should be helping around the house, when she should be doing dishes, chores, cleaning, and helping with the cooking and going shopping, you'll raise a girl who is unable to cope with married life. Nowadays, especially in Eretz Yisrael, children have to help their mothers. In previous generations in Europe, it was different. In Lithuania where I was born, even extremely poor people were able to afford live-in household help. For room and board, they were able to hire a peasant girl who did all the physical work in the home. Conditions now are not that easy, and everyone has to carry the burden in order for the mother to keep on going. Don't ruin your daughter's future, and don't indulge your children — including the boys. If you have only sons and no daughters, teach them to do everything — their wives will be forever grateful to you! A husband who can give a helping hand when it's necessary is a blessing.

You don't ask a child; you tell a child. Children can sense firmness and will soon understand that "this is the way it has to be." For instance, when it's time to get dressed you take out two things and give the child a choice: "You can wear this, or that. I'm going out of the room for two minutes while you decide." If they don't make a choice, then it becomes your choice. When you choose, don't let them override you. They have to know that yours is the final word. This is part of discipline. You allow your children choices, but within limits. Otherwise, the sky's the limit.

Teach them that bedtime is bedtime, that once you're in bed, you stay there. If they get out, be firm about getting them right back in. When you are putting the younger ones to bed, unplug the telephone so you can give them your full concentration. Some children are full of energy and won't go to bed without first reaching the limit of your patience. Sometimes it is necessary to be firm — they wait for that firmness.

You say *Shema* with them and put them in bed, you kiss them and give them the feeling that they're wonderful children and now it's time for bed and that's it, enough. And that you don't want to hear another word. They know that you're firm about it, that if Mommy said it's bedtime, then you go to bed and you don't come out. Children feel tension and they play on it. A relaxed mother, a calm mother, is in control.

Reb Yisrael Salanter used to say: "An angry face, but not an angry heart." Even if you sometimes have to show a child that you are annoyed with him, or if you have to punish a child or spank him, it shouldn't be from your heart, it should only be an outer expression. In your heart, you should be calm. Don't lose your temper and sacrifice your children to your mood — the damage is sometimes irreparable.

A mother's love is unconditional. Never tell your child he's "bad," or say, "I don't love you." You have to be very careful in the way you express yourself to children, and especially avoid shaming them (*halbanas panim*). The laws of speech apply to children as well. If you say to a two-year-old in front of other children, "Sarale, you're a bad little girl," you've destroyed that child's self-image and shamed her.

Be very careful to differentiate between the child and the deed. When you have to reprimand a child, stay calm. When the mother is tense, the children will automatically be tense, while if she's happy and calm, they will be that way too. If your voice isn't naturally calming, work on creating a calm voice.

As we discussed when we spoke of breaking patterns of behavior, it is a good idea to practice in advance your reaction if the children misbehave. Let's say your children are fighting. Instead of shouting at them, how will you react? First, you make sure to stay calm. Then you say to them, "My children can't be fighting. You're such good children." Sometimes the best approach will be to distract their attention and interest them in something else. A tense mother might shout and spank, and make the situation worse, but a wise mother will stay calm and appeal to her child's self-image, saying, "Yankele, you're such a good boy. It's not fitting for you to act this way. Why are you hitting him? He's smaller than you are." She will smile and say, "You're all such good children."

If you do need to punish a child, the best way is to use the surprise principle. Make it short and sweet; to the point. If you have to administer physical punishment, make it a spank and be finished. Be quick about it. **Never** threaten a child with punishment. Never tell a child, "You're going to get a spanking if...." Just give the spanking if need be. It's **terrible** to threaten a child.

Don't drive a child into a corner. Some people say, "The child told a lie and I'm going to get to the bottom of this." Give him a chance, give him an opening to save face, to restore his self-image. Actually, it's often the parents themselves who are to blame for the lie, for they are the ones who taught the child to lie. A child lies because he may have heard his parents lying, although the parents think they speak the truth. There may be a neighbor who knocks on the door ten times a day. One day the child's mother says, "I'm fed up. The next time she comes, tell her I'm asleep." Yet the next day, if the child tells a similarly blatant lie, his mother will become livid.

Another way of teaching children to lie is by being too strict. If you are a very strict mother who punishes a lot, then the child always has to have a good excuse. Even a husband starts lying to such a wife, for the sake of peace. If when he comes home she starts interrogating him with "It's already eight o'clock! You should have been home by 7:30! What have you been doing?" he'll "stretch the facts" as long as it keeps her quiet. A child learns to lie to *save his life*. He knows that otherwise, he'll get a spanking. If your child is lying, it's a sign that you're too strict and he's afraid of you. One should not instill fear into children.

One woman said that her four-year-old's teacher told him before Rosh Hashanah that if he didn't do what he told him to, he would be written in the Book of Wicked People (*sefer rashaim*). This is the wrong approach. Children should be taught that Hashem loves us, that He wants our good, and that He wants us to be good. They should feel that Hashem is everywhere, and that there are certain things He doesn't like us to do.

Never talk to a child about retribution. It's a terrible, terrible way to educate children. This is not a generation where you can say such things. People become fearful, they become upset easily. This is not a generation that can handle fear. We have enough fear as it is.

Remember: If you've punished a child and after ten minutes he's still crying inconsolably, make up with him. If you're not careful, you can break a child, and once you break the human spirit, it cannot be repaired. What will you achieve by destroying your child?! Never break the spirit of the child.

29
A Final Word

"**L**ife can be compared to a narrow path surrounded by danger," our Rabbis warn. "On one side, there is a tremendous fire burning; on the other side, an iceberg. If you walk too near the fire you'll get burned; if you walk too near the ice, you'll freeze. Where is the safest place to walk? In the middle."

In other words, you have to find what's important in life, what is a priority, and focus on it. Know what your destination is in life, and don't stray off the path until you reach your goal.

There once lived two men who were not only business partners, but close neighbors and good friends as well. Both passed away at the same time, and arrived at the Heavenly Court together.

The first one made his appearance before the Court, while his friend waited nearby and watched the proceedings.

"Did you pray and study Torah?"

"Yes, I did."

"Did you make brachos?"

"Yes."

The questions and answers continued in this fashion until the verdict was given:

"You are worthy of entering the World to Come."

His partner watching had been trembling with fear, yet now, when he heard the positive verdict given to his friend, he felt relieved. After all, weren't they friends, neighbors, and partners who did everything together?

When his turn came, he was asked exactly the same questions, and gave exactly the same answers. However, the verdict of the Heavenly Court left him shocked.

"You are to go to Gehinnom."

He started screaming in protest. "What kind of discrimination is this? My friend and I grew up together, lived next door to each other, worked together, and did the same things. We both gave the same answers. Why does he merit Heaven and I go there?"

"In this world," the Court answered, "there is no favoritism, there is only the absolute Truth. Yes, it is true that you were both neighbors and friends, that you did the same things and answered the questions the same way. But there was one small difference which makes all the difference: Whatever your friend did, he did for the sake of Heaven (l'shem shamayim). When he ate, he ate to gain strength to serve Hashem; when he drank, he drank for the sake of Heaven; when he slept, that too was for the sake of Heaven.

"You, on the other hand," continued the Court, "did everything for your own personal enjoyment. You enjoyed food, so you ate, and likewise with everything else. His actions earned him the World to Come, while even your mitzvos were done for your own personal enjoyment."

A person must take care to recognize his priorities while still in this world, and should always seek the middle way.[1] Rabbi Yehudah ben Ila'i, one of our great Sages, said: "A person for whom Torah is primary, and worldly affairs secondary, he himself becomes primary in this world; while he who makes worldly matters primary, and Torah secondary, he himself becomes merely secondary."

For a woman, what is the most primary thing in life? Our Sages give us the answer: "A man does not die except to his wife, and a woman does not die except to her husband."[2] To a wife, the most important person in the world is her husband. If, *chas v'shalom*, something happens to him, she is the one who feels it the most. And the same applies to him. To each other, they come first. That is why, as a woman, you have to try to find out what your husband wants from you, and then make yourself happy by making him happy.

When your husband comes home, you greet him with a radiant countenance. Always. If you have visitors, he comes first. Even if you have a very important visitor, excuse yourself. Give your guest a cup of coffee and some cake (you should always have some in the freezer), and, if you're a young married woman, let your guest look at your wedding album. If the sink isn't sky high with dishes and you're not shy about what's going on on top of the stove, you can invite her into the kitchen with you while you prepare. No matter who she is or from how far away she has come — even abroad — your husband comes first. He should not come home to a piece of bread for supper because you're busy with your friend.

> *One stormy afternoon, a woman came to visit her friend who kept a spotless home. As the two were sitting and talking, the hostess's husband walked in wearing boots covered with mud.*
>
> *"Look what's happening," said the guest. "Your husband is bringing all this mud into the house!"*
>
> *"Yes," said her hostess with a smile. "But along with the mud, my husband came home!"*

---

1. *Avos DeRabbi Nosson* 28:10.
2. *Sanhedrin* 22b.

The guest saw only the mud, but the wife saw her husband. It all depends on the way you look at things.

Make yourself beautiful for him. He should feel your welcome so warm, happy, and confident, that when he sees you he thinks you are the most beautiful person in the whole world.

Care for your husband. If you're going out to a wedding or other event, look at him *before* you leave the house. Are his shoes polished? Has he changed his shirt? Is his hat brushed? Does he look his best? Why wait until you get to the hall to notice that he needs a clean shirt? If he does, you have only yourself to blame. Where were you before, while there was still time to do something about it?

Respect your husband. Develop your sensitivity to the point where you are so careful that neither a word nor a sigh nor a sound nor even the blink of an eyelash will cause him pain or diminish his image. Every husband would very much like his wife to think highly of him. So show him that in your eyes, he is the most wonderful husband in the world.

Bring happiness to your husband. Look for the humorous side of everything, because to laugh together is happiness. Instead of making a fight, make a joke. When your husband comes home after a hard day, he needs warmth, a joke, and a smile. Even if you have a whole pack of problems to present to him, wait. He needs to feel surrounded by happiness, not to have someone add to his misery.

Every husband wants his wife to be happy; yours does too. Let him know what makes you happy, so that he will be able to bring you happiness in the future.

Be self-reliant. Make your own decisions and solve the problems that come up during the day. Major decisions are made together, but don't leave all the little things for him to solve. It will wear on his nerves and drain his energy. The image of the helpless female is not a Jewish concept. Jewish women have always been very self-reliant, especially in religious circles where the women ran businesses in order to provide for the family while their husbands sat and learned.

Be flexible. If you work outside the home and can't find a job in the field for which you were trained, be open and adaptable and look into other possibilities. Learn new skills. If you'd like to knit and don't know how, take a course in it. Hobbies and crafts — sewing, embroidery, tapestry work, painting — are not only relaxing, but give a woman a tremendous sense of satisfaction.

Keep yourself in perfect health. If you feel your muscles need strengthening, join an exercise class that meets once or twice a week. If you enjoy swimming, go out to swim once or twice a week. Find an activity that takes stress away, and stay healthy and relaxed in mind and body.

Above all, never make major decisions on your own. You and your husband should have a rabbi to whom you turn for advice. In times of uncertainty, everyone must have someone with whom they can discuss their problems. When it comes to deciding whether or not to move to a different place, accept a certain job, choose schools — any major decision — we don't make decisions like that on our own, we ask *Da'as Torah*.

Be honest with each other. Don't start telling each other lies, because it can become a habit. If it does, the other person will give up on the relationship. Be open and honest, and don't assume that the other person knows what you're thinking. Tell your husband exactly how you feel and what you think.

Focus on what you are bringing to the marriage, not what you are taking from it, and you'll never go wrong.

Avoid friction. Work together to look for the peaceful solution. Be considerate.

Share the burden of carrying the home — the rough and the smooth — together.

Don't blame your partner or the children for past mistakes. You yourself are not an angel, you're a human being. If you were an angel, you wouldn't be here, you'd already be up there. One of the problems of *shalom bayis* is that we expect everything from other people, forgetting to look at ourselves. What do we look like? How are we functioning? Perhaps others see *us* as less than perfect!

Learn to say, "I'm sorry. I made a mistake." It shows nobility of soul to admit that the other person is right. Not only will your marriage benefit, but your husband will admire you for admitting the truth, and feel good about himself for having truth on his side.

Make the most you can of each day. Each day is a gift. It should be something fantastic, a dream of happiness.

There are some wives who, when they are in the company of others along with their husband, for lack of a topic of conversation, speak about their husbands. They bring up his failings, wounding him in public. A husband who sees his wife destroy him in public — whether it be strangers, friends, or even family — will never forgive her disloyalty. Husband and wife should give each other the maximum amount of respect in front of other people, especially their children.

Your husband needs your attention. If he does something to irritate you, instead of getting annoyed, give him a little bit of extra attention.

Be a good listener, and be careful with your speech. Learn the art of avoiding criticism, cynicism, irony, nagging, and all the other verbal torments.

Make you husband's welfare a priority for you. Turn everything into one united "I." Don't think, "he wants and I want." Make "he" and "I" into one "I" wanting the same thing. Work towards the goal that what he wants matters so much to you that it becomes you; and that what you want matters so much to him that it becomes him — two halves of a single whole.

Pray for your husband's welfare. Follow Rabbeinu Yonah's advice: Whenever you feel you need Hashem's help first sanctify your hands, by washing them (*negel vasser*); give money to charity for the benefit of Klal Yisrael, because that way your prayers will be accepted; and finally, say the name of the person you are praying for. If your child has a difficult exam, teach him to give *tzedakah* and pray also. If you are going away on a journey, give *tzedakah* and pray before you leave the house. Prayer should be a basic part of the home.

You have to turn yourself into a beacon of light. My grandmother, for example, lived to the age of eighty-seven, and no one in the family, neither her children nor her grandchildren, ever thought of doing anything without first consulting her and hearing what she had to say. You are the mainstay of the home. Your children will come to ask your advice about friendships, about schoolwork, about everything. Your husband will ask you about his work. You are the essence, the shining light that guides them. Accept your job. By creating and turning your home into a miniature Beis HaMikdash, you will all together, *b'ezras Hashem*, bring the third Beis HaMikdash from Heaven into Yerushalayim and merit to see it.

Mashiach is on his way, there is no doubt about it, and everyone wants to be worthy. Work on becoming worthy of greeting the *Mashiach*. Wait for him every day. You can feel it — the world is shaking.

It's up to us, the women of Klal Yisrael, who have brought redemption and salvation so many times before. Let us be the ones who will, *b'ezras Hashem*, help bring *Mashiach*, speedily, in our days.

I Will Never Forget You

In memory of Rebbetzin Esther Greenberg,
on her first yahrzeit, 3 Tammuz 5752 [1]

*I*t is now nearly a year since I have seen you or spoken with you. Alas, you are no longer with us. As I listen to your cassette, I close my eyes and imagine I am once again sitting in Rebbetzin Gurwicz's living room in Mattersdorf, seeing you before us — inspiring, enlightening, and reeducating us to our role in life as Jewish women. In the background, I faintly hear the number 3 Egged bus careering down the winding road of Rechov Panim Meirot, and the laughter of the young *cheder* boys on their way home for the evening. Your voice rings out strong and clear: "You know, ladies, it is such a *z'chus* to be living in Yerushalayim — do you realize this? Do you feel this every single day that you are privileged to be here?

---

1. By S. Cohen. (Reprinted with permission from *Yated Ne'eman*, English Edition, 9 Tammuz 5752 / July 10, 1992.)

Do you wake up in the morning and tell Hashem how thankful you are to be living in Eretz Yisrael?"

As I open my eyes and realize that you are no longer here, I am left with questions. Rebbetzin, how did you make those tiring journeys in the late evening from Petach Tikvah to Yerushalayim? Didn't you ever feel too exhausted; weren't you ever too busy with other matters, or simply not in the mood? When did you find the time to prepare such perfectly organized, integrated lessons with deep content and profundity on such a wide range of topics? And my biggest question: How will I ever thank you?

I know that I am not alone in this sentiment. How many thousands of women wish they could acknowledge what you have done for their lives and for future generations! How many would tell you how they have changed their attitudes towards the world, towards their role as Jewish women, and towards Hashem!

Your awe is no longer with us, but the gifts you have left us endure. I have the many tapes of your lectures on the topic of "The Jewish Home." I also have your booklet, "The Key to Happiness," which you fondly called a workbook, and which we certainly treated as such. We found in it guidelines for basic Jewish living that need to be properly worked through and realized, rather than simply read as a piece of literature. Your ideas remain with us, and we carry them out in our lives.

Rebbetzin Greenberg, you brought me back to Hashem, and I am eternally grateful to you. It is true that I never left the fold — but returning to Hashem means deepening one's level of *yiras shamayim*, refining one's character traits, and strengthening one's commitment to *avodas Hashem* as a Jewish woman. Returning means the retrieval of a lost element.

Our Divine soul was once in close proximity with the *Shechinah*. However, this once strong feeling may have weakened over time. Have we soiled our souls with foreign impurities? Have we tried to model our role as women after the secular image of femininity? Have our homes become a hearth brewing controversy and conflict, rather than remain bastions of sanctity, sacredness, and beauty, as you often described? Rebbetzin Greenberg, you returned *kedushah* to our souls and homes, and so you have brought so many of us back to closeness to Hashem.

You not only wished to return us to Hashem, but also painted for us a picture of the glory of the days of yore, in contrast to the distorted image of the matriarchs and Biblical women which so dominated our thinking. How did you depict Ruth, the proselyte who married Boaz, the *Rosh Sanhedrin*?

"And she became his wife." [1] Immediately after she married she became his wife. She didn't need an adjustment period as we modern women need. Today they say that in the first year of marriage you must get adjusted to one another — after all, the different cultures, the background, and personalities. Some women even need four or five years for an adjustment period; they simply don't know what it means to be a wife. But Ruth married Boaz and immediately became his wife. This is the true example of Jewish marriage."

We all contemplated your wise words and smiled at our own distorted misconceptions, while chuckling at the jokes in the conversation about adjustments. With one story, you helped us see so much.

You also stressed your cherished theme of Jewish pride. You quoted Rabbi Yehuda HaLevi on this theme:

"The Jewish people indeed preserved the laws, but more than that, the laws preserved the Jewish people. Thanks to the commandments, the Jews have preserved their full spiritual and intellectual prowess as well as an inner vitality which has no parallel among the nations."

True, we Jews upheld and sacrificed for the observance of mitzvos. "But look what Yiddishkeit has done for us!" I can hear you exclaim.

And indeed, your shining countenance and full spiritual and intellectual prowess were living testimony to all you preached. In you, we saw a living example of inner vitality, inner strength, and thus . . . inner contentment.

Rebbetzin Greenberg, I will never forget you, and neither will many thousands of other women. Your voice lives on in the hearts and minds of all of us.

Your voice is still heard all over the country, and not just because of the cassettes that you left. You have penetrated our inner essence, and helped us "return." You have given our souls a taste of the heights a Jewish woman can reach in her life.

---

1. *Megillas Rus* 4:13.

This volume is part of
THE ARTSCROLL SERIES®
an ongoing project of
translations, commentaries and expositions
on Scripture, Mishnah, Talmud, Halachah,
liturgy, history and the classic Rabbinic writings;
and biographies, and thought.

For a brochure of current publications
visit your local Hebrew bookseller
or contact the publisher:

Mesorah Publications, ltd

4401 Second Avenue
Brooklyn, New York 11232
(718) 921-9000